What goes on beyond the pearly gates?

Communication with Angelic Healers

Miriam Bostwick

Robert D. Reed Publishers   Bandon, Oregon

Cover design by James Daniel Torlakson

ISBN 978-931741-83-5

Library of Congress Catalog Card Number
2006907515

Material in this book is intended to be used for educational and information purposes only. It should never be substituted for advice from physicians, psychiatrists, or other health care professionals.

ROBERT D. REED PUBLISHERS
PO Box 1992, Bandon, OR 97411
Phone: 541-347-9882 Fax 9883
E-Mail 4bobreed@msn.com
Web Site: www.rdrpublishers.com

Dedication

This book is dedicated to the many, many angelic healers who so enthusiastically enlightened me about the karmic implications of physical, mental, emotional, and social problems, and on the work they do in the hereafter to bring about healing through a change in attitude.

Acknowledgements

I am very grateful to the Reverend Rosemary Keith for her help in channeling some of the medical/karmic information.

My gratitude also goes to Carla Wong Gee, Elizabeth Mae Jordan, and Diane Messing for their invaluable editorial assistance.

A special thank you goes to James Daniel Torlakson for his inspiration and creation of the cover design.

Appreciation goes to the National Center for Biotechnology Information, a branch of the National Institutes of Health, for invaluable information on genes and the diseases that they cause.

Revelation 21:21—And the twelve gates were twelve pearls; every several gate was of one pearl:. . .

Other books by the author:
The Conquering Soul: the Key to Understanding Spiritual Psychology
More on the Conquering Soul

Books in preparation:
Another Peek Beyond the Pearly Gates
Mediations to Empower Your Soul
The Heavenly Abode of Our Friends in Fur Coats, Leather, Fins, and Feathers
The Empowered Soul: The Gospels for the New Millennium
The Empowered Soul: Acts and Epistles for the New Millennium
The Empowered Soul: Revelation for the New Millennium
Genesis Revisited
Biblical Profiles: As Told in Their Own Words

Contents

PART ONE: BACKGROUND

Preface / vii

1. The Case for Reincarnation/ 11
2. The Governing Power of Karma/ 23
3. The Etheric Body and Chakras/ 30
4. The Soul Plan or Contract/ 33
5. Implementing the Soul Contract:/ 36
   The Heart Seed Atom and
   Subconscious Mind
6. Facing the Fruits of Karma/ 38
7. Making our Transition and
   Viewing the Akashic Records/ 44
8. An Overview of the Nature of
   Attitudinal Healing in the Afterlife/ 53

PART TWO: THE PHYSICAL BODY

Introductory Statement/ 57
9. Heart and Blood Vessel Diseases/ 58
10. Circulatory System/ 75
11. Brain and Nervous System/ 92
12. Musculoskeletal System/ 124
13. Paralysis/ 143
14. Respiratory System/ 163
15. Digestive System/ 177
16. Endocrine System/ 184
17. Kidneys/ 194
18. Immune System/ 198

19. Nutritional-Metabolic System/ 205

20. Ear, Nose, and Throat/ 226

21. Eyes/ 242

22. False Growths/ 251

23. Leprosy/ 256

24. Skin/ 259

25. Sexually Transmitted Diseases
    and Deviant Behavior/ 270

26. Special Treatment of Children/ 275

27. Multiple Births, Miscarriages
    and Abortions/ 290

28. Alcohol and Drug Addiction/ 296

29. Chiropractic Care/ 305

PART THREE: MENTAL, EMOTIONAL
& SOCIAL PROBLEMS

Introductory Statement/ 307

30. Alzheimer's Disease/ 309

31. Paranoia and Schizophrenia/ 317

32. The Mentally Challenged/ 326

33. Possession/ 336

34. Multiple Personalities/ 341

35. Autism/ 345

36. Depression and Bipolar/ 351

37. Domestic Relations/ 359

38. Suicide/ 364

39. Learning to Bow the Ego/ 379

40. Coping with Pangs of Guilt, Regret, Grudges,
    and Bullying/ 390

PREFACE

This book contains information which will no doubt be controversial to some readers. Its intention, however, is to bring comfort by dispelling the fear of the unknown. One of its aims is to clarify misconceptions concerning death. It will, therefore, attempt to bring awareness to what we are doing to ourselves now, and what we can expect in our afterlife.

How did this book come about? A little over three years ago one of my spirit teachers asked if I would like to learn more about attitudinal healing in the afterlife. Naturally, my response was in the affirmative. Thus began a series of trance sessions to which angelic healers, many of whom were doctors and psychiatrists when on earth, came and told their unforgettable stories. As the word spread about this "project," as they called it, many other spirits asked if they could talk about their work also. They stated it was the first time anyone from earth had ever asked what they were doing in Spirit to help our friends and loved one who had passed over. Eventually, about 90 caring healers and group facilitators, covering a wide area of interests, participated. Their unedited contributions appear throughout this book under the title of *Enlightening Voices from the Other Side*. My master teacher was always present, and at times, offered his comments which are also included.

My spiritual quest began about 35 years ago, with trance developing as one of my phases of mediumship. So it was through my trance mediumship that the stories for this book were collected. I set a specific time twice weekly to hold sessions. With the exception of those few whom I personally invited, I never knew before the session who was coming, or what aspect of healing they would cover. They simply spoke through me into a recorder. I put my trust in my spirit teachers, with whom there is a close spiritual partnership, to protect me while in trance, and to permit only spiritually elevated spirits who were sincere and dedicated servants of the Light to come through me.

In order to carry on a dialog with my spirit teachers regarding important medical-karmic information included in this book, I turned to my long-time friend and teacher, the Reverend Rosemary Keith who is an unusually clear and dedicated channel for Spirit. She has had a profound influence on my spiritual growth. I feel confident that what she contributed to this book was accurately received from Spirit. I have been privileged over many years to have had at least 400 trance sessions with her. These were opportunities to converse with my own spirit teachers as well as numerous other highly evolved spirits who always patiently answered my endless questions about life here and in the hereafter.

I have drawn from some of those trance sessions with Rosemary to give some understanding of reincarnation and how it relates to karma. It will be shown that payments for bad karma incurred in past lives translate into many of our experiences, conditions, and genetically linked diseases that we suffer in this life. My master spirit teacher pointed out biblical references pertaining to reincarnation and karma and gave me his interpretation of those scriptures, as well as other scriptures elsewhere in the book. (King James version was used throughout.)

Again taking from "the Rosemary sessions," will be found answers to such questions as the purpose of life, why we have no memory of our soul contract, the function of the etheric body, how diseases serve as tools to work off karma, what happens at transition, attitudinal healing in the hereafter, reviewing the Book of Life, and other important points.

Intertwined with advice on how to avoid building more karma in the here, are the numerous aforementioned unedited communiques from spirit doctors and teachers on an infinite variety of topics describing how healing in the hereafter takes place by changing attitudes of mind. Many readers will be surprised to learn of the great care that is given our loved ones who have passed on. In fact, one of the spirit teachers commented, "I sometimes think that too many people on earth believe that afterlife, if they believe in it at all, is a life of idleness and listening to the playing of harps. This book should dissuade them of any such notion."

Progress on the other side of life is earned through selfless service, and this will be very evident in reading about the work of the angelic healers. Their therapeutic techniques include reversing mental retardation, Alzheimer's Disease, schizophrenia, bipolar, and other mental disorders. They help those who had physical illnesses and deformities accept their new and perfect bodies. Other spirit workers devote their efforts to trying to raise the consciousness of those who have brought over emotional problems, or who are consumed by guilt for leaving what could have, should have, or should not have been done while on earth.

Enlightening communiques from the other side also include helping bloated egos to bow in humility. The comments and views of the spirit contributors have in no way been altered, modified or slanted. They are presented just as they were received. It is understandable the reader may not be in agreement with some of their comments. They are viewing things from a different perspective than when on earth. In telling their stories, they have bared their hearts and souls to help us understand the continuity of life and the role karma has played in their individual lives.

May this book bring the consolation that loved ones will be reunited in the hereafter, and in the meantime, to know that communication is possible. When we understand death and its ramifications, we usually adopt a different philosophy toward life. In the words of a wise one, "To become learned concerning death is to become wise concerning life."

Miriam Bostwick

PART ONE

1.

THE CASE FOR REINCARNATION

Dating back thousands of years are the ancient mystical writings of **Hinduism**, the *Upanishads*, which contain references to reincarnation:

> "Under the hypnotic spell of pleasure
> And pain, we live for ourselves and are bound.
> Though master of ourselves, we roam about
> From birth to birth, driven by our own deeds."
> -*Shvetashvatara Upanishad*

In the second chapter of the *Bhagavad Gita*, Krishna explains some of the workings of reincarnation to the despondent Prince Arjuna before his momentous battle: "As the lord of this mortal frame experienceth therein infancy, youth, and old age, so in future incarnations will it meet the same. One who is confirmed in this belief is not disturbed by anything that may come to pass. As a man throweth away old garments and putteth on new, even so the dweller in the body, having quitted its old mortal frames, entereth into others which are new . . . Death is certain to all things which are born, and rebirth to all mortals; wherefore it doth not behoove thee to grieve about the inevitable."

Jainism "conceives the human body as a chariot on which the soul rides towards liberation. The conduct of the present life should be aimed to attain total freedom from which there is no return to the birth and death cycle."

Moksha (liberation from an endless succession of lives through reincarnation) is achieved by enlightenment.

Sikhism teaches: "The goal of human life is to break the cycle of births and deaths, and to merge with God." It shares their belief in this cycle of birth, life and rebirth with Buddhists, Hindus and Jains. **Buddhism** refers to it as "the wheel of rebirth." In fact, reincarnation is one of the central tenets of **Tibetan Buddhism**. There is also widespread belief in reincarnation among the **American Indian** tribes.

The *Chuang Tzu* (4th century B. C.) of **Taoism** states: "Birth is not a beginning; death is not an end. There is existence without limitation; there is continuity without a starting point."

Edgar Cayce, also known as the "sleeping prophet," brought reincarnation into mainstream consciousness with over 2,500 of his 14,0000 readings mentioning reincarnation. He had no difficulty blending these beliefs with his deeply-held Christian faith. Many Christians of today have accepted reincarnation as a result of his communication with the spirit realms.

While about 25% of Christians express some belief in reincarnation, the only group of any size promoting reincarnation from within official Christian circles has been the **Army of Mary**. This Catholic sect was founded by Marie-Paule Giguere, a mystic or medium. Based in Quebec, Canada, it claims to have 25,000 members around the world. The group includes some 60 nuns and priests who affirm that they are as dedicated to their faith as any other practicing Catholic. Despite pressure from Canadian Catholic authorities and the Vatican for teachings considered "heretical," the foundation has not only stood its ground against the authorities, but appears to be growing.

In our present day, **Spiritualism** not only openly teaches reincarnation, but affirms it through interdimensional communication. A large percentage of the membership of **Unity, Religious Science** and other New Thought religions also accept the possibility of the doctrine. It is also accepted by **Theosophy**. **Rosicrucians** have taught it from the time they were a secret society in Europe. The **Dead Sea Scrolls** and **Christian Gnostic Gospels** support reincarnation.

The **Sufi** mystical movement within **Islam** is very supportive of reincarnation. And the mystical school of **Judaism**, *Kabbalah*, has taught reincarnation (or *gilgul* as it is known in Hebrew) over the centuries.

In the *Old Testament*, Malachi foretold that God would send Elijah himself to reincarnate as the forerunner of the Messiah, and Elijah did come in the person of John the Baptist.

Malachi 4:5 "Behold, I will send you Elijah the prophet before the coming and dreadful day of the LORD".

It should be noted that sometimes references in the Bible to *Lord* should be interpreted as *law*. When Jesus came everything was changed because he brought spiritual law into the right perspective. So Malachi foretold it was to be a *dreadful* day because it would change everything. And, in fact, there was a change totally from one dispensation to another. It changed fear to love. Such change would be a dreadful day to the Jews, and others living at that time. By divine plan everything had to change, and changes do not come easily for any group or individual. On a personal level, the dreadful day of the law is when we have to go through the akashic records and review our life or lives in detail. We have to realize exactly what we have done and how good or bad it was, and what we can do to make amends, if we want to grow spiritually.

In the following passage, the angel tells Zacharias that his wife will bear a son and that he should be named John. "And he shall go before him in the spirit and power of Elijah," a promise made earlier by Malachi 3:1.

And again, in Malachi 4:5,6 it is prophesied that the ministry of John the Baptist will be the forerunner of Jesus.

Luke 1:11 And there appeared unto him an angel of the Lord standing on the right side of the altar of incense.
12 And when Zacharias saw him, he was troubled, and fear fell upon him.

13   But the angel said unto him, Fear not, Zacharias: for thy prayer is heard; and thy wife Elisabeth shall bear thee a son, and thou shalt call his name John.

14   And thou shalt have joy and gladness; and many shall rejoice at his birth.

15   For he shall be great in the sight of the Lord, and shall drink neither wine nor strong drink; and he shall be filled with the Holy Ghost, even from his mother's womb.

16   And many of the children of Israel shall he turn to the Lord their God.

17   And he shall go before him in the spirit and power of Elijah, to turn the hearts of the fathers to the children, and the disobedient to the wisdom of the just; to make ready a people prepared for the Lord.

Clearly in verse 17 above, "and he (John) shall go before him (Jesus) in the spirit and power of Elijah" means the actual return of the spirit, soul, and power of Elijah in the body of John. It is the spirit and soul which reincarnates, not the body nor the conscious mind nor the ministry.

At the time of Jesus, 2000 years ago, the Jewish sect known as the Pharisees gave every indication of their belief in reincarnation as shown in the following verses from the *New Testament*:

John 1:19   And this is the record of John, when the Jews sent priests and Levites from Jerusalem to ask him, Who art thou?

20   And he confessed, and denied not; but confessed, I am not the Christ.

21   And they asked him, What then? Art thou Elijah? And he saith, I am not. Art thou that prophet? And he answered, No.

22   Then said they unto him, Who art thou? that we may give an answer to them that sent us. What sayest thou of thyself?

23   He said, I am the voice of one crying in the wilderness, Make straight the way of the Lord, as said the prophet Isaiah.

24   And they which were sent were of the Pharisees.

25   And they asked him, and said unto him, Why baptizest thou then, if thou be not that Christ, nor Elijah, neither that prophet?

Here, John the Baptist is talking to the priests and Levites whom the Jews sent from Jerusalem to ask him who he was. Although he is in fact the reincarnation of Elijah, John flatly denied it. He did not tell an untruth; he simply did not know whether he was the reincarnation of Elijah. How many of us know who we were in a previous life? Even elevated souls like John do not always know. If John had known, he probably would have been hesitant in telling them because John was very humble. Elijah was held in high esteem by many Jews and John might not have wanted to detract in any way from the glory of the coming Messiah.

If there had not been acceptance of reincarnation among the Pharisees, it is highly unlikely they would have asked if he was the reincarnation of Elijah or one of the other prophets from the *Old Testament*. The priests no doubt had observed the striking similarities in dress and behavior between the description of Elijah given in the Scripture, and the man John the Baptist standing before them. Both were fiercely ascetic figures who were endowed with great eloquence in preaching.

John 1:29   The next day John seeth Jesus coming unto him, and saith, Behold the Lamb of God, which taketh away the sin of the world.
30   This is he of whom I said, After me cometh a man which is preferred before me: for he was before me.
31   And I knew him not: but that he should be made manifest to Israel, therefore am I come baptizing with water.

In verse 30 there is a clear reference to reincarnation. John is saying, "after me comes a man who ranks ahead of me because he was before me." In other words, Jesus had more incarnations than John. Jesus is more elevated than he, more evolved than he. In verse 31, John is saying that he did not know Jesus consciously in that former incarnation, but that he does know him in this one, naturally because he is his cousin.

In the passage below, Jesus clearly identifies John the Baptist as a reincarnation of Elijah the prophet.

Matt. 11:12 And from the days of John the Baptist until now the kingdom of heaven suffereth violence, and the violent take it by force.

13 For all the prophets and the law prophesied until John.

14 And if ye will receive it, this is Elijah, which was for to come.

15 He that hath ears to hear, let him hear.

Jesus says very plainly that Elijah is a prior incarnation of John. This is the doctrine of reincarnation which teaches that in life's great school, we come back into physical existence again and again until our lessons are learned. Jesus says, "if ye will receive it," meaning if you are able to understand and accept what I say. "He that hath ears to hear, let him hear" means those who are sufficiently awakened spiritually will hear. If your spiritual ears are not open, you will not understand.

Verse 12 regarding the suffering of violence, refers to some who seek shortcuts to higher consciousness. They try to force entry through black magical methods to a plane they are not qualified to enter. There are no shortcuts. Slow steps are sure steps under the guiding hand of reason.

Later in the *Gospel of Matthew*, Jesus reiterates that John the Baptist is a reincarnation of the prophet Elijah:

Matthew 17: 10 And his disciples asked him, saying, Why then say the scribes that Elijah must first come?

11 And Jesus answered and said unto them, Elijah truly shall first come, and restore all things.

12 But I say unto you, That Elijah is come already, and they knew him not, but have done unto him whatsoever they listed. Likewise shall also the Son of man suffer of them.

13 Then the disciples understood that he spake unto them of John the Baptist.

The disciples asked Jesus why the prophets had said that Elijah would return before the Messiah comes. Jesus told them the prophets were correct and that Elijah had come to prepare the way and was not recognized, or well treated by many. Likewise, he knew he, too, would suffer at their hands. Then the disciples understood that John the Baptist was the reincarnation of Elijah.

Another reference to reincarnation appears in the *Gospel of Matthew* when Jesus asked his disciples who the people thought he was:

Matt. 16:13   When Jesus came into the coasts of Caesarea Philippi, he asked his disciples, saying, Whom do men say that I the Son of man am?
14   And they said, Some say that thou art John the Baptist: some, Elijah; and others, Jeremiah, or one of the prophets.

If reincarnation had not been a common belief among the general population, it is obvious they would not have speculated that Jesus was an old prophet reborn in a new body. They certainly were not referring to the reanimation of a corpse.

In the *Book of Amos* is another reference to reincarnation. It describes God taking the dead to heaven then bringing them back to earth.

Amos 9:2 Though they dig down to the depths of the grave, from there my hand will take them. Though they climb up to the heavens, from there I will bring them down.

In the following verse from the *Gospel of John,* Jesus is confirming the preexistence of our soul:

John 8:56   Your father Abraham rejoiced to see my day: and he saw it, and was glad.
57   Then said the Jews unto him, Thou art not yet fifty years old, and hast thou seen Abraham?
58   Jesus said unto them, Verily, verily, I say unto you, Before Abraham was, I am.

In the above scripture, Jesus is saying, "Abraham predicted long ago that I was coming, and rejoiced from the land of spirit to see my day had come." Jesus saw and conversed with Abraham clairvoyantly. And Joseph, being the father of Jesus and the reincarnation of Abraham, Joseph did see Jesus's day. But Joseph also knew from the time he was Abraham that he would be the father of the Christed man. He knew it in his soul consciousness. Jesus was talking about the soul consciousness. This is a wonderful revelation of how many incarnations are required to prepare us for our mission. From our soul memory, we know exactly where we are going. Our conscious level, as far as our personality is concerned, does not know.

"Before Abraham was, I am." The Christ is the I AM, not Jesus per se, and was in existence before anyone was born. Jesus personified the Christ Spirit.

Below, in the *Parable of the Talents*, Jesus gives wise guidance concerning how we should make the most of our talents:

Parable of the Talents

Matthew 25:14   For the kingdom of heaven is as a man travelling into a far country, who called his own servants, and delivered unto them his goods.

15   And unto one he gave five talents, to another two, and to another one; to every man according to his several ability; and straightway took his journey.

16   Then he that had received the five talents went and traded with the same, and made them other five talents.

17   And likewise he that had received two, he also gained other two.

18   But he that had received one went and digged in the earth, and hid his lord's money.

19   After a long time the lord of those servants cometh, and reckoneth with them.

20   And so he that had received five talents came and brought other five talents, saying, Lord, thou deliveredst unto me five talents: behold, I have gained beside them five talents more.

21 His lord said unto him, Well done, thou good and faithful servant: thou hast been faithful over a few things, I will make thee ruler over many things: enter thou into the joy of thy lord.

22 He also that had received two talents came and said, Lord, thou deliveredst unto me two talents: behold, I have gained two other talents beside them.

23 His lord said unto him, Well done, good and faithful servant; thou hast been faithful over a few things, I will make thee ruler over many things: enter thou into the joy of thy lord.

24 Then he which had received the one talent came and said, Lord, I knew thee that thou art an hard man, reaping where thou hast not sown, and gathering where thou hast not strawed:

25 And I was afraid, and went and hid thy talent in the earth: lo, there thou hast that is thine.

26 His lord answered and said unto him, Thou wicked and slothful servant, thou knewest that I reap where I sowed not, and gather where I have not strawed:

27 Thou oughtest therefore to have put my money to the exchangers, and then at my coming I should have received mine own with usury.

28 Take therefore the talent from him, and give it unto him which hath ten talents.

29 For unto every one that hath shall be given, and he shall have abundance: but from him that hath not shall be taken away even that which he hath.

30 And cast ye the unprofitable servant into outer darkness: there shall be weeping and gnashing of teeth.

There is a reference here to the talents earned in our various incarnations. Jesus uses the word "talent," a unit of currency, to symbolize skills, abilities, talents, soul lessons, and opportunities which we are to use to enhance and enrich and evolve our soul ever upwards.

We work to develop our talents and God sees that we come back to another life with the potential to use those talents. We can gain other talents, strengths, or abilities if we work hard to develop them. Jesus was trying to teach here that we cannot take our talents or any of our abilities and hide them (not use them) because that will not do us any good. We must share them. That is the service we render to the universe.

"After a long time the lord of those servants cometh, and reckoneth with them." In a sense, we take an accounting of what we have done in our life. To those who have, more will be given because the more we work and the more we use what we have, the more that is going to be given to us.

"And unto one he gave five talents, to another two, and to another one" simply indicates that each of us brings into this incarnation varying abilities and soul lessons in varying degree. The one with the one talent who is afraid to use it for fear he is not going to have anything else, hides it. And that is like us sometimes. We are afraid that God is not going to take care of us. If we are afraid, we will hoard things. We have not learned to use our minds to create for ourselves, and so that which we have shall be taken away. The Lord in this parable is actually the law. "Hard man" means the law is difficult. That is, you cannot break the law without paying the price. Jesus is saying you cannot reap where you have not sown.

In verse 30, it seems harsh to say that for your finite failings you will be cast into the outer darkness where there will be weeping and gnashing of teeth. At that time, the belief in hell was so common that Jesus was simply reflecting the values of his time. The people had always been taught hell fire. The *Old Testament* religion was the religion based on fear. When Jesus came, he was showing the people how to live, but he was also appealing to them from the standpoint of where they were in consciousness. Matthew in particular did seem to draw out that kind of darkness because he drew so much on the *Old Testament*. Matthew was definitely a product of the Jewish people. Apparently, it was hard for him to turn off that kind of yoke. Many people raised in a strong faith find it difficult to give up all aspects of the old when they do change to a different belief.

It is believed that in the early Church Father Origen used this parable when referring to reincarnation. In his *De Principiis,* he stated that we "come into this world strengthened by the victories or weakened by the defeats of our previous lives."

Still another reference to reincarnation can be found in the *Book of Revelation:*

Revelation 3:12 Him that overcometh will I make a pillar in the temple of my God, and he shall go no more out; and I will write upon him the name of my God, and the name of the city of my God, which is new Jerusalem, which cometh down out of heaven from my God; and I will write upon him my new name.

"He shall go no more out" means to be free of the wheel of reincarnation. "Pillar in the temple" is an evolved soul. The "new Jerusalem" is not actually a city. It is the new consciousness which will be the consciousness for the Aquarian Age. "I will write upon him my new name" means our consciousness is now raised to the point where our perception of the nature of God is more refined and accurate.

A Creed
The British poet laureate, John Masefield, penned a poem entitled, *A Creed* which beautifully and correctly describes the process of reincarnation:

"I hold that when a person dies
His soul returns again to earth;
Arrayed in some new flesh disguise
Another mother gives him birth
With sturdier limbs and brighter brain
The old soul takes the road again."

Reincarnation under Christianity
The belief in reincarnation flourished during the time of early Christianity. Under the Roman Emperor Constantine, the First Council of Nicaea was convened in 325. This first ecumenical council held by the church is best known for its formulation of the Nicene Creed, the earliest dogmatic statement of Christian ortho-

doxy. It was an attempt to settle the controversy raised by Arianism over the nature of the Trinity. At that time Christianity became the official state religion.

Disagreements over various points of doctrine continued, and in the year 553 A.D. ideas concerning reincarnation were repudiated. The Byzantine emperor Justinian banned the teachings of pre-existence of the soul which Origen taught. This removed the possibility of acceptance of reincarnation within Christian belief. Despite the anathemas, Origen's influence did not completely die out.

Many writings of the Roman Catholic Church were destroyed, and with the exception of a few, references to reincarnation were purged from the scriptures. Some historians believe the decision was intended to enable the church to increase its power. The new doctrine stated that we have just one life in which to accomplish our salvation or be dammed. The idea of having only one chance at salvation is totally and completely incorrect.

While still on earth, how can we find out who we were in a past life?

To be sure of reincarnation, you have to feel it deep within yourself. It has to be something that you truly believe is right. For some people, it comes in a dream state. They will have a dream and it will be very, very real, and they will know they are in a certain place, and will know various things about it. It is best when a knowing comes to you, rather than having someone tell you. Many times past life regressions are not true because they come from the medium's subconscious. A good medium will not tell you who you were, but will guide you through the process of feeling it for yourself. One way the medium begins is by having their relaxed client look down at his or her feet, and describe the kind of shoes he/she is wearing in a past life and which country he/she lived in. This opens up to some of the events of that life, and the client is actually feeling as the person he/she was then. ♦

2.

THE GOVERNING POWER OF KARMA

In the realm of spiritual science, the place of karma (the accumulated good and evil that one has done) occupies an even higher position than the place of the law of gravitation in physical science. The doctrine of karma is considered the backbone of the spiritual life of followers of several of the major religions mentioned in the preceding chapter. Buddha said, "the law of karma governs all things."

Everyone is bound within the universe by his or her karma. The theory of karma explains how, why, and what happens to us. It also explains the role that karma plays in our lives, how we accumulate karma, and how we get rid of negative karma. "The ultimate end, and purpose of all life and activity is to realize the free and blissful state of our true being" is the philosophy of Jainism. Our life should result in removing all bondages (karmas) in the process of purifying our soul. Our experiences provide that opportunity to gain insight and to apply our soul faculties, such as love, understanding, tolerance, peace, generosity, trust, and the like so that the soul will unfold to a higher level of consciousness.

We go on as a human. We never come back as an animal. It is ever an eternal progression of the soul toward higher levels of spiritual existence. As Rumi, a famous Sufi poet, writes,

> I died as a mineral and became a plant,
> I died as a plant and rose to animal,
> I died as animal and I was man.
> Why should I fear? When was I less by dying.

If we accumulate a great deal of bad karma, we will be reincarnated in a less desirable state, but always with the opportunity to work off or balance out our negative actions. Shirley MacLaine's book, *Out on a Limb*, sums it up: "Reincarnation is like show business. You just keep doing it until you get it right."

The question has been asked many times: **Why does one get punished because of bad karma for something he or she cannot remember having done in a previous life?** That is how the divine plan operates. The soul *does* have the memory of what we have done, but that memory is not available to us consciously. Before we incarnate, we make a soul contract to work off accumulated karma and to accomplish certain things for soul growth. During our earth life we are prompted at appropriate times to work on these things. It is up to us to perceive these "nudges" and to follow through. If we had conscious memory of our soul plan at birth, how could we grow? Prov.25:1-2 states, "It is the glory of God to conceal a thing, but the honor of kings is to search out a matter." Ecclesiastes 1:11 puts it this way: "There is no remembrance of former things; neither shall there be any remembrance of things that are to come with those that shall come after."

Working off karma should be viewed as a learning experience, not as a punishment. God or the Universal Teacher does not punish us. We punish ourselves by violating divine spiritual laws. Suppose a very mean person in a former life reincarnated with the plan to be very kind. If that person brought conscious memory of her soul contract into this life, she would perhaps be "kind" because she knew that was expected of her. Her "kindness" would not be sincere. Rather it would be perfunctory or mechanical. It would not be because she was listening to the inner prompting of her soul and did what was right because it was right to do. No one comes into this life with the conscious memory of his/her soul plan, not even the great Avatars knew exactly what was expected of them. They were elevated enough to perceive the promptings from within and to receive the impressions from above and to act upon them, and that is how they accomplished what they came to do.

How can we learn from our past mistakes if we cannot remember them? We can know what our lessons are by shining the lamp of honesty over our thoughts and acts. Is it patience, tolerance, kindness, or some other soul faculty that we need to unfold? The things that we do not do well are the things we should work on, When we have an experience not to our liking, ask *why this and why now?* The reason why humanity has been slow to exhibit noticeable improvement over the millennia of reincarnations on earth is because people are very reluctant to make the effort to accept personal responsibility for all their thoughts, acts, and deeds and to make the necessary changes in their lives.

A good example of karma is shown in the healing by Jesus of the man born blind. In this *Gospel of John* scripture, it clearly indicates the blind man was working off a karmic debt.

John 9:1   And as Jesus passed by, he saw a man which was blind from his birth.

2   And his disciples asked him, saying, Master, who did sin, this man, or his parents, that he was born blind?

3   Jesus answered, Neither hath this man sinned, nor his parents: but that the works of God should be made manifest in him.

4   I must work the works of him that sent me, while it is day: the night cometh, when no man can work.

5   As long as I am in the world, I am the light of the world.

6   When he had thus spoken, he spat on the ground, and made clay of the spittle, and he anointed the eyes of the blind man with the clay,

7   And said unto him, Go, wash in the pool of Siloam, (which is by interpretation, Sent.) He went his way therefore, and washed, and came seeing.

8   The neighbours therefore, and they which before had seen him that he was blind, said, Is not this he that sat and begged?

9   Some said, This is he: others said, He is like him: but he said, I am he.

10   Therefore said they unto him, How were thine eyes opened?

11   He answered and said, A man that is called Jesus made clay, and anointed mine eyes, and said unto me, Go to the pool of Siloam, and wash: and I went and washed, and I received sight.

When his disciples asked Jesus if this man was born blind as a result of his own sins or those of his parents, Jesus answered that the condition was not from "sin" committed in this lifetime by either his parents or himself. It was a karmic debt that had to be paid from sin or errors created in a past incarnation. This case affirms the law of cause and effect in operation. Whatever we sow, we reap the effects thereof. It is an inescapable law and operates equally as well in good or negative situations. Our motive or intention sets a law into motion, and as like attracts like, it returns like kind to us in the here or hereafter. This case refutes the idea of inherited weaknesses. Certain conditions may appear to run through families, but actually are related more to working off karmic debts. We choose a family that will provide the propensity for a particular disease or condition. This reference is a proof of reincarnation which the early fathers evidently overlooked when they were omitting reincarnation from the scriptures in 553 A.D.

Other references to karma include the following:
Matthew 26:52 Put up thy sword into his place; for all they that take the sword shall perish with the sword.

2 Corinthians 9:6 But this I say, He which soweth sparingly shall reap also sparingly; and he which soweth bountifully shall reap also bountifully.
Galatians 6:7 Be not deceived; God is not mocked: whatsoever a man soweth, that shall he also reap.

James 3:18 And the fruit of righteousness is sown in peace of them that make peace.

These are clear statements of the law of cause and effect. As we do unto others, it shall be done unto us in the here or in the hereafter. The seeds that we plant today become the flowers of tomorrow. Divine justice will prevail.

Does reincarnation insure justice? God is a God of absolute justice. This Infinite Intelligence does not give to one and take from another. Some people are very rich, have excellent health and beautiful homes. Others are born in poverty or have severe handicaps. We start out equally due to pre-existence of the soul, but through our own choices and/or our abuse of spiritual law, we find ourselves in unequal positions. In other words, while it may appear that some people have more than others, it is all balanced out through the laws of reincarnation, which operate impartially to award each living being what he/she has earned by his/her actions. The circumstances of our life are basically determined by how we have used or abused the law of karma, which is an impersonal and unchangeable rule of the universe. It is through reincarnation that we can satisfy the divine justice of reaping what we have sown, and to be given another chance to live within divine law.

Many people mistakenly believe that under the law of karma there is no unjust suffering, that we deserve everything that happens to us. That is not true. There is unjust suffering at times. Everything bad that happens to us is not necessarily caused by what we have done in this life or in a previous life. There are innocent people and innocent situations. Bad things can happen to good people. For example, a woman who was raped may never have done anything to deserve it. The rapist is the one who is going to pay the karma for having done something to the innocent woman. If that were not so, it would simply give people the message, why should they try to be good? If everything bad is going to happen to them, why should they even try? That is saying there is predestination. It would be believing that we come to earth destined for everything that happens to us. That is absolutely not true. We have free will at all times. Some suffering is definitely undeserved, and all suffering deserves our empathy and action to enable the sufferer to help himself or herself. There is grace, forgiveness, and mercy. In the *Book of Lamentations* 3:31-32 it says, "For men are not cast off by the Lord forever. Though he brings grief, he will show compassion, so great is his unfailing love."

Frequently the question is asked: **What is the purpose of life?** We are here for soul unfoldment and to become free of karma. We utilize our relationships, circumstances, environmental factors, situations, responsibilities, duties, and work as opportunities to apply spiritual principles—not religious dogma. In other words, the purpose of our experiences is to gain insight and to apply our soul faculties, such as love, understanding, tolerance, peace, generosity, trust, truth, and the like in all we do so that the soul will unfold to a higher level of consciousness.

Too often people think if they do not have a position of power and influence or social standing, they are failures and are just marking time with no purpose in life. Some of the most spiritual people are in humble positions. It is how we perform every task, and every relationship. Do we put good into them? Some people find the unity and upliftment in attending a church, synagogue, or mosque of great support, but for others it does not take belonging to a particular religious faith to be ethical and in tune with the higher values of the universe. When we reach the other side of life, we will go through a review of our life, at which time we will judge ourselves. The question to ask ourselves now is, will we be reasonably content with the contents of this review? It will show us very clearly the purpose of our own very personal life and the soul growth we have made. It may surprise many to know how much the little thoughtful things done with sincerity really count.

Another question frequently asked is: **Why is there such widespread poverty, starvation, disease, and horrible suffering in India, especially, where reincarnation has been systematically taught throughout its history?** People are drawn to certain countries to learn the lessons that come only through experiencing the particular group consciousness of that geographical area. Each country has a soul, in a sense, with its unique wisdom, traditions, achievements and ideas that have existed for centuries. In our many incarnations, we live in many different countries that will provide for us what we need to grow.

India has always been spiritual, and the religions of India will give the people, if they turn to their religion, the understanding and support they need to go through the misery that exists there. Many of these souls have not really progressed much in past lives so they are there to experience the things that they need to work on, and they have a religious structure that will help them achieve this. Others may be drawn to Russia, or to Italy, or any place in the world where the culture grants the unique opportunity required by the soul during a particular incarnation.

Another important point which should not be overlooked is that individuals could have some particular dislike of people who live in a particular area. They probably lived in that area in a past life, so they reincarnate to learn to like the people they disliked before. They keep coming back until the karma is worked out. Usually we are surrounded by people with whom we have karma. Certain diseases seem to affect only certain groups of people, which indicates they are purposely drawn together for karmic reasons.♦

3.

THE ETHERIC BODY AND THE CHAKRAS

In the *New Testament,* 1 Corinthians 15:44, St. Paul wrote, "There is a natural body, and there is a spiritual body." The natural body, of course, is the physical body. By spiritual body, St. Paul was referring to our etheric body which is on a higher plane than the physical. It is with us on earth, and it goes with us at transition. It is the body that is seen in spirit.

There are seven major chakras located in the etheric body. The etheric body or double, is an energy field which is invisible to the physical eye. It is the exact pattern from which the physical body is formed. Actually, it is constructed according to your past karma. This etheric body, which interpenetrates or interconnects with the physical, plays a vital role in keeping the physical body alive for it is the vehicle through which streams of vitality flow. The chakras, therefore, are vortices or points of connection which indraw energy from the ethers to flow into the physical body. They may be thought of as energy plugs which fit into the sockets of the physical endocrine system.

Each of the centers has special links with certain glands of the body, as well as with certain states of consciousness. They have been called chakras because they resemble a wheel in motion, with the central core acting as the hub, around which petal-like structures revolve. In each of these energy centers, the number of spokes or petals differs, as indicated below:

Chakra	Gland	Petals
Root	Gonads	4
Spleen	Lyden Gland	6
Solar Plexus	Adrenals	10
Heart	Thymus Gland	12
Throat	Thyroid Gland	16
Brow	Pineal Gland	96
Crown	Pituitary	972

As the solar and earth energies are indrawn, there is a rhythmic pulsation, so that the whole resembles a flower whose petals are in constant harmonic motion. As we raise our consciousness, these centers open wider.

The chakras play a vital role in the hereafter also. There are no functional lungs in the etheric body, therefore; a spirit is dependent upon indrawing energies from the ethers. As the degree of the opening of the chakras is a measurement of one's spiritual unfoldment, it follows that the amount of energy that can be taken in is ever commensurate with the elevation of the soul. The light of the spirit body, therefore, bears a direct relationship to the opening of the chakras.

As stated above, the etheric body resembles the physical. The etheric body or pattern comes first because the soul decides what kind of body it is going to need for the purpose of what it wants to accomplish during its incarnation on earth. Just as needing a pattern in order to cut out fabric to make a dress or shirt, the soul has to have a pattern of what it is looking for in order to form the required type of body. The strengths and weaknesses of past lives are utilized in the construction of the future body, programming into the body a tendency toward some ailment or condition which may be required to provide karmic workouts. The poison of past lives must be changed into pureness.

The etheric body is composed of the four ethers which are all around us. So it is the ethers which take form as a body. It contains no blood and the skin cannot be penetrated. In spirit, it is very pliable according to one's thoughts. A spirit can think their body younger and thinner, if they wish.

We check out our prospective parents to determine whether they can genetically provide the kind of body needed to work out our karma, for karma plays a big part in this decision. If we have been with these people in other incarnations—and most of us have—we are going to have the kind of parents who will supply our needs. This accounts for certain diseases or physical defects seemingly to run in certain families. The gene for the propensity to develop a particular disease is present, therefore, we select those parents. When children blame their parents for passing on a physical problem, they need to stop and realize that they chose those parents, usually for that reason. The exception to this occurs when the parents possess other genes for something not needed by us, and we pick up those gene as well. So some diseases are only "karmic to a point." Depending on how we live our life prior to the proposed onset of a disorder, we may not develop it at all, having already worked off our karma in another way. Or, the case may be mild, and we are very responsive to treatment. In the case of a child, a serious condition is always karmic, either for the soul of the child to work off karma, or as a very sad growth lesson for the parents. No matter how difficult, we must keep the proper perspective by seeing karma as enlightenment and not punishment. The scales of the universe will be balanced fairly and unemotionally. Divine justice will prevail.

Genetic counseling may effect the decision of some not to bear children for fear of passing on certain diseases. However, new diseases will always come into existence as long as we need ways to balance our karma. For example, the ancient disease of leprosy has been replaced by cancer. As we evolve, the magnitude of our karmic debts will decrease, and proportionately so will the severity of our afflictions.

If a person is born with a missing limb or is deformed, that means for karmic reasons the etheric mold was designed that way as a pattern for the physical. However, upon transition, the etheric will become whole, complete and perfect. In spirit, the etheric body is always perfect regardless of what we go through here. An amputation will only affect the physical and the etheric counterpart will remain intact.

As spirits progress spiritually, their etheric body will change. It will be more full of light, but there will not be a change as far as features. It will have greater mobility and energy. Because the etheric body is so pliable, and thoughts are things, spirits can change their age to be younger, and they can scale back their weight, if they so desire. ◆

4.

THE SOUL PLAN OR CONTRACT

In each of our many incarnations there are certain things which our soul wants to develop. To accomplish these things, we bring to earth a plan or soul contract which has been carefully worked out with the help of the higher spirit teachers. It is a plan to maximize our opportunities to unfold our soul. In addition to specifically and intentionally choosing a family who can provide the necessary genetic factors discussed in the previous chapter on the etheric body, it takes into consideration the unseen influences which will provide tools that we can either use or abuse. Each of us is born with an individual pattern of attunement to these influences. One of these influences by which we are affected is the Seven Rays, those radiating streams of energy coming from the God Head—cosmic, solar, and planetary—from which there is no escape. These energies are transmitted from cosmic sources through the zodiacal constellations to our Sun, to the planets of our solar system, to the earth, and to each living thing on earth. That consciousness works through various energy centers in us. These spiritual centers are known as the chakras. It behooves us to educate ourselves as to the nature of these energies.

Another strong influence is astrological in nature and plays a larger role in our lives than many want to accept. If we do not succeed in conquering the characteristics of a zodiacal sign under which we are born, we repeat somewhat the same thing again and again in our subsequent earthly sojourns. Regardless of which sign we are born under, if we do not control the negative aspects, or live up to the positive characteristics of that sign, we must come back to that sign and face it anew. All the traits of the sign are generally present within a person, although some may be dormant because that person has conquered those aspects and only needs to work on those which are more apparent. Under the influence of our sign, we do broadcast, through our actions, how past life experiences are affecting our functioning in this life. Each of the zodiacal signs affects at least one or more of our chakras. The sign also indicates the strengths a person should try to achieve in this life time. For example, Pisces is an advanced sign which affects all the chakras. In a past life, there was little or no religious training or spirituality. So the strength a Piscean should achieve in this lifetime is to learn to develop spiritually and become a living symbol of faith. If not achieved, it is carried over to another lifetime.

Our ideal plan also includes numerological calculations which establish our basic vibration at birth. The day we are born is no accident, and the name we are given at birth is critically important. Numerology is a science of vibration and is as old as recorded history. Everything is in motion. We move constantly in an inner and outer world of motion. Thus, numerology can guide us in making the significant choices we face in life, such as picking the right job or the right mate. It can also be used to better understand friends, business associates and other interests. It can provide a timetable for determining when the vibrations are best for pursuing particular endeavors. Karma from past lives is revealed.

The numbers do not interfere with free will, for free choice is our birthright. A correct interpretation of the numbers guides us rather than compels us to take a specific course of action. We resonate with certain numbers which define our life path, soul urge, personality, character or expression, as well as our karma. A chart done by a professional numerologist can be amazingly revealing and very accurate as another tool to guide us on our life's path. But with all tools, it is only with conscious awareness that we can wisely utilize these influences in a positive way. As we pause a moment to reflect on these various tools that the Infinite Intelligence has given us to analyze and measure our strengths and weaknesses, we realize that the universe is a great teacher. Our spirit guides and teachers are knowledgeable about our mission in life, and they try to impress us to stay on course. They take into consideration all influencing components.

Factored into the soul contract must be the important element of how to work off karma accumulated in past lives. If a person has committed heinous crimes of great magnitude, the karma cannot be satisfied in one life time. It may require multiple life times of intense suffering to satisfy the debt incurred. Normally, however, retribution for the average person can be achieved in one life time. We work out the past only to build more karma during the present life which has to be erased in the future, until eventually we get it right and get off the wheel of reincarnation. The severity of the karma must fit the debt. It does not necessarily follow that we erase particular karma of one incarnation in the very next incarnation. There may be many intervening incarnations before we work on a given thing. This may be due to several reasons: we may not be strong enough to deal with the infraction at an earlier time, and/or the return of others involved must be synchronized with our return. It takes a great deal of planning if one truly wants to accomplish much. The more elevated a soul is, the more carefully the plan is thought out. Those souls who come back without regard to what they wish to accomplish, actually accomplish little. Although they are counseled by high spirit teachers not to do so, it is their right and they are allowed to carry out their wishes.

Consideration has to be given to what kind of personality and physical body will be required for the soul to do its job. The soul remains the same, but the personality and appearance and state of health change with each incarnation. There may be a thread of similarity running through successive incarnations, but the etheric bodies are never identical. So that brings us to the next consideration—finding the parents who are going to provide the type of body and the propensity for the particular disease or condition necessary for us to work off our karma. Many times we go to families that we have been with previously.

In view of the foregoing, it is obvious that no one can truthfully lament, "I didn't ask to be born!" The soul definitely chooses its own destiny.♦

5.

IMPLEMENTING THE SOUL CONTRACT:
THE HEART SEED ATOM AND
THE SUBCONSCIOUS MIND

The heart seed atom and the subconscious mind act to prompt us when to implement certain phases of the soul contract. If we are receptive to these cues, the soul can accomplish much. The soul is a spark of God, or whatever name the reader assigns to this Infinite Intelligence. The personality or ego is the energy tool which the soul uses to function within the physical world. The personality is in a superiority struggle with the soul to run the show, so to speak. But when it is sufficiently disciplined, it listens to the still small inner voice and follows its guidance.

The subconscious mind is the storehouse of everything that we have thought and done in this lifetime as well as in past incarnations. When we make our transition to spirit, we take with us that memory, and it is deposited in the akashic records, or as some call it, the Book of Life in the Spirit World. In spirit life, we draw from soul memory as there is no subconscious mind in the spirit body once we review the akashic records. In other words, after going through a reflection of the last life on earth, there is no further need to dredge up the contents of the subconscious.

Upon our return to earth, we are again given a subconscious mind. And in that subconscious mind of the newborn is stored all of our past incarnations, in addition to the plans we hope to accomplish on our earthly sojourn—plans which we worked out while still in spirit. These include the lessons we want to learn, the circumstances which will provide the best learning environment, and opportunities to work off our karma. The knowledge that we need as we go through life is then dispensed at the appropriate intervals. We receive these impressions ever in keeping with our spiritual elevation. There is no conscious awareness of the role of the subconscious mind as the causal factor in letting us know what we must go through to achieve maximum soul growth.

The heart seed atom is located in the etheric body. It is the storage unit which contains the memory of all of our incarnations. It goes with us from incarnation to incarnation. As that information is needed, it is released into the blood stream. The blood stream uses it by awakening special cells which will, in turn, take that information to the designated chakra which will utilize it. This is what provides the physical body the direction that will best accomplish what the soul desires for its unfoldment. The heart seed atom also works in conjunction with the subconscious mind. When releasing information into the blood stream, it simultaneously makes an imprint on the subconscious. We have to be spiritually developed to some extent for that to transpire, or we would not be receptive.

It is the subconscious mind that brings up the actual experiences that we have to go through. The conscious mind then reacts to the subconscious promptings and works to carry these out. The personality must cooperate and not interfere. It is clear that the subconscious mind and the heart seed atom work in concert with each other to prompt us to follow our plan of incarnation or soul contract—one working on the mental level and the other on the physical level.

Actually the subconscious has two functions. It is not only programmed to bring back those experiences that we have to go through, but it is also storing the thoughts and experiences of this life time. The subconscious mind very definitely does not begin life on earth as an empty vessel, so to speak. In what must be an incredibly delicate operation, the subconscious is programmed by transferring from the akashic records in spirit all of our records from our past incarnations. This is how our karmic conditions are revealed.♦

6.

FACING THE FRUITS OF KARMA

It is one thing to accept intellectually that karma is a reality of life, but it is an entirely different situation when we are actually in the process of paying off the bonds. Even when we know there is divine justice, to the mind the payment always seems high, especially if we do not want to face personal responsibility for our thoughts and actions. When we are ill or deformed, to whom do many turn to place the blame? God, Allah, parents? Actually, karma may be considered just an exchange of energy which balances those scales of justice. The afflictions or deformities are the tools by which the law of karma is dispensed.

The soul is drawn intentionally to a family who can meet the necessary conditions for that soul to free itself from karmic bonds incurred in a past life. These conditions may include a wide variety of experiences that the soul needs for growth. A person may choose to incarnate as mentally challenged or physically deformed. An alcoholic from a previous life may need to come to a family with alcoholic problems in order to face and overcome the need to drink to excess. Some conditions are definitely genetic in nature, such as blindness from birth, diabetes, cancer and many others. If the soul decides to work off karma using an inheritable disorder, it would naturally choose the parents who carry the gene to provide that propensity. Depending upon how we live our life prior to the proposed onset of a disorder, we may not develop it at all, having already worked off our karma in another way. Or, the case may be mild and we are very responsive to treatment. Some diseases may only be "karmic to a point." In other words, we may have chosen a family to pick up one disease, but the predisposition for another disease or deformity existed, and we simply pick up that gene as well. It may or may not actually develop, however.

Some people think because a disease is karmic, they cannot do anything about it. Many times they think, "I am just going to die with it, so why bother?" That is not necessarily the case. We do need to accept the condition in order to grow, but we can and should seek available treatment. If the karma is about worked off, we may be healed. If not, our condition will not respond. Again, keep in mind that it is the disease or condition that is giving us the opportunity to go through whatever it is that we have to do in order to be karma free. It is not the disease we get that is karmic; it is by working through that particular disease that we can get rid of the karma that we have brought with us.

The Spirit teachers tell us that many of the diseases we currently see will eventually be cured. However, others will take their place until people get their act together and raise their consciousness so they no longer need disease and poverty as avenues to pay karmic debts. As mankind evolves spiritually, the replacement diseases will not exact as heavy a toll on the body. One does not have to believe in God in a formal way to be very kind and ethical, but believing in *good* is essential. Atheists are not held back if they live this way.

Sometimes we come to families for things they can supply for us although we did not have actual karma with them. In other words, a family can supply things for a person's soul growth although they did not actually have a karmic reason to be there with them.

Some children need to come just to go through the birth experience, or maybe to stay for a very short time and then go back to Spirit. If they only come to have the birth experience, then it is the parent's karma. In that case, the soul of the baby only needs to come for that particular reason.

Many different karmic things do come from a particular place. We keep coming back there until we work out the karma there. It could be that we have some particular dislike of people that live in that area. Very probably we were living in that area in a past life. And also, we came back to finish out the karma or to learn to like the people we disliked before, because usually we are surrounded by people with whom we have karma.

Some conditions are only karmic in the sense that we have not been living the kind of life that we should be living in this incarnation. We have caused it by our actions in this life.

What the future holds in understanding and treating the whole person who has karmic related problems remains to be seen. One such physician, however, Auroleus Phillipus Theostratus Bombastus von Hohenheim, immortalized as "Paracelsus," was born in 1493. A Swiss alchemist and physician who was very much ahead of his time, he was the first to establish pharmaceutical chemistry in medicine to eliminate the practice of bleeding and purging people. He shed much light on the problem of disease in relation to reincarnation.

In a trance session, Paracelsus, in a very direct manner, related:

> I realized that many of the diseases that people had did come from karmic things that had happened in past lives. I was a firm believer in that. And I also was a firm believer that if you did not cope with things very well, and you did not believe in past lives, there was very much a chance you were not going to get over that disease.

> I definitely believed I was in contact with Spirit Teachers who helped me make that connection. Definitely. I do not know who, but I would sit down and see a patient—it is not always karma—let's say a person is born and has been very good in a past life and that person chooses to help someone else go through their karma. They are ill or become ill in order for someone or a family member to get stronger. Many times that happens, but these are very old souls. There is a karmic relationship with the family they come to. It is not someone picked out of thin air. They are trying to help someone close to them to complete their karma. Many times that is the case.

I used to sit down with a patient and if I didn't know exactly what the problem was, I would mentally concentrate on the patient, and most of the time I would receive in my head the answer. I knew I was talking to Spirit. I knew it was a doctor or someone who had been on the earth not too long before and had realized the importance of medical help, not so much medicine. I would tune in, and I would receive many answers.

I worked with many mentally disturbed people. I very definitely did, and that is usually caused by being very harsh, very unsupportive in a past life. You know, you say, *you are driving me crazy.* You can drive someone crazy if you keep after them long enough. You can drive them into a mental condition. Those people are going to come back and have a mental condition themselves so they can experience it. That is their karma. Sometimes it is very difficult to help these people. Because if they do not want help, and there are so many people upon your earth who like the attention of being sick, and if you find that kind, you are not going to be able to help them. They do not want it. And they can take medicine after medicine and not get any better because they are not allowing themselves to get well. Even people with karmic conditions can get relief. They may not get completely over the condition, but they can get relief if they want it. With karma, you have to work it out. It kind of goes in cycles. A person may have some illness for three years, and all of a sudden it seems to be better because they have worked off their karma. I knew that when I was practicing. If you have not worked it out, and you go back and do the same thing again, well, here we come again.

I spent a great deal of time with each of my patients. I used to talk and talk and talk and talk and try to get them to understand what was going on. A lot depends on the individual and how willing he is to listen and take advice. I ran into problems with the medical profession because I was too advanced for them. And you know, if you can tell somebody that something is causing a problem, something they either did in the past, or something they are doing now, and if you can get that person to realize that, then they can do a lot to stop it themselves. The thinking starts changing. So what is going to happen? The doctor is not going to make the money, is he? The patient is starting to help himself. What do they do; they fight it. Even eating properly can help a great many things.

Paracelsus did write some papers which were published by the Rosicrucian Society, a secret society in his day. As a member, he gained much spiritual enlightenment. A few excerpts from his papers housed in the Rosicrucian library at San Jose, California, include the following:

An intimate tie binds the generator to that which is generated. Past generations are utilized in the construction of the future body; they are woven into the body as a tendency to some ailment, affecting either disposition or the life forces. This poison of past lives must somewhere be changed into healthfulness. This struggle comes through infections. Epidemics of races are materialized evils of the past.

No physician should presume to know the hour of recovery because it is not given to man to judge the offense of another and the inner temple containing mysteries in which no uninitiated stranger is permitted to spy.

In the wisdom of the future all disease will have an end.

The true physician must both understand and perceive. If he does not see the patient's astrality, he cannot prescribe that which being the curative opposing force, must be roused within the patient's spirit. The true healer looks not for causes in the visible, but seeks to understand the invisible.♦

7.

MAKING OUR TRANSITION AND
VIEWING THE AKASHIC RECORDS

What happens at the point of death on the physical plane? After the silver cord breaks, the soul and etheric body are freed from the physical body. The normal process for the average person is to spend the next three days following death near the earth around loved ones, and often times people have reported seeing them. That is why some religions teach not to bury the dead or cremate them until the third day. Usually the silver cord does not get totally severed until the third day. If a person dies at 9 a.m. on Monday, cremation, autopsy, or burial should not take place before Wednesday morning. The same holds true for a pet.

When death has come very suddenly, it is especially difficult for the dead to comprehend that they are gone. They need the time to understand they are no longer in their physical body, otherwise, they are going to be very disturbed. In fact, a spirit reported to this author that he had been cremated immediately following his death. He did not know what was going on. It was a terrible experience with the soul still being connected to the body. He went to Spirit very upset, very discouraged, and very mixed up. So it is better to wait until approximately three days to get a person prepared to go to the other side, and to let the silver cord sever naturally. This gives one time to view his etheric body which is more translucent than the physical one and to be able to realize within himself that he is physically dead. That does not mean that he is left in limbo. Generally someone from a person's family already in Spirit comes to greet him/her. If, however, a person passes away in a car accident, or has a heart attack, or in some other way goes very, very quickly, and the family in Spirit has not been notified to come, the spirit guides will be there. The problem is that so many, many will not understand what a guide is; so they cannot immediately recognize those who are there to help. In the case of a more elevated soul, the guides will be acknowledged. All people have spirit guides and teachers, whether Christian, Jewish, Hindu, Buddhist, Muslim, or another belief or unbelief.

The author's husband immediately recognized someone was with him, and when he was told, "You are dead, but now you are *really* alive," he accepted it. His first concern was how his family was taking it, and he stayed close until the silver cord severed, and then he went on. His transition went smoothly because he had some understanding, but many, many, many people do not have the realization of what goes on after death of the physical body. They may not realize they are no longer in the physical body. They will try to make contact with those who are left behind, but usually they are unable to do so, and this is very upsetting to them. It is definitely recommended to wait until the third day to bury or cremate a body.

Many who are dying are very frightened. They do not know what to expect, and they do not want to leave their family. If there is someone in whom they have great faith, that person can walk with them and help them to release. Spiritualist ministers or good mediums have walked with individuals many times—on occasion actually going part way through the tunnel with them. And then the departing soul will see the light ahead and approach what looks almost like a forest. At that point, everyone has to go on alone. We walk through the forest alone; even the spirit guides and teachers leave us at that point. They go on ahead and wait for us, but we have to go through the forest alone. It is not very far, but it is like a darkness. It has been described as similar to going out into the woods. It can be pretty dark out there if there is only a little light coming through the trees, or none at all. It all depends upon the elevation of the soul. The point of being taken out into the forest and left alone is for us to look within ourselves. We do a super fast review of the last few weeks of our life. It is a judgment, in a sense, but we judge ourselves. Our conscience is our judge.

For some, going through the forest is a very scary experience, especially for those who believe in hell fire and damnation. Some will turn back and not go through right away. They have "died" but will stay around the environment that they knew and where they feel comfortable. At some point they still have to go through that self-judgment before they can really go on. No one is standing there saying they have to go through it right away. But for reunion with their loved ones, they have to go through self-judgment in order to go higher into the Astral Plane.

As we walk on in the forest, we can see the guiding light at the end. We can look up and see spirits lined up ready to greet us. When we look up and see that light, we should no longer be afraid because we are moving toward it. As we get to the light and to this beautiful band of spirits, we are taken by the spirits and walk on with them. This is the same experience for all regardless of their religious faith or lack of one.

There are seven planes in the Spirit World, each registering a certain level of consciousness. Each of those seven is subdivided by seven, creating a total of forty-nine levels or realms. As like attracts like, we go to the realm that we have merited—the place we have prepared for ourselves based on how we have lived on earth. Each realm is a level of consciousness. And each realm has what is called an intensive care unit. We are taken to the appropriate intensive care unit to be watched over by our guides and teachers and the angelic forces. Even elevated people need some orientation, but people who have many layers of negative energy in their aura are in special need of love and light. And it is literally poured into them. While they are there, subconsciously every negative thought form that they have created, everything they have done that was wrong, does come to greet them. They have to meet this negativity and cope with it.

There has to be this total review of this life because we take our auric field along with us, and everything is there in that auric field. It is also transcribed into the akashic records. Sometimes people are very aware of where they are, and they know some of the things they have done or left undone. But before we ever get to review the akashic records, or Book of Life, where a record of all incarnations is kept, we have to review the entire life just lived on earth. It can be very painful to examine every thought, every word, every action that we have performed in this particular life. Many people think that God is a person sitting up on a throne and when we die, He is going to judge us. No, it is the Book of Life— the book of our entire life that is going to be opened. It will be opened to the current incarnation.

This reflection of our entire life takes quite some time. For some people, it takes a very long time in earth terms. Everyone has to go through this, but the more elevated we are and the more good we have done, the easier we accept being in Spirit and the less painful are the reflections. We are going to realize what we have done or have not done or should have done. Maybe we have already cleaned out some of the "garbage" in our subconscious prior to making our transition. This reflection can be considered a second judgment of ourselves. We are the only one who will ever judge us. God does not judge.

One spirit commented that "Progression is not something everyone is ready to consider when they come to this side. They have not been exposed to spirituality, and they do not understand how important it is. It is not easy to get people to embark upon a spiritual journey. They do not want to make the effort. And why should they make the effort, they think, when they are over here. Because they do not have to go out and make a living; they do not have to worry about food in their tummy. They do not have to worry about a roof over their head. They can just have a perpetual vacation. And that is the way it is for about half of them. It takes a bit of turning the key inside to want to open the door and to be receptive to the understanding that they can receive and the light they can reach."

When people do the review of this life, it truly is about the same as going on a spiritual path while still on earth. It takes a lot of time to get the "hang" of it all. It can be overwhelming because we suddenly realize there is a bill to pay—karma—for all the things we have done. We never thought these things carried a price tag. It really makes one stop and think about what he or she had been doing. When we are on the other side and we come to this awareness, it is much more difficult than when we are here. There is no buffer, and we find ourselves with like-minded people, so it is harder to rise above that vibration. However, there is much help available in Spirit. We can go to our guides and teachers and get their advice. But we have to build confidence in them, if we do not know about them. That takes time too. It is not something that happens overnight.

If someone expresses the desire to return to earth without having done a review of this life, they are counseled against doing so. If they insist, they are permitted, of course. It takes the intervention of the higher ones to bring this about. By going back to earth too soon, not having come to terms with what transpired in this life, they are only compounding their inability to pay off karmic debts. After another life here, they will return with a bigger mess to straighten out. This can go on and on. If, however, the soul says enough is enough, and it is time to grow, a review of multiple lives could be overwhelming, and the guides would no doubt help them in taking it in small doses.

People who are elevated definitely want to do a total review of this life and to go into the akashic records to see what they have done in past lives and how it has affected them. It is called reflection. The review of this life will make a big difference in how they are going to feel after they see the akashic records. These records contain a record of all of our lives, and we may review as many as we would like. Let's say there is a particular life we know we have lived, and we want to see just what we have accomplished or did not accomplish in that life; then we can review the entire life because there is a record of every thought, and every action on record. No escape. We do not have to look at the akashic records if we do not wish to. But we absolutely have to look at the record that we just lived at some point in time. That is very definite. That we cannot escape, if we are to progress. We have to go through it day by day, piece by piece. Then we decide what we should do or what we feel we need to do in another life, or what we need to do while in Spirit. Some people do not have to do all that much. We have time. We can do whatever we really want to do. Some people decide never to return to earth, working off their karma in the Spirit World.

Many of our records in the Book of Life may never be opened if we have finished with them and no longer need to view them. If certain aspects or lessons have been learned, that part of the book is closed. But, let us say, while on earth we did not give healing or we did not give help or comfort when we could have. These may be very definite things our soul needs. Then in the next incarnation, we will probably come back to work in the health field or something akin to it, or whatever our karma is connected with.

If we truly desire to grow, our spirit guides and teachers, and even higher spiritual mentors, will come to help us make a new plan or diagram of what we should do and should not do, how we can learn, and how we can serve now that we are in Spirit. The selfless service chosen in Spirit is guided by our past, as well as our planning for another incarnation. This takes quite some time. For some people it can take years and years of equivalent earth time before being ready to review the akashic records. There is no time in Spirit, however.

The akashic records are like a diagram, and everything that we have done in every life that we have lived is definitely recorded. After having gone through this particular life we have just lived, all elevated people want to know: *why did I go through this, why did this or that happen, what am I learning from that? What am I supposed to remember from that?* They want to go to the akashic records to look and see. We do not have to look at all of them, only the ones that interest us. It is usually the life before this one that people most often want to review. They want to know what they worked out in this life. *What did I do in the last life that I needed to work out in this one?* But if we wanted to go back to the fourth or fifth previous life, etc. we could.

When we are actually reviewing the akashic records, it is kind of like a movie. We tune into whatever life we are interested in, and it all goes before us because every single thing is on record.

For example, if we went back to the days of Moses, we would see ourselves as we looked in the dress of that day. We would see all the good we did, and also all the bad we did. Then we would go from there and view the next life to gain an understanding of why this happened or that happened. In other words, each lifetime is based on what transpired in a previous life and what aspects of it we choose to work out or improve upon. The review would be a movie of our life in which we are not only the main actor but the only actor. We would only see ourselves. We do not see ourselves in relation to anyone else, but we will *feel* the relationship with someone else. It is a matter of sensing it, and it can be painfully strong. We retain the subconscious mind until we actually go through the akashic records. We really need it for reviewing our immediate past life, after which it no longer serves a purpose. From that time forward we have only our soul memory while we are in spirit.

The akashic records are very personal and private. No one has the right to look up anyone else's akashic record unless they are given permission. In some cases, the guides and teachers will be given permission to look at the akashic records so they can help an individual who is not yet ready to view them, or to help someone on earth. Let us say that a person still living here had something happen in a past life that is really affecting this life. A medium could tune in and get the help from the guide or teacher of that individual. Sometimes if a person knows what happened in a past life, it can really help that person to understand better what they are experiencing in this life.

It should be clearer to the reader now that heaven and hell are states of consciousness. The Spirit World is not a place of endless worship, or eternal rest. There are no angels playing their harps. There is no fiery furnace where the spirits of those who had led an evil life on earth are condemned to suffer endless agonies from heat. Those who have been extremely cruel while on earth go to a realm of darkness. Their bodies emit no light. They live in darkness until they are remorseful and work on elevating themselves. Although only about 5% of the population on earth make the effort to go on a spiritual path, the majority do manage to get to a realm of light. Those, however, who have walked a spiritual path go to a much higher plane of light, as like attracts like. And they have greater mobility. The door to reformation, to climb to a higher realm, is never closed, but why not make the effort here and now to balance the material with the spiritual? It is easier to make spiritual progress while on earth.

Whenever we have a dream that we can remember, it is usually a dream when spirit has been with us. If we dream about our mother who has passed over, our mother would have been there. Some times we may have a dream which will tell us something that happened in a past life—that is our guides and teachers working for our advancement, so we will understand why such and such has happened. This is different from meeting someone on the Astral plane and remembering. In other words, if we can dream that we are out with somebody who has passed over, we are definitely out with them. If they are still on earth, we are astrally travelling to them.

When there are loved ones on earth who are on a spiritual path, their light helps those in Spirit. It gives them energy, as well as encouragement and inspiration. The light and the love are what help anyone to grow. That is why those who are in the hospital or in the intensive care unit are showered with love and light by the guides, teachers and higher forces; for it is the love and the light that is going to uplift them.

Most religions teach some misconceptions about the afterlife, if they teach anything at all. Some tell people that it is going to be just perfect on the other side. They can rest eternally. Well, that is not so. In Spirit we can do what we want, truly we can, within the realm to which we have gravitated. We are building our house over there right now while on earth. We are building where we are going right now. And speaking literally of houses, let's say we have a very small house when we get there. We built that. That is what we merited. Then as we grow, we simply build another one, or add on to it, or change it. Our neighbors would change as we grow to another realm. It is kind of like a tornado that comes and picks the house up and moves it, because everything we do is by thought. And all we have to do is think it. It is going to happen if we are ready for it. If we are ready for a better place, then all we have to do is create it. But we have to be ready for it in consciousness, or we cannot make the change.

It is understandable why it takes about 200 of our earth years to really get ourselves in shape to come back and to understand what the pattern of the next life is going to be. Of course, we are going to forget the plan as soon as we get back here. However, that pattern will be etched in our soul. We possibly would attract new guides and teachers depending upon what we wish to accomplish in the new plan, but our old guides and teachers will never, ever be too far from us. They still would be interested in what they have accomplished with us and how we are working it out in another life.

Each time we reincarnate, we progress a little faster while still a child, depending on how elevated we were in the previous life. However, if we bring back much so-called garbage, this is because we took much with us when we left. ◆

8.

AN OVERVIEW OF THE NATURE OF ATTITUDINAL HEALING IN THE AFTERLIFE

Attitudinal healing is very important in the Spirit World and there are many, many helpers to assist anyone in need.

Dr. Waltham on attitudinal healing techniques

I know a little bit about the treatment techniques of awakening one who has had a long illness or disability on earth. When they come to this side, those who are not aware of where they are, as well as those who do know a little bit about the afterlife, are both taken to our intensive care units or convalescent centers. We try initially to get across to the newcomers that although they have passed from a physical dimension, they really are more alive than ever. They have arrived in the Spirit World and they will be taken care of. They need to rest. Very few people come over here who do not require at least a little rest. It is a bit too much to absorb it all at once.

When people are very sick on earth, or have had some physical disability for much of their life, they have it in their head that they still have that condition when they come over. The memory of the pain and/or disability is there; so it takes time to convince them to move on in consciousness. We teach them they no longer have a heart problem. They no longer have dysfunctional kidneys and need dialysis, and so forth. It does take very gradual steps to get across the fact they are now healthy and no longer need to experience the sensation of pain. All of the physical pain has been alleviated in the Spirit World unless you insist upon bringing it with you by your thoughts and attitudes. Thoughts are things.

Holding onto illness or disabilities of the earth results from overidentification with the physical body. When individuals can truly accept that they are spirit clothed in a physical body while still on earth, then, of course, the transition is much, much easier. Many earth people will say they accept they are spirit, but frequently this acceptance is only on an intellectual level. It requires a great change in thinking to look in the mirror and see a physical body, yet identify as a spirit while on earth.

The spirit or etheric body is strengthened by the ability to indraw the spiritual power which is limitless. Those who have done a great deal of Astral travel may make a rather quick recovery of strength. That comes about with the acceptance of a new body. There has to be a reidentification of the body one is wearing. When that fully occurs, then the pain and the disability of the old body fades. It really is as simple as that. However, going from Step A to Step B is not so easily accomplished. Attitudes must be changed. The soul memory of the old has to be replaced with the image of the new. In time, most of these new arrivals do accept that they are in a new body and that it is perfect and they will not have any pain or physical disabilities in that body.

The higher they are progressed and the higher their consciousness, the easier will be their transition. That is, if they truly and honestly believe there is no pain in the next life, despite the terrible pain they may have suffered while on earth, they will be put to rest for a little while, but they will not have the difficulty of adjusting that the average person would have who has no understanding of the conditions of the Spirit World.

We talk to people who have no understanding of an afterlife and very basically tell them about having been on this side of life before. This is their real home. We explain that they went to earth to have some experiences which would help them to progress their soul. We explain why certain things have happened to them. These conditions may have been karmic in nature, and if so, that debt has been paid. They no longer need to struggle with it.

Spirits who have had amputations on their physical body look down at their etheric body and see that they are whole. Amputations only affect the physical while on earth. The etheric body remains intact. That is why many amputees will say they feel sensation or pain in the area of the lost arm or leg although that limb has been physically removed. We explain to them this probably was a karmic thing, and when they are strong enough their spirit teacher will help them to understand why that happened.

As far as someone continuing to use crutches, we firmly discourage that. If you see that, or see a spirit insisting upon keeping his peg leg, we want them to get over those remnants of disability carried over from the earth plane. They cannot move on spiritually as long as they retain such close ties of that sort with the earth realm which is lower. So we encourage them to let the past go, that this is a new life and to get on the "road to recovery." It is an important step to take.

The same applies to one who was born without a limb. The physical body was imperfect but that was the form of the etheric body which is the pattern for the physical. Parents should not feel a sense of guilt in having a physically deformed child. Their function was to provide the incoming soul with a body that would enable that soul to work off a karmic debt. Usually, however, there is a karmic tie with the parents or caregiver which affords them the opportunity to erase karma, as well.

When it comes to sight, it is more difficult for the blind person to accept the restoration of sight than for an amputee to accept the wholeness of his or her body. We encourage them to open their eyes and to tell us what they see. At first, they will say that it is all black. They see nothing because it is in their head that they cannot see. We tell them no, it is only because you think it is black. Thoughts are things. This is especially observable in the Spirit World.

We patiently encourage them to open their eyes again and they will see there is light. And so, we work with them that way. They do not need glasses over here, although many times spirits will continue to wear glasses with no magnification, strictly for identification. That is their choice.

Usually the hearing impaired do not require as long a recovery period to know that he or she is perfectly capable of hearing. In fact, hearing rarely presents a problem. They are receiving impressions even when they may think their hearing has not been restored to the ear. This is because we work through thought, mainly. They pick up telepathically what is going on because that is a very natural function of the spirit body. They can communicate without speaking a word regardless of what language is spoken. The thoughts come just as plainly as if it were something one was hearing. In other words, thought is so strong on the spirit side of life, one hears it as a voice.

If a disease seems to run in a family, it is because that family can provide the appropriate genes for that to take place. But when people go over without an understanding, they frequently feel much anger and resentment toward their parents. In fact, this can be the case while still on earth because so much is blamed on genetics. The truth of the matter is they would not have chosen those particular parents if they had not needed the experience of a disease or affliction to work off karma.

The various aspects of attitudinal healing and the enlightening stories from the angelic healers comprise the remainder of this book.♦

PART TWO

THE PHYSICAL BODY

In this section, I have drawn, with permission, technical information mainly from a collection of articles on the website of the National Center for Biotechnology Information (www.ncbi.com), which is a branch of the National Institutes of Health. It is a national resource for molecular biology information. NCBI conducts research to give us a better understanding of genes and the diseases that they cause. It is not the aim of this book to delve into a study of the human genome, the "blueprint" containing all of the information and instructions necessary for defining a human being. "Learning the language in which God created life" is for the scientists. Our interest is in the identification of genetic disorders and their karmic implications.

In the following chapters I have used the description and organizational structure of NCBI in classifying genetic disorders by the parts of the body which they affect. Some diseases affect several body systems; therefore, they are listed in the charts of more than one chapter.

Spiritual knowledge regarding the karmic implication of genetic disorders has come down from the higher spirit planes through trance mediumship. These disorders act as tools to work off karma. This information is given for the sole purpose of bringing about a better understanding of the underlying basis of suffering. Through awareness, individuals will be enabled to make better choices in consciousness, which in turn, will determine their destiny. Through communication with the other side of life, we are enlightened as to how attitudinal healing takes place when a person crosses over. ✦

9.

HEART and BLOOD VESSEL DISEASES

Function of the Heart and Blood Vessels

The heart is the most durable and efficient pump in all of nature! It is the center of perfect circulation. The action of the normal heart is very adequate and very complete. Its function is to provide oxygen and nutrient rich blood to every cell in the body. When its vessels become clogged with plaque, it cannot perform its vital role.

Diseases and Karma Associated with the Heart and Blood Vessels

We know that the seeds that we plant today become the flowers of tomorrow. So what are we doing today that will cause us problems tomorrow? If we do not change our attitudes and really try to resolve conflicts, work on our weaknesses, and make an effort to achieve the goals of the soul, we build karma which we take with us when we make our transition to Spirit. This means we carry karma over to yet another incarnation. This book is to help people realize that many of their physical problems are directly related to past lives, and that we accumulate more karma in this life if we do not understand how we are building it.

The heart symbolizes love

Love is truly the center of a person's being. King Solomon from the *Book of Proverbs* Ch. 4:23. said, "Keep thy heart with all diligence for out of it are the issues of life." And when we stop to think about that, it does go to all issues. It goes to health. It goes to everything. It all comes from the heart.

The critically important thing to remember is that anything that touches our sympathetic nature has the power to either build up or destroy our physical body. When we let hate dominate, when we let negativity dominate, we can destroy our physical body. Conversely, when we express universal love, harmony flows through our veins and arteries. When we are intensely selfish and place personal love above all, failing to regard the welfare of others, we set ourselves up for heart trouble. Many heart conditions are caused by a lack of love in a past life. For example, a man who did not show any love or appreciation for his wife and children, went out and did whatever he wanted to do, did not make time to spend with his family, was very controlling of them, as well as of friends and co-workers, surely did not use love in the right way. He will come back and probably have a heart problem. We are talking about love, not sex, and that through intense selfish and personal love, a person like this failed to regard the welfare of others.

We must learn to love universally and unconditionally

When individuals pass over to the Spirit side of life never having really loved others, they find themselves in a state of darkness and loneliness. So, the one thing that everyone has to learn is unconditional love, and it is much, much more difficult to achieve in Spirit than it is on the earth plane. It is more difficult because like attracts like and one is drawn magnetically to spirits of like mind. Whereas, on earth we have an opportunity to mingle with people other than those on our own level of consciousness. We can choose to be around people who are more elevated spiritually who will demonstrate love. If we learn unconditional love, we are going to take it with us. We will not have a heart problem in our next life if we can work out a love problem in this life. In universal love we love all humankind and all other creatures in God's kingdom. In unconditional love we love without expecting anything in return for ourselves. Emmet Fox taught, "There is no difficulty that enough love will not conquer; no disease that enough love will not heal; no door that enough love will not open; no gulf that enough love will not bridge; no wall that enough love will not throw down; no sin that enough love will not redeem."

Fear manifests in the body as heart trouble

Many deaths are attributed to heart diseases. Heart problems are among the most prevalent of all diseases. What can cause a heart attack? A sudden shock can, so can a terrible loss of a loved one or someone close, and all kinds of fear. Fear manifests in the body as heart trouble, and the remedy for that is love. The opposite of love, of course, is hatred, which is love distorted by fear.

Unfortunately, fear seems to be the basis of almost everything for many people. Fear is sometimes very subtle, but many times it is very strong. Fear is negative faith and keeps us where we are. Faith puts us where we want to be. As one Spirit teacher expressed it, "Fear is the brain's control of the soul; faith is the beauty of the soul's expression."

Fear is dependent upon the lack of understanding. When understanding is gained, fear disappears. Therefore, we must make the effort to understand what it is that we fear. With understanding, which opens when we exercise self-control, the power of faith expresses. The only way we gain faith is through understanding. What understanding brings is an awareness of the way the Divine truly works—how the spiritual laws of the Universe truly work. When we see something work, we most certainly have faith in it. Emerson said it this way, "All I have seen teaches me to trust the creator for all I have not seen."

Fear may rise when we have a project to do—fear that we will not do it right or that we might not finish it on time. Rather than being overwhelmed by trying to tackle the whole thing, take it in small sections or amounts and just know and accept we will receive inspiration to work it all out. Fear is something that everyone has at times, but with some people it is constant. They think this is not going to work out, or that is not going to work out. How am I going to survive? "Perfect love casteth out fear." (1 John 4:18) So, if we have a love of God and we have a love of Spirit, we are going to depend upon Spirit and know that Spirit is working with us. It is going to work out! And it does because we have many heads (spirit guides) with their input. Do not look at the whole picture. Look at it piece by piece. That truly is the key. Sit down sometime by yourself and quietly think, *I want to do this and I want to do that, but what is the best way to do it?* If we concentrate on it, we will get the thought coming through our mind as to the best way to do it. Do one little bit at a time. Never let fear over take us. Fear immobilizes and we are rendered unproductive.

People also have to fight depression, but they do not always know how. Why do they get depressed? Because they are scared to death that something is going to happen. When the personality rises in dissatisfaction with the way their lives are going, instead of expressing love, peace, and joy, they become frustrated which leads to depression. They are too wrapped up in themselves.

We have all heard people say that things are going so well, they just know that everything is going to fall apart. If we truly believe, "In Him we live and move and have our being," then we know that Infinite Spirit is within. It gives us all the security that we possibly need. If we truly believe that, then we accept that our life is governed by divine law and harmony within ourselves. We only have to cooperate mentally with the law of life! That is all we have to do. The spirit is within us—the life force is within us—and it is a very wonderful life force or power and it is not going to go anywhere, but we must cooperate with it. When we have loving thoughts, it sends new life to every part of our body which will stimulate the heart into healthy action.

Fear may rise when we do not seem to have any control over that which is going on outside. We cannot control others. When you have a decision to make, go in consciousness to perfect peace and the light of consideration will shine on the situation and reveal the truth. You can cross all bridges and stay in the light by never registering fear in your consciousness, no matter what the threat is. And in the words of a great spirit teacher, "That that is yours only your fear will take away. And that that is not yours nothing you do can hold it."

Faith is the light that guides us to God because faith is the power of the soul over the force of the personality. When we choose not to allow fear to control us, our soul is expressing itself. We must then ask ourselves the question, *How often in my life is my soul expressing? How often am I truly free of fear?* Whatever is free is filled with the spirit of joy.

We are spirit here and now

Know that Infinite Intelligence is with us. *I am spirit here and now and it is going to work out.* We cannot allow ourselves to be so frustrated that we are almost afraid to get up in the morning. And that can happen. So if we are trying to treat heart trouble or any other condition, there has to be a determination to think only good, positive thoughts. A great deal of strain, inharmony, many disappointments, family disagreements, disagreements with a spouse and partner—can all actually cause heart trouble. There can be financial reverses that will cause it because they create fear. People really need to work to keep themselves in a good mood, in a happy mood, in a joyful mood. They are not going to be as likely to have a bad heart if they have love in their hearts and truly try to love other people—really use love and not hate. Joy is from the soul and joy is felt on a deeper level of consciousness than happiness. We must realize that there is but one mind working through each individual. That is a universal mind.

Love is stronger than any other force in the universe; so express universal love and do not fear. Remember that it is Infinite Spirit that is flowing in and through our bodies. We are spirit here and now. That is a point few people seem to understand. We are spirit here and now enrobed in a physical body, and it is the spirit that is working through us. Understanding it intellectually is not enough. We must really feel it—feel the spirit working through us. Of course, we cannot discount that there are diseases and conditions that, because of karma, we have either brought with us, or we have caused in this life. But these are experiences we have had to go through. We have to learn to cope with them and work through them. We do this by controlling our thoughts and our emotions and seeking the needed treatment.

Hardening of the arteries can be karmic

So when we have thoughts of depression, fear, or thoughts of imperfection, this can lead to hardening of the arteries. We are not getting the blood to flow properly because of a build up of fatty deposits along the inside of arteries. Atherosclerosis or hardening of the arteries can be karmic in that we can attract stressful situations to bring it about: for example, when we are not flexible enough and cannot cope with two things at once. Let us say that in a past life, a person was an employer and made life miserable for those under him. He will come back and have to be an employee under an employer who will treat him in like manner. It is not going to help for the man to quit his job because he will just go into another one that is just the same. The karma causes the situation. That is a stressful situation, very stressful, so his karma is to learn to handle the stress. So the disease is not as karmic as the situation. By handling a situation in the right way, a person will learn to rise above it. If we can find peace within, all things around us will become harmoniously arranged.

Hardening of the arteries is also often caused by race suggestion. As we get older, the race suggestion is that the heart is going to wear out. *I can't do this and I can't do that.* Believing this, people are going to develop hardening of the arteries. This hinders the free flow of the blood. When we fear, we bring this condition about.

Karma may be associated with high blood pressure

High blood pressure usually is seen with a person who either has a bad temper, has a lot of anxiety, or is unable to control his/her thoughts and attitudes. And, of course, high blood pressure can be karmic. It could affect a person who treated others very badly in a past life. At the extreme, it could be a person who killed someone in a former life, and who came back and found a parent who could provide the necessary predisposition. Although the predisposition may exist, one really does not have to get the condition. A drastic change in one's thinking and ways can prevent having to go through a particular condition, or the condition will be milder.

Congenital heart defects have karmic connection

With congenital heart defects, there is generally karma with the family one is coming into. It does not have to be all of an individual's own karma, but is a matter of coming to parents whom one would not come to if he or she did not need to go through it—not a loving situation. Possibly there are other things in that family that he or she had to straighten out, or to be of help with.

Whole families may have heart problems

If a child is born with a bad heart that requires surgery, it is definitely a karmic situation. The soul of that child has attracted a particular family where there are heart problems in order to work out the reason for his or her own heart disease. If we can love unconditionally, we are not going to have to face this problem in another life. Many times we find a father, a mother, a brother, or a sister with a heart condition. That indicates that they did not show the right kind of love in a past life and may not be showing it in this life. So they are adding to their karma in this life. When a person hates a certain situation or a certain disease that he or she has, and so many people do, they are just making it worse. They are holding it to themselves.

Familial hypercholesterolemia stems from lack of love in past life

A type of high blood cholesterol known as familial hyperchoesterolemia appears early in life and often leads to heart attack during young adulthood. It stems from a lack of being loving in a past life. The heart is the love chakra (the spiritual energy center in the etheric body), so we can generalize that anything that has to do with the heart means we have not worked at being loving in a universal way. We may have been aggressive, very judgmental and so forth, and are coming back into this life to change, but we will suffer now because of those past attitudes.

The soul will release in sudden cardiac arrest

When sudden cardiac death occurs, this is usually when the soul feels that the person can no longer do what he/she is supposed to do. The physical body cannot be used to produce what has to be done, or to do what it should be doing to achieve its goal. It is a situation where the personality is not trying to work with the soul to go on a spiritual path to fulfill the soul contract. When the soul realizes there really is no effort being made to do anything to go on a more spiritual path, the soul will release in cardiac arrest, rather than build up more karma while here.

Sending out loving thoughts does make a difference

The spirit teachers tell us that if we would sit down for at least five minutes a day and **send out loving thoughts to the entire world,** what a difference it would make. Even if it is difficult to send loving thoughts to some leaders, we can still ask God to bless them and bring out the good that is within them. "Blessed are the pure in heart for they shall see God." (Mt. 5:8) We see God within ourselves. We are seeing the Principle. We are seeing the Love. We are seeing that which God manifests. There is a little bit of good in everyone. We may have to look very hard to find it in some individuals, but there is good there.

Chart of Heart and Blood Vessel Diseases

The major heart and blood vessel diseases are included in the chart in the following pages. The spirit doctors have indicated whether they are genetic and/or karmic in nature. At present, the four most common types of vascular diseases are high blood pressure, coronary heart disease, stroke, and rheumatic heart disease.

Note: On the following chart are listed diseases which can be inherited, but some are only karmic "to a point." In other words, in keeping with our soul contract, we may have specifically and intentionally chosen a family who could provide the gene to develop a particular "karmic" disease or condition. This is our way of balancing our karma. The predisposition also existed in that family for one of the "karmic to a point" diseases, and we simply picked up that gene as well. Depending on how we live our life prior to the proposed onset of a disorder, we may not develop a "karmic" or a "karmic to a point" disease at all, having already worked off our karma in another way. Or, the disease may be mild and very responsive to treatment.

Disease	Description	Genetic	Karmic
Angina	Term for pain behind the breastbone (sternum). Caused by reduced blood flow to a segment of heart muscle, a common manifestation of coronary artery disease. Pain only of a few minutes duration. Usually brought on by what is going on currently in a person's life.	no	no
Aneurysms	A weakened segment of an artery fills with blood, causing it to balloon outward. One possible cause is congenital weakness in the arterial wall.	yes	Karmic to a point
Ataxia Telangiectasia	Usually appears in second year of life as a lack of balance and slurred speech. A progressive disease characterized by cerebellar degeneration and predisposition to cancer. Early childhood diseases which are genetic are usually karmic	yes	yes
Arteriosclerosis obliterans	Lower limbs are affected by occlusive arterial disease. Major arteries carrying blood to legs and feet become progressively narrowed by fatty deposits. Poor circulation.	yes	yes
Atherosclerosis	Hardening of the arteries involves the progressive narrowing and loss of elasticity of the artery walls due to a build up of fatty deposits. Karma causes the stressful situation to bring it about.	possibly	yes

Disease	Description	Genetic	Karmic
Cardiac Arrhythmias	Irregular heartbeats.Disturbances in the normal beating pattern of the heart.	yes	no
Cerebral Hemorrhage	Blood vessel in brain ruptures. High mortality rate. Survivors are likely to be permanently disabled. Build up of stress and worry over long period of years	no	no
Cerebral Thrombosis	A condition where the blood clots in a narrowed vessel causing further obstruction in blood vessel.	yes	Karmic to a point
Congenital Heart Defects	Involves an obstruction to blood flow or an abnormal routing of blood through the heart chambers present at birth. Some may correct themselves in time; others may be life-threatening or interfere with normal growth and development. It is the karma in the family that has to be worked out .	yes	yes
Congestive Heart Failure	Characterized by an inability of the heart to pump efficiently. Lack of care of heart to point of condition being irreversible.	no	no
Familial Hyper-cholesterolemia	High blood cholesterol appearing early in life. Often leads to heart attack during young adulthood. Karma is due to lack of expressing love in a past life.	yes	yes

Disease	Description	Genetic	Karmic
Friedreich's Ataxia	A rare inherited disease characterized by the progressive loss of voluntary muscular coordination (ataxia) and heart enlargement. Generally diagnosed in childhood and affects both males and females, but females more.	yes	yes
Heart Valve Disease	Leads to heart muscle damage. Rheumatic Heart Disease is one example. Working out individual karma.	sometimes	yes
Hypertension	High Blood Pressure. In a small number of cases due to congenital narrowing of the aorta. A lot of anxiety in this lifetime.	yes, but rarely	Karmic to a point
Long QT Syndrome	Results from structural abnormalities in the potassium channels of the heart, which predispose affected persons to an accelerated heart rhythm (arrhythmia). This can lead to sudden loss of consciousness and may cause sudden cardiac death in teenagers and young adults who are faced with stressors ranging from exercise to loud sounds.	yes	yes

Disease	Description	Genetic	Karmic
Myocardial Infarction or Heart Attack	Coronary heart disease which involves the progressive narrowing of the arteries that nourish the heart muscle. It is the death of part of the heart muscle due to its sudden loss of blood supply. Typically, the loss of blood supply is caused by a complete blockage of a coronary artery by a blood clot. Heart attack is common manifestation. Pain usually does not recede with rest—lasting 30 minutes or more. Pain varies from mild to excruciating. Karma is usually related to current stress. Watch diet, exercise, avoid stress, and take other preventative measures.	yes	no
Phlebitis	Inflammation of a vein accompanied by formation of a clot.	no	yes
Progeria	A congenital disorder characterized by striking premature senility, with many children dying of coronary artery disease before the age of 10 years.	yes	yes
Stroke	Usually caused by a marked reduction in blood flow to the brain, leading to brain-tissue death. Associated with hgh blood pressure, diabetes, arteriosclerosis, smoking. Lots of stress. Definite anger problem—gets upset easily. Coming to family that will provide stressful conditions to work out karma, but has failed to cope.	yes	yes

Disease	Description	Genetic	Karmic
Sudden Cardiac Death	Result of ventricular fibrillation —reversible if treated in time. When the soul feels the physical body can no longer do what it is supposed to be doing, then the soul releases in cardiac arrest.	no	yes
Varicose Veins	Large veins in legs become distended, due to inherent weakness or malfunction of some of the one-way valves, permitting a backflow and pooling of blood. Can be treated.	yes	Karmic to a point
Von Hippel-Lindau Syndrome	Von Hippel-Lindau syndrome is an inherited multi-system disorder characterized by abnormal growth of blood vessels. While blood vessels normally grow like trees, in people with VHL little knots of blood capillaries sometimes occur. These knots are called angiomas or hemangioblastomas. Growths may develop in the retina, certain areas of the brain, the spinal cord, the adrenal glands and other parts of the body.	yes	yes
Williams Syndrome	Williams syndrome is a rare congenital disorder characterized by physical and development problems. Common features include characteristic "elfin-like" facial features, heart and blood vessel problems, irritability during infancy, dental and kidney problems, hyperacusis (sensitive hearing) and musculoskeletal abnormalities. Although individuals with Williams syndrome may show remarkable competence in areas such as language, music and interpersonal relations, their IQs are usually low.	yes	yes

Enlightening Voices from the Other Side

Dr. Monroe connects withholding love with heart problems
I was a heart specialist on earth, and I know from personal experience about heart conditions. When I reviewed my akashic records, I learned that in a previous life I had been a very withholding person. I was very strict and stern with my children and I was rather aloof with my wife. I did not show the love that I should have. I was very proud of them and wanted them to do well. In fact, I wanted my children to do very well. And I provided well for my family. But the tenderness I should have shown my wife, I did not show. And so when it was time to come back in this last life on earth, we decided to all come back together and try the same family configuration. I had two sons in the previous life, and the only change this time was to add a daughter who had been a niece in the previous life. And it turned out to be a very beautiful family relationship. We had our ups and our downs, but we were a loving close family.

I chose to be a heart specialist. I had been a doctor in a previous life. This time I wanted to treat people in a way that would truly express my love for them, and to help them with their expression of love. I wasn't terribly consciously aware of the connections between heart problems and the expression of love, but sometimes I would say to a patient, "Are you showing your children love? Let your heart express." See, I would say these things but I did not consciously realize that our thinking and expression of love would affect the heart. I really didn't. It was there and yet it was like it was not there.

Now I did not live to be an old, old man. Sometimes when we have these happy situations, they get broken up because we need to go on, and those that we leave behind need to grow. So I came to this side when I was about 47 years old. I had a heart attack which was a karmic thing, of course, but I had not only worked to help repair the hearts of others, but I had to suffer my own condition. I did not suffer too long with it before I came to this side of life.

I work with people over here. So it is a matter of working with them, telling them, look, I was a specialist. I know what I am talking about. You are perfectly well now. You do not have to restrict any of your movements. You can do whatever you like. The more you get around and the more you learn things, and the more you mix with other spirits, the healthier you are going to be in terms of your spiritual growth because that is what we work for here. We are not concerned about physical growth any longer, or our physical well-being. We have that. We have just got to get mental and spiritual health and elevate ourselves as high as we possibly can.

So I am enjoying my work very much. I have been able to see from both sides of the veil what happens to people who do not show enough love. You have a lot of heart problems on earth, so you know what the condition is. That is a barometer of love. We show it first to ourselves. We have to love ourselves, not selfish love, but the love of knowing that we are a part of God. Then we can reach out and love those who are close to us. When we can do that, we can reach to a higher dimension and love those who are in the world universally. We can recognize the levels that they are on, the things that they do that are not right, but we still can love them for the love of God that is in them. And we can love nature because nature is part of God's creation.

I have truly enjoyed coming and talking to you. I would like to say one other thing. When I first came over, I thought people should be waiting on me because I was a heart specialist and had nurses and other staff at my beck and command on earth. I could order them about, and I found that I could not do it here. The doctors are not gods and I had to become humble. And that was a little hard at first, but when I was able to do it, my love for others increased immensely because I did not separate myself from them. I may have had more knowledge about some things, but that did not make me a better person than someone else.

Miss Sunshine and her delicate heart
They call me Miss Sunshine because I go around and am just a bright and happy spot in the life of any one that I can reach. I

was a spinster; so I am dating myself because they don't use that term much anymore. I had suitors in my youth, but I had so many physical problems, real and imagined, that it was a deterrent to a long relationship. My parents really did not want to let me go. Actually, they made me feel guilty to even think about leaving. Especially after my father died, my mother held on to me. I was her companion and she discouraged me from getting married because I had a heart condition, and I had an eye problem. I wore glasses. I had a congenital abnormality of the heart and later died of heart failure. When I was on earth, we did not have the knowledge you have today to treat these conditions. That is what I finally died of.

I was the one with the delicate heart, so I was pampered a lot, and I thought everything on earth had to be done for me. My family made me a lifetime patient, which was very wrong, because with most heart conditions you can do something. You do not have to be a total invalid. My mother made me a patient. And when I finally died and came to this side, I found that I did not need to have that condition at all. When I reviewed the akashic records, I learned that in the previous life I had not given love and care to others like I should have, and so I chose coming to a family with a congenital heart problem to give love. And I think that I really did, because despite the fact that I was constantly reminded of my heart condition, I nevertheless was very, very upbeat. I guess my soul had reached the point in consciousness that it knew I had to rise above my circumstances. I was a very cheerful soul. And my mother did not want to lose me because I cheered her up. I was little Miss Sunshine.

When I came to this side, I realized that I had worked off my karma and that I did have a perfect etheric body, and that I had gone to the right family to have had the circumstances that I needed to do this. And I think that is about all I can say. I am still very upbeat and very happy. That is my nature. I try to cheer up others, but not everybody wants to be cheered up. So it takes a while to break that down. So I hope I have given you a different little slant on things.

Dr. R. came to talk about his attitudinal healing of patients who still think they have heart conditions

I especially work with people who have had trouble with their arteries and veins. I know that you have already received something on the problems connected with the heart and the clogging of the arteries and the veins. This is a very serious situation when this material which is a form of cholesterolrich plaques of the immune system cells clog the arteries. Hardening of the arteries is definitely caused by a lack of flexibility.

To work effectively in attitudinal healing, you take the anatomy that you are interested in, you see what the condition is, and then you look for the opposite. So if the arteries are all clogged and hardened, it certainly is not caused by flexibility in thinking. It was caused by narrow, constricted opinions about things. And it seems to run in families simply because we grow up with these narrow prejudiced restricted ways of viewing life. Kids are inculcated or indoctrinated with it. And they grow and indoctrinate the next generation. And if they have teachers or others around them with the same thinking, it just reinforces that kind of thinking.

So when we get them over here, they think they have got physical problems, and we assure them, they do not. They must identify with their new, perfect etheric body. And they have to change their thinking. We find it most helpful to work with them in groups before they go through the akashic records because people have narrow ways of looking at particular things. In a group setting, if someone is expressing an opinionated, rigid view, there may be someone in that group who is more open about that particular thing and can quickly point out to the first person the error in his/her thinking. So we find groups helpful initially in breaking down the ideas. We work also individually, of course.

We have no great problems to deal with except the stubbornness of some of these people. They do not want to budge. We ask them why they hold onto something. Let it go. Well, it takes time, but we work on it. I hope that has helped you to understand how we work over here with spirits who think they still have heart related problems. ✦

10.

THE CIRCULATORY SYSTEM

Function of the Circulatory System

Two distinct fluids move through the circulatory system: blood and lymph. Blood carries oxygen and nutrients to the body's cells, and carries waste materials away. Blood also carries hormones which control body processes, and antibodies, to fight invading germs. The blood consists of two basic parts: the formed cells, or corpuscles, and the fluid plasma in which they are carried. The heart is the pump that keeps this transport system moving. Together, the blood, heart, and blood vessels form the circulatory system.

The lymphatic system (lymph, lymph nodes and lymph vessels) supports the circulatory system by draining excess fluids and proteins from tissues back into the bloodstream, thereby preventing tissue swelling. It also serves as a defense system for the body, filtering out organisms that cause disease, producing white blood cells, and generating antibodies.

There are four main blood types. In Type A only Type A special protein (antigen) is present. Type B is composed only of Type B special protein. Type AB contains both Types A and B. Type O has neither Types A nor B special proteins present.

Diseases and Karma Associated with the
Circulatory System

The blood stream or blood system is so very important because it represents the spiritual flow of life, pure and perfect—the circulation of pure thought. So considered from a spiritual standpoint, the body is pure spirit substance and the blood is the perfect life stream. When our blood starts flowing, it is perfect and it fills every blood vessel. It circulates freely and it circulates sufficiently. However, negative thoughts—envy, malice, selfishness, and above all, hatred, can lodge in our consciousness. The more we think such thoughts, the more deeply they become embedded in the consciousness, and this will poison the life that flows in and through all of mankind. There are people who are so full of hatred and malice and envy and all negativity, that it is very hard for them to rise above that level. Such thoughts and emotions poison the life force that is going through them.

Blood disorders can range from relatively benign to serious and can be acquired or inherited. All blood diseases are correlated to the element of fire. While we actually poison this pure stream of ours by our thoughts, we use other labels in identifying the condition, such as leukemia when the poisoning from our thoughts could cause more white corpuscles to increase than can be handled, or, hemophilia when there is a lack of coagulating ability, or anemia, etc., for other kinds of blood problems due to these thoughts that are lodged in the consciousness. This applies to people who have a constant negative outlook. To them, everything is negative. They are not positive about anything. So in lodging this constant negativity, they create the poison which goes through their blood stream.

Negative thinking can affect any part of the body. What determines which part is going to be affected? If the negative thinking goes to the legs and feet, it is because you are not standing up straight for what you believe. If it goes to the arms and hands, you are not reaching out to gain the truth. You are submerged in negativity. If it goes to the blood, it is very serious because you must be constantly in a state of negativity which creates poison. When you poison your blood, there is very little likelihood that you are going to be consciously aware of what the heart seed atom, which contains your soul contract, is releasing into the blood stream. The heart seed atom, along with the subconscious, plays a critical role in prompting us when to work on certain aspects of our soul plan.

The basic cause of anemia is the lack of love, not personal love, but a consciousness of universal love. When we do not have that, it can produce anemia. Of course, there are other causes of anemia as well, such as iron deficiency, hemorrhaging, liver or kidney diseases, and many others. There is a type of anemia that is sometimes inherited—hemolytic anemia. Blood problems can also be a result of karma created in a past life through the wrong use of love—not applying unconditional love at all. That is, by trying to get all the love for self and not expressing that love for other people. It is not that individuals are bringing anemia with them; it is that they come to the earth plane because they probably have problems with love, and so they are attracted to parents who can provide the predisposition for anemia in order to work out their karma. If a person is anemic and there is no medical reason for it, it would behoove him/her to gain a better understanding of the heart, because what is the heart? The heart is the controller of love.

The life stream is renewed daily. It is important to understand that. And the blood stream is not material. It is spiritual and is constantly renewed as it converts spiritual substance into material benefits. The blood is the spiritual part of us. When we make our transition to the Spirit World, it is the heart seed atom that goes with us. It is the record of everything we ever thought or did while on earth. So actually everything is going through the blood stream. It will convert spiritual substance into material benefits because it is working in conjunction with the subconscious mind in directing us. What is meant is that the spiritual substance which is in the blood brings material benefits as far as the body is concerned. The benefits to the body would be better health, better attitudes and better things all around.

So, let us say that we are under constant irritation at work and we cannot adjust ourselves to this stress—we have probably all heard people say they are constantly irritated at work—then it is going to manifest as a physical condition sooner or later. We are talking about a consistent thing, not about something occurring one day a month, or one day a year. We are referring to people who are constantly irritated. This will bring on a physical condition sooner or later. Criticism and the inability to get along brings about many disorders. Some people do not seem to be able to get along with anyone. To them, everybody is doing something wrong. They are constantly criticizing them and finding fault.

Sometimes there is even a very deep seated resentment of certain people and certain ethnic groups. That is the cause of sickle cell anemia which affects blacks primarily. It has also been found among those of Greek, Spanish, Turkish, Italian, Asiatic, and Mediterranean descent. People who were very prejudiced against the black race are coming back as blacks to overcome their disagreements, upsets, or prejudice against the race. When we are intolerant, we are guaranteed the experience to gain understanding. The same applies to those with thalassemia which mainly affects people of Mediterranean background.

These are good reasons why everyone should honestly take stock of his/her habitual feelings toward people around them. If people live as they see fit and we do the same, that is fine. Let them alone. We should not keep criticizing and judging others. Do not try to change them because we are not going to be able to do that. The key can only be turned from the inside. That is their problem. Our problem is not to have these habitual negative feelings toward them. Sometimes we listen to too much news, and we let it control our thinking. And sometimes we can even become obsessed with the terrible conditions that are going on. It helps when a person can affirm, "I am calm. I am poised. I am at peace with the world." Concentrate on better conditions, not on bad conditions that are going on. "I am calm. I am poised. I am at peace with the world." As we become at peace within, all things around us become more harmoniously arranged.

St. Paul gave us a beautiful way to view life when he wrote: "I have learned that in whatsoever state I am, therewith to be content." (Phil. 4:11)

It does not mean that we have to like it, nor does it mean that it is not going away. It means that whatever the experience is now, if we can be content and know that it is going to pass, and if we do everything we can to get it to pass, we are going to be all right.

Chart of Blood and Lymph Diseases

Note: In the following chart are listed diseases which can be inherited, but some are only karmic "to a point." In other words, in keeping with our soul contract, we may have specifically and intentionally chosen a family who could provide the gene to develop a particular "karmic" disease or condition. This is our way of balancing our karma. The predisposition also existed in that family for one of the "karmic to a point" diseases, and we simply picked up that gene as well. Depending on how we live our life prior to the proposed onset of a disorder, we may not develop a "karmic" or a "karmic to a point" disease at all, having already worked off our karma in another way. Or, the disease may be mild and very responsive to treatment.

Disease	Description	Genetic	Karmic
Agammaglobulin-emia	Very low levels of protective immunoglobulins, affecting only males who develop repeated infections.	yes	yes
Gaucher Disease	The body is not able to properly produce the enzyme needed to break down a particular kind of fat. It then accumulates, mostly in the liver, spleen, and bone marrow. Can result in pain, fatigue, jaundice, bone damage, anemia, and even death. Common in the descendants of Jewish people from Eastern Europe (Ashkenazi). Other ethnic groups may be affected.	yes	yes
Hemophilia	Coagulation factor deficiency. The blood does not clot normally.	yes	yes
Hemolytic Anemia	Red blood cells are broken down at a faster rate than normal, before they can be replaced. While possibly genetic, it could also be due to other causes.	possibly	Karmic to a point
Hodgkin's Disease	A form of lymphoma.	yes	Karmic to a point

Disease	Description	Genetic	Karmic
Leukemia	A type of cancer in which the blood has too many white blood cells. The white cells produced continually multiply, even though they are not needed, spreading throughout the body and interfering with body functions. Karmic to a point in adults, definitely karmic in children.	yes	Karmic to a point
Lymphomas	Cancers of the lymphatic system, especially of the lymph nodes.	yes	Karmic to a point
Myelodysplasia	A group of disorders in which the bone marrow does not function normally and produces immature blood cells. MDS affects the production of any, and occasionally all, types of blood cells including red blood cells, platelets, and white blood cells. Most often found in adults over the age of 50. Slightly higher incidence in males.	yes	yes
Niemann-Pick Disease	Cells are defective in releasing cholesterol from lysosomes, leading to excessive build-up of cholesterol inside lysosomes. Can cause death in children.	yes	yes
Non-Hodgkin's Lymphomas	Frequently has spread before initial diagnosis is made.	yes	Karmic to a point

Disease	Description	Genetic	Karmic
Paroxysmal Nocturnal Hemoglobinuria	Characterized by a decreased number of red blood cells (anemia) and the presence of blood in the urine and plasma, which is evident after sleeping. Associated with a high risk of thrombosis of large intra-abdominal veins.	yes	yes
Polycythemia Vera	A blood disorder that usually results in an increase in all blood cells, with the red cells being the most severely affected. The counterpart to anemia.	yes	Karmic to a point
Porphyria	When heme production is faulty, porphyrins are overproduced and lend a reddish-purple color to urine. Heme is the oxygen-binding part of hemoglobin, giving red blood cells their color. Can cause abdominal pain, nausea, personality changes, seizures at the outset. With time can involve weakness in many different muscles.	yes	yes
Septicemia	Blood poisoning—an infection affecting the blood or its components. Bacteria invades the blood and multiplies.	no	no
Sickle Cell Anemia	Hemoglobin disorder that affects Blacks primarily. Red blood cells collapse into sickle shapes which entangle with one another and block circulation in small blood vessels. Vital organs can be damaged by lack of circulation. Strokes are common.	yes	yes

Disease	Description	Genetic	Karmic
Thalassemia Anemia	Found most often in people of Mediterranean background. Affects a person's ability to produce hemoglobin, the protein in the red blood cells that carries oxygen and nutrients to all parts of the body.	yes	yes

Enlightening Voices from the Other Side:

Dr. Ligget sharing knowledge about blood diseases

Spiritually, the blood plays a very important role because it has the function of taking memory from the heart seed atom. You have your soul contract in that heart seed atom, and at certain intervals, it releases into the blood stream the next phase of your plan or operation. And so, it gathers information and takes it back. As you know, it works in conjunction with the subconscious mind, in playing its critical role. There are other seed atoms which collect information and distribute the information as well, but the heart seed atom is the main and most important one. When you poison your blood, there is very little likelihood that you are going to be consciously aware of what the heart seed atom is releasing into the blood stream.

The blood has always been known to symbolize wisdom because of this function. It stores the information on the progress of the soul. And when Jesus performed the Last Supper, and he said, "Do this in remembrance of me," he really was talking about the advanced teachings that he had given that he wanted stored in the heart seed atom of his disciples. For Christians who reenact the Last Supper, it is to remind Christians that they are to apply the beautiful teachings that he gave—to apply this knowledge and wisdom in everyday life. The Buddha, Mohammed, Zoroaster and other avatars taught the same basic beautiful teachings, using other words, and they are all stored in the same place. It is just that in Christianity there is a sacrament of the Last Supper or Communion in which this is an outward sign or an invisible transaction that is taking place.

When we have problems with our blood, it really means that somewhere along the way that blood got tainted. The wisdom teachings got tainted, and they are not being purely expressed. So when we come back in this incarnation, and we bring with us the tendency to have something go wrong with the blood, that could be by selecting the parents who have the predisposition toward this. Normally, on the physical level, the blood gets purified by going through the liver. So we could also have a liver problem associated with the blood problems, and frequently they do go hand-in-hand, because that filtering, purifying mechanism of the liver is not working properly.

Many illnesses on earth do not always show up, so to speak, until later in life. It is true that children can have Leukemia at a very early age. But with blood diseases, usually, they do not show up immediately because people are given a chance to straighten out their thinking. And if they do not, this is the way their karma is paid. We do not always have to work off the karma that we agree to in our soul contract. It depends on how hard we work on ourselves before the onset is scheduled to occur.

When they get to this side of life, they no longer have that problem. But they do usually have the problem of getting their thoughts purified. And we work on them so that they get correct knowledge about spirituality. And when they do, naturally they become functioning people or spirits at a very much higher level.

Blood diseases are not nearly as common as some other diseases. I would say that they occur more with people who have really taken whatever wisdom or whatever spiritual teachings they have had in past lives and totally distorted them for self-gain and are now paying the price. Having a blood disease is a very debilitating kind of thing. If the blood does not do its job properly, if it is so clogged with toxins, and the liver is not clearing it up, then this is what is being sent through the arteries, through the veins, through the capillaries to all parts of the body. You are not sending pure, clean blood. You are sending polluted blood. And it is that pollution that we work with when they come to this side. It is the pollution consciousness, not the blood, for there is no blood in the etheric body.

We work a lot in groups because this seems to be a very helpful way to do it. What we do is work in small groups, very small groups, maybe only 3 or 4, or there may be 10, but no more. We regress these spirits to a former life when this pollution took place.

We let everyone in the group listen and observe, and they each take turns, maybe not all at one sitting. But they take turns. And we try to keep the group together so that the same people meet and develop a harmony, a comraderie so that they feel very comfortable and they begin to see the similarities in their thinking. This is what really helps to bring it all out. Each one is agreeable, of course, to having their privacy exposed. Normally, we would not just put them in a group and say, "This is what you are going to do." No, it has to be by consent and the desire to be helped. It is beautiful how it emerges. Many of them form very deep relationships as a part of this. Much is worked out and they feel and say, "I feel clean, I feel clean inside because I am no longer carrying that. I am free. I am lighter." They can see each other's growth. That is the beauty of it. The light becomes brighter, and they can observe this.

The blood is very, very important from a spiritual standpoint; so we have to watch how we poison it, how we corrupt it. I believe that Paracelsus explained to you that in his day and long after, they used to bleed a person because they really felt that it was the impurities in the blood that caused all the problems. They sometimes allowed people to bleed to death. Now, it is true that impurities in that blood will affect the organs. As the practice of medicine continued, the doctors were willing to try other techniques, and found that it is not the blood that needs to be purged.

Dr. Owen also wanted to talk about blood poisoning

This is a pleasure and a new experience for me, but I will try to do my best. I want to talk to you about blood poisoning. Now, I am aware that Dr. Blake spoke to you last night and he told you about the purity of the blood which we contaminate, which we poison with poisonous thinking—with the feelings that he described to you of hatred, envy, and really any poisonous feelings, and so a person suffers. We cannot have these feelings and not feel the negative effects of them. It just is not possible. When the person does not learn to clean up his or her act, so to speak, before leaving earth, they come over here with so much poison, not in the body, but in their attitude of mind.

If they have been to any kind of church, especially the fundamentalists, they have been taught that you either go to heaven or to hell. But somehow some people justify that others deserve the negative thoughts they have directed toward them. So despite their judgments of others, they think they are going to heaven when they pass over. They are very surprised when they get here and it is not a bright, sunny place with angels playing harps and where the streets are paved of gold. It is very disillusioning to them to have to face reality. They do not want to accept personal responsibility for having engaged in any kind of negative thinking. We have a very difficult job with them.

And it is the kind of work in which we find we have to stop occasionally and renew ourselves in order to work effectively with them. Although there is no time here in the Spirit World, in your earth time it is not a 24 hour 7 days a week experience for us. We do have the opportunity to take breaks and we encourage people on earth to take breaks. You come back with more strength and renewed vigor. And you can go at it again. We do burn out over here, too. When we feel we are not getting anywhere, we go back to our home realm or plane and refresh. Then we come back and we work more with these people to try to get them to see that you cannot survive on negativity. There is absolutely no way under the sun that it can be done.

We do give them some background, an orientation course, in a sense, to being in Spirit. We try to get them to the akashic records as quickly as we can to take a look at themselves. Of course, they have to reflect on the present life first. When they rationalize they have not done anything really wrong, that their thoughts have been justified, then we work with them more and we take them back again to review the akashic records. And this is the process.

As you have been told by other teachers, it is very helpful to work in a group. It seems to break through the malarkey more quickly. Some religious practices are very prejudiced against certain groups unfortunately. They might deny this but the truth of the matter is that they feel a lot of hatred toward people who are very,

very different from them. It is helpful many times when they reach a certain point of growth to bring spirits into the group for whom they have had such an antagonistic attitude. For instance, maybe a gay or a minority or one of a different faith, or whoever. We bring in spirits who are elevated but have that kind of background. We bring them into the group, and we are there to support them and we have discussions. It is through understanding that tolerance is gained, accepting that these are human beings just like themselves. They are spirit, a part of God, and this does help break down some of that prejudice and discrimination that they feel. They have to be willing and ready to want to change. We cannot force them. They might at some point, when they are really elevated, come back to a group and talk about it. *Look, I went through this and I learned that this was not true, and that was not true.* They help us. So this is how we work. These are people who primarily have literally poisoned their blood with their outrageous hatred of those who are different or who do not agree with them, or they are envious or jealous of.

I was attracted to working with this group of spirits because I had done the same thing in a previous life and when I came back, I did have much more tolerance than I had in the previous life, but I still had to work on that. So when I came to this side and grew out of such thinking and changed, then I felt that I could be of benefit because I know what it is like, and I know how miserable a person can be. They are not happy people, believe me. God has a foolproof system. You cannot be happy, you cannot know joy, you cannot know love when you have such negative thinking as a part of your everyday diet.

Dr. Rice on working with hemophiliacs

I have come to talk to you about hemophiliacs. This does not happen to too many people but it is related to a lack of control mentally. As you know, the blood represents wisdom. And when we allow our wisdom, our spiritual thinking, as in a past life, to be polluted, it is that pollution of our thinking that brings us back into this life (reincarnation) where there is a propensity for something lacking in wisdom. Symbolically, it is worked out this time by the inability of the blood to coagulate, a defect in the blood-clotting mechanism, and therefore, inability to stop the free flow of the blood. In the past life, these individuals polluted their thinking so that their wisdom did not run purely. I am speaking symbolically. This time it is running without control. These people live a life where they are constantly in fear of injuring themselves, of getting a cut or something to cause bleeding. Extra precautions must be taken in engaging in sports, surgery, dental care and even in everyday living. Frequent treatment for bleeding can take its toll physically and emotionally for the patient and the family. Bleeding is not always external. It can occur internally as a result of a blow to an area of the body or to undue stress to a joint. This is passed from mother to son.

So hemophilia has a combination of fear carried over from a past life, actually a fear of the teachings they had received in the past. They had allowed these teachings to become polluted. The truth was not there. It was way, way off. And there may have been some who indulged in witchcraft, and so now they are trying to allow the wisdom to flow, but it is overflowing.

I do believe that if people on earth who are suffering from hemophilia would truly go on a spiritual path, that this could be controlled to a great extent. When they come over here, they bring fear of bleeding and want to be protected. And we have to work to get them to understand that they are now whole and complete and cannot be hurt or harmed by anything to their body. We work with them to help them see what brought this about and how to correct their thinking. We encourage them to go to the various schools that are over here and to learn different things, and of course, we teach them also. Their guides and teachers work with them to help them in every way possible to understand how the soul wants to grow. Some tell us that they lived a very tense life because they could not relax. They were always on edge, but they certainly are curable over here. They learned that having gone through their earthly experience, they have worked off the karma related to their medical problem.

Dr. Morehouse on Sickle Cell Anemia

Sickle cell anemia is a very debilitating kind of thing. And it occurs, as you probably know, mainly with Blacks and those living in the Mediterranean area. It affects them because in a previous life they were very intolerant of Blacks and those living in the Mediterranean areas, and a few other areas of the world. But mainly it is associated with those of African origin. It is really balancing out the karma. That is what it is all about because these people who are afflicted were Whites. They did not like the dark skin, or they just thought these people were inferior. And so they had to come back to be the very race that they had put down. And that is what it is all about. To tell them this, I am not sure they would believe it. But there is a wonderful scale that balances out everything in life. There is absolutely no escaping.

I, myself, suffered from sickle cell anemia. I am a Black man, though, we really are simply souls on this side of life. But I was Black on earth and I resented being Black, and I certainly resented the fact that sickle cell anemia affects so many Black people. I thought why should we be saddled with a disease, almost like a stigma, when we were suffering enough from segregation, from discrimination, and from total inequality. Why have this on top of all that?

There were times when I was on earth that I was a very bitter man. I was determined, despite my illness, that I would get an education. And I did. I wanted to be a medical doctor to see if I could do some research and help my people, but I was not accepted in medical school because of my health. So I became a chemist, and I thought in that way, I could do medical research, and that probably would be better anyway. I did actually go through graduate school, and my doctoral thesis was on sickle cell anemia. But I did not live very long after receiving my doctorate.

I came to this side frustrated and angry because I could not accomplish what I really wanted to do. At first, I was pretty lethargic over here. It took me awhile to really accept that I had a perfect body and that I did not need to lay in a grave, and that is where I was. My people did not believe in cremation and I was in that grave and I just thought I was supposed to stay there. You know, we were all taught—I was a Southern Baptist—Gabriel comes and blows his horn and he will get you out of that grave, and he will take you to heaven. And I really believed that. I truly did. It took a lot of persuasion to get me to come out. My grandfather was the one who really helped me. He told me he had done the same thing and someone helped him get out of the grave. He said, "come on with me," and I did go with him and my grandmother. They really helped me to want to be more elevated. So with my guides, teachers, and grandparents, I got over my resentment when I understood that I had paid my dues for being so intolerant in a past life. I paid that part of it, but because I carried over my resentment of having the disease, I still have work to do. I felt that I could best work it out by elevating myself.

I have tried many times to come through to someone to tell my story but I was not very successful. I am very happy to have had this opportunity today, and I would be so glad to come back and to talk to someone who is working in the field. If a medical researcher were at all receptive, I would work night and day trying to impress him or her. I really would like to see help given. I realize that we need opportunities or tools through which to work off karma, but we could lessen the problem of those who are suffering. Goodness knows, people really need to understand about these problems.

Comments by the Master Teacher:

If we had more mediumistic scientists working on various problems, they certainly would make greater progress. There are so many knowledgeable spirits on this side who would really give their right arm, as your earthly expression goes, to help. They truly would totally dedicate themselves. They try so hard now but their impressions are not always received. ◆

12.

THE BRAIN AND NERVOUS SYSTEM

Function of the Brain and Nervous System

The brain and nervous system form an intricate network of electrical signals that are responsible for coordinating muscles, the senses, speech, memories, thought and emotion. The nerves represent the mind or highest form of intelligence that is running through the flesh. As the nerves control the body, then it is the mind that is working at its very highest form.

Diseases, Karma, and Type of Thoughts
Affecting the Brain and Nervous System

We have to keep a harmonious vibration in our body. If there is harmony, the nerves will react immediately in a positive way. If there is a struggle or a strain, then the nerves are going to respond in a negative way.

Thought is always creative and once thought is sent out, we cannot change it, nor can we escape from its effects on our life. The nerves are especially responsive to thought, therefore, thoughts of peace, thoughts of poise, and thoughts of power will keep the nerves working properly. As applied to the nerves, power represents the ability to take care of the entire body. We have to give the nervous system the power to do its job.

The nerves control the whole body, so when we are very nervous, always uptight, just about fit to be tied, we begin to get shoulder and neck problems, or feel a tightness in our stomach. Also, depression and discouragement and indecision must be neutralized. People who are very, very depressed have problems with their nerves. The same thing applies if they are very discouraged. They find it very difficult to make a decision about anything, so naturally, they are going to have a lot of trouble. This then manifests in the way the life force expresses. The nerves are the life force flowing freely through every atom, every cell, and every organ of the body. We have to get rid of worry, for it is one of the main things that will cause nerve problems. We must have faith in the God power that is within us. Every person has that same God power, but do they use it?

Dwelling on the past is detrimental to nerve health
The important thing is to erase the thoughts of the past that could rob us of happiness. To hold on to the past causes great tightness of the nerves, therefore, we must not dwell on the past. Individuals with nerve problems should learn to live in the present and have no fear of the future. Let the past go. Live in the present. Have no fear of the future. That will make for healthy nerves.

Especially when people get older, they tend to live in the past. They are thinking about this thing that happened, or that thing that happened, and much of it may not be all that great. We cannot change the past, so do not dwell on what we did or did not do, what we should have or could have done, or what was done to us. We should view what happened as a level of consciousness we were on at that particular time. We are now on a different level and can view what happened from a different perspective, so let the past go. Put it all to rest and move on in consciousness.

Some nerve conditions stem from past life negative expression
The nerves in the body react to the soul qualities. Most nerve problems are generally brought on in the present life rather than being associated with a past life. However, if we were not expressing the soul qualities in the right way in a past life, we could come back and have problems with our nerves. In other words, the karma that we bring into this life affects the nerves if it is very negative. Let us say a person in a past life seemed to have a very difficult life, never expressed themselves on a positive note, always looked for bad things to happen, and those bad things did happen. That person passes on, comes back to earth and brings those prob-

lems with him/her in order to work out that karma, but instead of getting rid of the negativity, creates more karma by living the same way in this life.

A person who was very uptight, or who did not stand up for principle, did not stand up for himself/herself or for what was right, could come back and suffer from sciatica or other spinal problems. Or, as one spirit described, he was a very muscular man who was constantly on the go, constantly moving and doing heavy work. As the boss, he expected the same performance from those under him, and they could not keep up with him. And so he came back to pay for his unrealistic expectations and total lack of empathy for his employees by choosing a delicate woman's body and parents who would provide the predisposition to sciatica. She was unable to lift anything heavy—the total opposite of the former life. The pain of sciatica or other nerve problems acts as a reminder to work on the problem we had in a past life. And even though it may be karmic, that does not mean that we have to live in constant pain. We can do as much as we can to get over that in this life by seeking treatment, changing our attitude, and not dwelling on our condition.

Nerves can affect everything. The nerves in our ears can be affected causing Tinnitus, a ringing in the ear. If we were insensitive in a past life, we could have a lot of problems in this life. Sometimes we come to families for things they can supply for us although we did not have actual karma with them. In other words, a family can supply things for a person's soul growth although they did not actually have a karmic reason to be there with them.

Removing nervous tension by projecting peace
If a person with a lot of nerve problems can think peace, and send out words of peace, and speak that right to the nervous system, "Thank you, God, I am at peace," that will remove tension which produces pain. It will also get rid of irritations to the nervous system. That is the point that we are trying to make with all of these things, that our thought brings about most of our physical problems. Of course, some injuries do cause restrictions of the nerves. If we

have an injury, sometimes the nerve will be damaged. Then we do the very best we can by going to a physician, or by going to a chiropractor, or by doing something to try to help the situation. Also, we do not dwell on the condition.

Let us say that one has a problem and he/she does not know the outcome of that problem—we all go through that at times—if the anxiety continues over a period of time, then the muscles will twitch. Sometimes this occurs around the mouth. Or, one can get an upset stomach, or the nerves all tighten up. That can produce a tension headache, tightness of the neck, and even shortness of breath. This is because the nerves are not functioning properly. So we need to control our thoughts to arrive at a state of calmness so these problems will ease up or cease. People do not realize how much thoughts can produce all kinds of diseases and problems in the human body. People will not believe it because it means accepting personal responsibility and they do not want to accept that and make changes.

Spina Bifida and Hydrocephalus are karmic tools

Spina bifida (open spine) is definitely a karmic condition. As the spine helps to keep us upright, evidently a person suffering from spina bifida had a weak spine in a past life. In other words, they would not stand up for their own beliefs or principles, or had no beliefs. They reincarnated with a spinal problem which they may have chosen in order to be reminded to stand up for principle. It should be mentioned that everything that is karmic is not necessarily consciously chosen to endure when we make our soul contract. It may just happen to us to provide a learning experience rather than a punishment for the past weakness.

Hydrocephalus, water on the brain, is karmic, and is frequently associated with spina bifida. In a past life, the intellect was violated by using it for immoral purposes, thinking of physical things, passion, and sex. It is anticipated this condition will be seen more frequently when the present generation reincarnates due to their lack of morals.

Scoliosis may be related to parental karma

In cases of scoliosis, a progressive lateral curvature of the spine, the soul chose its parents. There may have been developmental problems during the period in the womb or during labor or actual childbirth. Frequently, it is more a karmic situation for the parents than for the child. With degenerative lumbar scoliosis seen in elderly persons, that is something going on in this life. It could be due to an injury, or tumors in the vertebrae or adjacent ribs, or bone dysplasia.

Parkinson's and Huntington's may be triggered in the present life

While the propensity for Parkinson's Disease is inherited, and may be karmic from a past life, it is usually brought on by what we have done in this life. There is an enormous rigidity and tremor characteristically involving the hands which mirrors a very rigid person, one not going to give an inch. Medically, strides are being made to find a cure. In fact, many diseases will eventually be cured. As they are brought under control, new diseases will appear on the horizon for people to work off their karma. As we evolve spiritually, the replacement diseases will be less severe. If suitable parents are not available to provide the necessary propensity to develop a particular disorder, a substitute will be used. It will be a matter of balancing the scales so that the degree of karma is satisfied. For example, in the case of someone who might have been very mean, that person may not necessarily come back and have a disorder of the brain, but something entirely different.

With Huntington's disease, a progressive degenerative disease of the nervous system, it can be karmic to an extent because the person has come to a family that provided the opportunity to develop it. But it is mainly karmic because a person is not living the way he/she should be living at this time. In fact, when there is a degenerative condition with the nervous system, it is generally triggered by present conditions—putting the desire for money and the material things ahead of any kind of emphasis on spirituality. Having a predisposition for a disease does not mean that we actually have to develop it.

The degree of physical disability is commensurate with karma to be erased

Cerebral palsy is caused by a permanent brain injury that occurs before, during, or shortly after birth. It is characterized by a lack of muscle control and body movement. While it is not a progressive disease of the brain, the effects of cerebral palsy may change gradually over the years. Everyone with cerebral palsy has problems with body movement and posture, although the degree of physical disability varies. Some people have only a slight limp or an uncoordinated walk. Others have little or no control over their arms and legs or other parts of their body, such as their mouths and tongues. Brain injury related to prematurity often is involved. Whatever the cause, the person chose the mother who could provide something for his/her soul's growth. Perhaps the mother could not have a normal delivery. The degree of physical disability would be commensurate with the degree of karma to be erased.

Death occurs in infancy for babies affected by Zellweger Syndrome or Menkes Syndrome. Some children need to come just to go through the birth experience, or maybe to stay for a very short time and then go to Spirit. If they only come to have the birth experience, then it is the parent's karma. In that case, the soul of the baby only needs to come for that particular thing.

Tumors of the brain are indicators of incorrect thinking in a past life

Tumors of the brain are growths. That indicates that something went on in a past life which the individual did not solve, and it just grew and grew and grew and was brought over into this life. With all conditions, the part of the body that is affected puts a little more description on what the person did not take care of. Anything going on in the brain relates to an abuse—not thinking correctly. These people let their thoughts and desires overpower them. They came back into this life to have something like a tumor on the brain so they would go through a period when they could not think properly or clearly.

Head injuries may give opportunity to work off karma

People who have suffered severe head injuries, and are unable to function on earth as a consequence, have an opportunity to work off karma while in that condition. When they pass over it is a matter of working with them to convince them that the injury was only to the physical brain. The brain was no longer able to serve as a tuning fork for the mind to function. They worked off karma with no memory of that non-functioning time going into the soul memory. So those years are somewhat lost. They go to Spirit confused, but they learn to function well by drawing from memory prior to the accident. They are encouraged to go to school and spend time with their guides and teachers who will help them.

Untying mental knots

Also included here is the headache which is a congestion in the head. It is caused by confusion, worry and tense thoughts. Most people who have bad headaches worry about all kinds of trifles and the conditions that surround them and they do not know what to do about them. Sometimes there is nothing that we can do about them except put them all in God's hands.

Everything that is back of nearly every disorder is what can be called a mental knot. Those mental knots have to be untied, especially with headaches. A migraine headache is a more severe form, and people really do get sick. But generally it is because of all the strain and the tension that they have allowed themselves to experience. It can also be from a suppressed emotion, especially, if it centers around affection. For example, a man and wife who are having problems and the emotions are suppressed can experience migraines very easily. Or, it can occur when parents and children have their disagreements or upsets. They cannot make the other person do what they want them to do, or what they think they should do; so they are suppressing that, and are reacting. They are trying to control someone and we cannot control anyone. They get so tensed up when they cannot control the other person that it manifests as a headache. Headaches seem to recur on a regular basis because the person has not learned to get rid of the desire to control. Sinus and other conditions cause headaches, but here we are talking about the very bad headaches that stem from stress, strain, tension and suppressed emotion. The stress may be karmic. That is, the situations might be karmic. We may have several different situations come up in our life because of things we did in our past life. The karma is to see if we can work through them. If we cannot handle the situations correctly, we can get migraine headaches. There is not much relief for migraines. We have to learn how to handle these different things in life without allowing ourselves to become all stressed out.

A lesson from the Good Book.
"Whatsoever things are true,
Whatsoever things are honorable,
Whatsoever things are just,
Whatsoever things are pure,
Whatsoever things are lovely,
Whatsoever things are of good report;
If there be any virtue, and
If there be any praise,
Think on these things. . .(Phil. 4:8)
And the God of peace shall be with you."(Phil. 4:9)

If we would sit down every day and try to think on those things, we would find that much of our stress and many of our concerns would be gone. If we would really concentrate on the good things, we would find that we would be freed from a lot of pain and disease because we would not be attracting it to us.

Mankind must look at something besides the physical. They have to look at the inner self. Go back to God and a belief in a supernatural power—something higher than the ego or personality. Even people who do not believe in God can be spiritual in the sense that they are very kind and ethical. The important thing is we must believe in goodness.

Chart of Brain and Nerve Disorders

There are a number of diseases which affect the brain and nervous system which have a genetic component and/or karmic relationship, as shown in the following chart.

Note: In the following chart are listed diseases which can be inherited, but some are only karmic "to a point." In other words, in keeping with our soul contract, we may have specifically and intentionally chosen a family who could provide the gene to develop a particular "karmic" disease or condition. This is our way of balancing our karma. The predisposition also existed in that family for one of the "karmic to a point" diseases, and we simply picked up that gene as well. Depending on how we live our life prior to the proposed onset of a disorder, we may not develop a "karmic" or a "karmic to a point" disease at all, having already worked off our karma in another way. Or, the disease may be mild and very responsive to treatment.

Disease	Description	Genetic	Karmic
Adrenoleuk-odystrophy	The fatty covering (myelin sheath) on nerve fibers in the brain is lost, the adrenal gland degenerates, leading to progressive neurological disability and death.	yes	yes
Alzheimer's Disease	Progressive inability to remember facts and events, and later, to recognize family and friends. (See chapter under Part III for details on why it develops and how it is treated.)	yes	yes
Amyotrophic Lateral Sclerosis	Characterized by progressive degeneration of motor neuron cells in the spinal cord and brain, which ultimately results in paralysis and death. Known as Lou Gehrig disease.	yes	Karmic to a point
Angelman Syndrome	Characterized by mental retardation, abnormal gait, speech impairment, seizures, and inappropriate happy demeanor that includes frequent laughing, smiling, and excitability. Known as "happy puppet" syndrome.	yes	Karmic to a point
Autism	A devastating neurological disorder with a strong genetic component. Impairs ability to interact with other people. (See chapter under Part III for case histories)	yes	yes

Disease	Description	Genetic	Karmic
Ataxia Telangiectasia	A-T usually appears in second year of life as lack of balance and slurred speech. Progressive, leading to cerebellar degeneration, immuno-deficiency, radiosensitivity, and predisposition to cancer.	yes	yes
Brain Tumors	Can develop only in the brain or can originate elsewhere in body but spread through the bloodstream to involve the brain secondarily.	no	yes
Charcot-Marie-Tooth Syndrome	Most common inherited peripheral neuropathy in the world, characterized by a slowly progressive degeneration of the muscles in the foot, lower leg, hand, and forearm and a mild loss of sensation in the limbs, fingers, and toes.	yes	Karmic to a point
Cerebral Palsy	A group of motor problems and physical disorders that result from a brain injury or abnormal brain development that may occur during fetal growth, at the time of birth, or within the first 2 or 3 years of a child's life. Although permanent, the brain abnormality does not get worse over time.	no	Karmic to a point
Cockayne Syndrome	Mainly inherited disease of children. Sensitive to sunlight, short stature and appearance of premature aging.	yes	yes

Disease	Description	Genetic	Karmic
Congenital Brain Defects	A group of disorders of brain development beginning shortly after conception and continuing throughout the growth of a fetus.	Yes and other causes	yes
Epilepsy	Disorder is characterized by recurring seizures resulting from abnormal cell firing in the brain.	yes	yes
Essential Tremor	Tremor or uncontrollable shaking mainly affecting hands and head.	yes	Karmic to a point
Familial Mediterranean Fever	Characterized by recurrent episodes of fever and peritonitis (inflammation of the abdominal membrane). Most commonly occurs in non-Ashkenazi Jewish, Armenian, Arab, and Turkish background.	yes	Karmic to a point
Fragile X Syndrome	The most common form of inherited mental retardation	yes	yes
Friedreich's Ataxia	Characterized by the progressive loss of voluntary muscular coordination (ataxia) and heart enlargement. Generally diagnosed in childhood.	yes	yes

Disease	Description	Genetic	Karmic
Gaucher Disease	The body is not able to properly produce the enzyme needed to break down a particular kind of fat. It then accumulates, mostly in the liver, spleen, and bone marrow. Can result in pain, fatigue, jaundice, bone damage, anemia, and even death. Common in the descendants of Jewish people from Eastern Europe (Ashkenazi). Other ethnic groups may be affected.	yes	yes
Headache	Congestion in the head	no	no
Head Trauma	Severe head traumas in which patients have lost much of their reasoning ability, and they do not recognize people and are just vegetating.	no	Some times
Huntington's Disease	Degenerative neurological disease which begins with occasional jerks or spasms due to brain cell deterioration and ultimately leads to dementia. Onset between 35 and 40.	yes	Karmic to a point
Hydrocephalus	Inability of the cerebro-spinal fluid to circulate. Water on the brain. Most babies born with spina bifida have it.	Cannot always be determined	yes

Disease	Description	Genetic	Karmic
Maple Syrup Urine Disease	The underlying defect disrupts the metabolism of certain amino acids which accumulate in the urine to give the distinctive smell of maple syrup. If untreated leads to progressive neurodegeneration and death within the first months of life. Mennonite community of Lancaster County, Pennsylvania is particularly afflicted by MSUD.	yes	yes
Menkes Syndrome	An inborn error of the metabolism that markedly decreases the cell's ability to absorb copper. Death in infancy.	yes	yes
Multiple Sclerosis	Degenerative disease which attacks the brain, spinal cord and nerves.	yes	yes
Myotonic Dystrophy	Inherited disorder in which muscles contract but have decreasing power to relax. Muscles become weak and waste away.	yes	Karmic to a point
Narcolepsy	Sleep disorder. Affected individuals are extremely drowsy during the daytime and may fall into a deep sleep at any time. After a short nap, the patient may feel refreshed, but it is only a short period of time before drowsiness returns.	Sometimes	Karmic to a point if inherited, otherwise reacting to this life.

Disease	Description	Genetic	Karmic
Neurofibromato-sis	Rare inherited disorder characterized by the development of benign tumors on both auditory nerves (acoustic neuromas). Also characterized by the development of malignant central nervous system tumors as well.	yes	yes
Niemann-Pick Disease	Brain and nervous system impairment. Affects children.	yes	yes
Parkinson Disease	A neurodegenerative disease that manifests as a tremor, muscular stiffness and difficulty with balance and walking. Called shaking palsy.	yes	Karmic to a point
Phenylketonuria	(PKU) is an inherited error of metabolism caused by a deficiency in the enzyme phenylalanine hydroxylase. Loss of this enzyme results in mental retardation, organ damage, unusual posture and can, in cases of maternal PKU, severely compromise pregnancy.	yes	yes
Prader-Willi Syndrome	Inherited disorder characterized by mental retardation, decreased muscle tone, short stature, emotional lability and an insatiable appetite which can lead to life-threatening obesity.	yes	Karmic to a point

Disease	Description	Genetic	Karmic
Refsum Disease	Rare Disorder of lipid metabolism. May include a degenerative nerve disease, failure of muscle coordination, vision disorder and bone and skin changes.	yes	yes
Rett Syndrome	A progressive neurodevelopmental disorder mainly affecting females. Severe mental retardation, autistic-like behavior and seizures.	yes	yes
Sciatica	Characterized by a bulging or herniated disk pressing on the sciatic nerve.	yes	yes
Sensorineural Deafness	Hearing impairment. Sometimes due to loud noises as working in a factory or boom boxes playing loud music. Can also be a karmic condition.	yes	Sometimes
Scoliosis	A progressive lateral curvature of the spine occurring either in the thoracic region or in the lumbar spine. Onset may occur during infancy, between 4 and 9, or in adolescence.	yes	yes
Spina Bifida	Baby is born with opening in the spine allowing the spinal cord to protrude. Degree of paralysis depends on where opening is on baby's back.	Uncertain	yes

Disease	Description	Genetic	Karmic
Spinal Muscular Atrophy	Death of spinal motor neurons and subsequent muscle paralysis. Infantile onset form causes early death from respiratory failure. Rare. If begins in adulthoodl, it is usually milder in form and due to what is going on in life at that particular time which may cause changes in spine.	yes	Definitely if occurs in child-hood
Spinocerebellar Ataxia	Degeneration of spinal cord and a "wasting away" of cerebellum resulting in loss of muscle coordination.	yes	Karmic to a point
Stroke	Sudden neurological disorder due to interruption of the blood supply to part of the brain.	yes	Karmic to a point
Tay-Sachs Disease	A heritable metabolic disorder commonly associated with Ashkenazi Jews, French Canadians of Southeastern Quebec, Cajuns of Southwest Louisiana, and other places in world. Varies from infantile and juvenile forms that exhibit paralysis, dementia, blindness and early death to a chronic adult form that exhibits neuron dysfunction and psychosis.	yes	yes
Tinnitus	Sensation of sound in the ear when there is no sound. May take the form of ringing, buzzing, whistling, or hissing and may be intermittent or continuous.	yes	Karmic to a point

Disease	Description	Genetic	Karmic
Tuberous Sclerosis	Characterized by benign, tumor-like nodules of the brain and/or retinas, skin lesions, seizures and/or mental retardation. Patients may experience a few or all of the symptoms with varying degrees of severity.	yes	Karmic to a point
Von Hippel - Lindau Syndrome	An inherited multi-system disorder characterized by abnormal growth of blood vessels. Growths may develop in the retina, certain areas of the brain, the spinal cord, the adrenal glands and other parts of the body.	yes	yes
Williams Syndrome	Characterized by physical and development problems. Their remarkable musical and verbal abilities, and their tendency to be very sociable, has lead to the suggestion that children with the syndrome were an inspiration for folktales and legends. IQs are usually low.	yes	yes
Wilson's Disease	Copper accumulation and toxicity of the liver and brain. Liver disease is the most common symptom in children; neurological disease is most common in young adults.	yes	yes
Zellweger Syndrome	Affects infants. Enlarged liver, high levels of iron and copper in the blood and vision disturbances. Usually results in death.	yes	yes

Enlightening Voices from the Other Side

Dr. Nelson on working with those who had brain problems
I was a brain specialist when I was on earth. Now, we know that the physical brain is what some call a tuning fork for the mind. Everything that we think and do is recorded in the heart seed atom, and there is, of course, another seed atom. The subconscious mind has one; and there are others. But let's concentrate on the heart seed atom because that is the main one. The others may be considered as kind of backups.

The brain represents our thought process, so when something of a karmic nature affects the brain, it usually has to do with thinking of a degenerative nature in a past life. It could be due to manifesting thoughts of debased sexual acts, it could be meanness, feeling superior or arrogant, or being a know-it-all, etc. It has to do with something in the thought process that has not been pure. A tumor on the brain is an abnormal growth, so you know that things are not pure. If they are not pure in this life or in a past life, it becomes a karmic situation. It is karmic in either sense because it is a payment. You can make karma for yourself whether it is here or hereafter. You may not pay for it in one lifetime. It may be carried over and worked out in another lifetime. We are constantly making karma for ourselves by our thinking or acting. Sometimes it is good, sometimes not so good. As we sow, so shall we reap.

When I got to this side of life, I understood better the various problems with the brain. I even had a patient on earth whose brain was born on the outside, and of course, that infant could not live very long. This was extremely difficult for the parents. It certainly was a karmic thing. I did not have the knowledge to explain this to them. There are other conditions that can take place in the brain and cause problems, even an accident or something of that sort can cause great loss of functioning. Usually when something like this happens, it is karmic.

When they come to this side of life, I have worked with those who have had problems with the brain. I do other things as well.

Art was my hobby on earth; so I teach some classes in art over here. Part of my work is to help people who need to work through what has happened to them. Perhaps they have died as a result of a tumor. So, as soon as we can, we try to convince them that they no longer have anything wrong. We teach that they are now in the etheric body which is perfect and that their tumor and the pain were a part of the physical body which is rapidly deteriorating and to let it go. I talk to them about what has happened and together we do view the akashic records as soon as it is deemed wise. And depending on the person, they move pretty rapidly.

We do try very hard to get them into spiritual awareness classes so they can learn about this side. When we say classes, it is not always a formal class as such. It may be just introducing or assigning them to someone who can work with them on an individualized basis. Those who have been on a spiritual path on earth can help these individuals, and also serve as a guide or teacher with some aspects of their orientation.

And so I just wanted to leave that with you. We do not require or have anything connected with brain surgery over here. The surgery that we perform over here is getting some of those negative, limited ideas out of their heads, and to replace them with the pure spirituality that we teach and demonstrate and observe on this side of life.

M.B.

In one of my lives I was a man. I was very muscular, constantly on the go, constantly moving and doing heavy work. As the boss, I expected the same performance from the people who worked under me, and some of them really could not keep up with me. This life I paid for it by suffering excruciating sciatica and not being able to lift anything heavy or do hard physical work. It appeared to be cyclic, flaring up at times when I did not stand up for principle. Chiropractic did help, and I know that we should take advantage of the treatment that is available to us. We can get relief even though the condition may be karmic. Coming to this side, it was hard to believe at first that I no longer had back and leg pain, but it was wonderful. And my karma was paid.

Dr. Greenberg on his work with Spina Bifida

This is certainly a pleasure and a surprise for me to be able to come and talk to someone about the work that I am doing. I work with children and the older ones who come over with spina bifida. That is my chosen field. My name is Dr. Greenberg. My name is not important but the work that I do I feel is very important and could bring a great deal of comfort to the parents who have borne children who have this condition.

I am aware that your Master Joseph very briefly explained to you that this is a condition that affects the spine. And it is a very serious condition on earth. It goes back to a former incarnation in which the people were very, very wishy washy and they showed no spine at all in standing up for principle. They got into personality and whatever pleased a particular personality on earth, and then they went in that direction. So if there was some real stand or position to be taken about something, they were easily swayed by the personality of someone that they either liked or felt was important. And that is not the way to do it. We all have to have some really strong beliefs. There has to be character. And if we cannot express that character and are totally wishy washy, then we live a life that is not very satisfactory to the soul at all.

When they come to this side and do a review of the akashic records, they see where they have just allowed their learning opportunities to go by the wayside because they were not strong enough to speak up and say what was right. So these people choose to come back in a state which is symbolically spineless. It is really punishment. Now, they could have chosen to do it differently because we are never without choice. They could have chosen to make a soul plan to come back with a soul commitment where they would be in a position to have to make strong decisions. They could have gone that route, or they could take the opportunity for self-correction. It is not a punishment from God, but a result of their own doing.

And in many cases of spina bifida, in a former life these people have not really had strong spiritual convictions because the spine does keep us upright. It is very important. So much activity goes on in that spinal column, with impulses being sent from the brain all the way down. When this is not operating correctly, as in spina bifida, then they do not have the control at all. They are without control. They were not taking control in the previous incarnation, and in this one that has been taken away from them completely. They are being punished, in a sense, but this is what they deserve. And we are truly taught by our actions and reactions. So the soul is here to grow one way or the other. Finally, we learn through bitter experiences—I believe more often than through good ones. But we have to learn.

I do enjoy working with these individuals that come over because we do have a perfect etheric body, and it is a matter of regressing them to that former life to see what they did, and we do review the akashic records. We are able to get through this and they understand, " O. K., now I have paid the price for being that way." And hopefully, they will be stronger in the future and they will attract guides and teachers who are also more elevated to work with them, if they were not elevated enough before. That all depends. Many times we continue with the same guides and teachers in incarnation after incarnation because they are elevated sufficiently to guide us as we grow along.

If these individuals come over as children, we do provide a lot of wonderful activity and play for them so they can enjoy life again. And if they are older, there are musicals and plays and art, and all kinds of wonderful, wonderful entertainment so that they can get out. They can travel and go places where they never had an opportunity to go to in their last lifetime. So I do hope I have given you something of interest. If not, do call on me. This has been a lovely experience and I really enjoyed coming and talking to you about it. I never thought I would have this opportunity and I am so pleased.

Comments by the Master Teacher:
I think Dr. Greenberg did a beautiful job. There is really nothing much that I could possibly add; except to tell you that

usually these individuals do not have very long, long lives on earth because their karma is done. And when their karma is finished, then they pass over. So it really depends on the degree of their wishy washiness (I like that expression) that they have to work through. They learn a great deal and they learn so much about life. They have their spiritual studies over here. They have classes. I don't believe Dr. Greenberg mentioned that they also work with them frequently on an individual basis as well as in groups. With the spina bifida, they require more individual work than group work, but the group does help a great deal. We believe very much in group therapy over here.

Dr. Hennessey on head traumas

I have come in today because I wanted to talk to you a little bit about head traumas. We are going to try to bring Lawrence in to tell you about his experiences. First, I will briefly say that in our therapeutic efforts we go back to the time before the trauma occurred. I am talking about people who have had severe head traumas. They have lost much of their reasoning ability, and they do not recognize people and they really are just vegetating. These are usually karmic conditions, not accidents, but that is not always the case. It may be an accident which provides an opportunity to work off karma. They are as much karmic for the person as they are for the family. This is true.

Lawrence on recovering in Spirit from head trauma

Well, I am very pleased to be able to come in and to tell you a little bit of what happened to me on both sides. When I was on earth, I liked to amateur box and I sustained a very heavy blow which damaged my brain. I was no longer able to use the brain except in a very limited way. As you know, the mind uses the brain as a tuning fork, and when that is no longer available then you have limitation ever in keeping with the damage that was done. When I passed over in the later 40's, I believe, I had spent many years in an institutional setting because I was no longer able to take care of myself.

When I got to this side, I had no memory of those years that I had spent in the institution. I went back in time prior to the boxing match and it was a time that was very different on earth. When I tried to relate and just pick up where I left off, I looked at my mother and she was much, much older than when I had left her. I looked at my brothers and they were much, much older. It was a weird experience. I had wonderful helpers who explained to me what had happened and that I had chosen this thing to happen to me. It was not an accident. It was by plan and that it was my way to work off karma and to help my family with their karma. No one on earth understood why this had happened to me. The person that I was boxing with had a deep sense of guilt and he is now on this side of life, and he had to be worked with also, to explain to him why it took place and there was nothing to forgive him for.

I thought I was going to have a great future right up until the time the accident occurred. I have now gone on and am doing work with teenagers, helping them with athletics because I was a very athletic person. And so I think that is about all I can say. It did not take me a long time to get over and make an adjustment as long as I understood what was taking place. I had to be filled in with the new inventions and progress that were being made on earth. It is like going to sleep. It is almost like a Rip van Winkle experience. So I am happy that I could share this with you.

Comment by the Master Teacher:
It is not always the soul that chooses because the personality has free will. Lawrence chose boxing and, therefore, this happened. It was necessary for him to understand this and why it happened. It was not necessarily karmic that it happened, but the fact that it did happen worked off a lot of karma. If we choose to go a certain pathway, it does not necessarily mean that we have to go that pathway, because we all have several different pathways that we could go. Some people say, *I had to do this or that, it was forced on me to do that.* No, you still have freewill. We can even change our karmic direction if we have free will and use it. If we change our karmic direction and we do not work off our karma, we are going to carry it over to another lifetime. But on the other hand, if we elevate ourselves, we change the karmic direction because it is finished.

Everything is like a scale. All our good is on one side and our bad is on the other. If the good overpowers the bad, then much of the karma is worked out. We do not have to go through it. But if not paid, we are going to have to pay here, or in another life, or while in the Spirit World.

Dr. Nielsen on working with brain diseases

I was a brain specialist on earth. There are a number of diseases of the brain, as you know. The brain is difficult to treat. The tumor is really the tool used to work off the karma. And it really depends on how well or how progressed or elevated the soul is whether we can really do much for the person or not. I did believe very much in spiritual healing when I was on your earth and that was approximately 35 years ago.

I would encourage a person to see a Christian Science practitioner. They did not believe in medicine. They wanted to do the whole thing on their own, and so I would tell the patient, "Do not tell the practitioner you are seeking medical help." Those of my patients who listened to me and came to me for help, as well as getting help from the practitioner, did receive help if the karma was being worked off. If the karma was finished, they would respond. Now, I did not know this when I was on earth. I did not know that it was connected with karma. I knew nothing about that, but I can see in retrospect that is what was happening. I do know that the practitioner was able to reduce the pain and that worked very well. Had I gone to a Spiritualist, I probably would have gained a much greater understanding about reincarnation and karma and would have been able to follow things better. But I did believe in the possibility of healing. I know now that I had healing ability and that I was able, apparently, to be helpful to some extent.

We know that problems of the brain do relate to past lives and not using the mental faculties in the right way. They may have been totally materialistic. They may have thought about very debased kinds of things. They may have been unscrupulous in some ways, or turned down and discredited, or looked with disdain on spirituality. Something in the thought processes that were not pure brings about an abnormal growth. Healthy thinking produces healthy cells. It is unhealthy thinking that causes the cells to mutate and grow. So a person comes back into the life, their life on earth, with that propensity for the mutation to take place. It is all built in. However, it does not have to occur. None of the karmic situations that come in later life really have to occur if we can work off our karma in some other ways prior to the time that a karmic condition would normally take place.

I thought that this would give you a little understanding of how this really takes place. The parents of a child who has a brain tumor have to gain the understanding that this is karmic, and that the child only needed a short time on earth to work out certain karma. If parents would only understand they are vehicles for souls to come to earth to grow. If we had no karma, we would not need to come to earth. However, there will always be wonderful spirits who would elect to come back for the sole purpose of serving and helping to elevate those around them.

So we need vehicles, and there must be greater understanding. Yes, we realize there is an attachment to flesh and blood, especially to a child. It is not mechanical by any means. And yes, they are going to feel a great sense of loss when their child or a loved one at an older age is taken away. However, it is easier to go through a grieving process knowing that you were helping to do God's work by bringing that soul to earth. We are not talking about having promiscuous sex, and not caring about whether you bring a child into the world or not. We are talking about children that are planned for and that are wanted and loved. If only doctors and others who work with people could understand this added dimension of the true purpose on earth!

Dr. Barnes on working with those who had a stroke

I think things are just humming. And I am very, very pleased to be a part of this project, and that is truly what it is. Never before has anyone really asked me to talk about my work, at least not anyone from earth. We do get together over here. You may not be aware, but we have—it is an informal sort of thing—associations, very loose associations. And so people who work with different situations will come to meetings and we share our ideas, our work, and the progress we are making or not making. So it would be like a paralysis society. That is not exactly what we call it, but that would suffice to give you a general idea. And maybe somebody else works with heart problems and they call that the Lovebugs because they like to get little lovebugs right into the workings of those minds so they can make some changes. That is something.

It is very, very difficult for these people when they first come over, having had a stroke. We work with those who have had strokes and who have regained some awareness and are able to speak. We also work with those who are so paralyzed that they do not regain facility of speech. The ones who are able to talk come over in a perfect body but they are still feeling the mental effects of having been partially paralyzed from it. Some people have only suffered ministrokes or temporary spells of impaired brain function due to brief reduction in the blood flow to the brain. Some of them are so minor the person may only be slightly aware, or maybe not aware at all. We work with all of them, but the intensive work certainly is done with those cases that are more severe. So, if they have some paralysis but are able to speak and to get around, when they come over it is a matter of convincing them that their body is whole and perfect and there is absolutely no problem any longer.

They are in intensive care over here and what we do is work with the conditions that brought about the stroke in the first place. Usually, it does go back to living a life with a rather explosive temperment, not really being calm, not thinking things out, developing high blood pressure. The high blood pressure can then progress to a stroke. A lot of stress on the job can bring it about. But we do see people who on the surface appear to be calm, but yet inwardly just boiling over. They do not know how to let that steam out. So we work on a safety valve over here. We wish they could develop a safety valve while on earth. We do talk about these things that they can see in their own lives that really made them so upset.

We work a lot in groups where the members share and see that the others in the group have had similar problems. It is very comforting and it gives them the strength to see that they are not alone, and that they can work these things out. I think the propensity for not being very calm is there, and usually they are in families where there is a little more than normal emotional expression, shall we say.

If they were paralyzed at the time they crossed over, they can understand our thoughts very readily because this is our natural form of communication. They could understand people talking to them when on earth, but they were not always able to respond. We have to work with them for quite awhile to get them to understand that they can speak because they are in a perfect etheric body. We encourage them to send their thoughts to us first before they even try to speak. The first thing is to communicate by thought. We work very hard on that because some of them have been paralyzed for years and they do not realize that they can communicate. They still think they are totally and completely shut off from the world. We really have to explain to them that is not the case, and so it does take time. It does really take time. And sometimes we put them in a pool and use water therapy to get them to start using their limbs, and to know they do have control over them. That is very, very important.

I got into this work because I, myself, had a stroke. I do feel I was a very high-strung person in the previous life. That is the connection that I want to make here, that sometimes we can bring that propensity with us in order to be calmer individuals in our next life to work through it. I obviously did not work through while on earth this last time. I was in a family where there was emotional violence, not physical, but emotional. We screamed at each other and did such things. My parents got into real emotional fights. Instead of rising above that—I was given the opportunity to rise above it—I did not. I just had a life of being a very emotional person. And so I had to learn when I came over here to be very calm and that was not an easy thing for me to do. But I did settle down, go through my life bit by bit, and then go through the akashic records. I did see what was going on. That is why I thought I could be very helpful to other stroke patients, having experienced it. I know what it is like to be shut out and be absolutely helpless, not being able to do for yourself. If there are any question, please call on me. I am so grateful to have had the opportunity to come today.

Sarah on being paralyzed as a karmic condition

My name is Sarah and I have come to tell you a little bit about myself. I was a cripple when I was on earth. I had cerebral palsy and I was in very, very bad shape. I was very, very demanding. And I can see, from looking back from this side of life, that I made things worse by my attitude. I was very unhappy. I was absolutely miserable. I was angry at God. I was angry at my parents. I was angry at the world. And I became more and more helpless as I dwelt on my miserable condition. And the more helpless I became, the more I was resented by my family. It was a bad, bad situation. I prayed to die. I did not want to live another minute.

We did not have much money. We were just a very average family. My father was a fireman and was not home every day, and so care fell mostly to my mother. I think under other circumstances, she would have been a very different person. I tried her to the very, very limit of her patience and endurance, and she did resent taking care of me. It was a karmic situation for both of us, and neither of us did a very good job of it.

I believe that I still have a little karma left to work out because of the way I acted. Most of it is gone, but I do believe there is still a little residue because I could have been a much better patient and daughter.

I had really misused my body in a previous life. I did things that I should not have done. I abused my body in ways that I don't want to go into. Suffice it to say, that I came back to be a paralytic for very justifiable reasons. It was a miserable life on earth to be helpless. I did not care about people who were helpless in my former life. I did not care at all, and I never lent a helping hand to them. I had a grandmother then who needed help, and I totally ignored her pleas and cries. So that combined with what I did to my body led me to a pretty miserable life this time around. My grandmother has forgiven me and now I am working on forgiving myself. We don't escape from anything. It is amazing how the score is kept, and how divine justice unfailingly balances it all out eventually. Divine Justice is the only justice that truly prevails in an non-judgmental, perfectly balanced way.

I am trying now to work under doctors and teachers here to help others who come over who have been paralyzed. I try to get through to them not to be bitter, but to understand what is going on. I do hope that your book will reach people who work with those who are paralyzed to explain to them that it is a karmic condition, and to really welcome that opportunity to get out of that prison and to be free. When you do not do it right, you have to do it over, and the second time is more difficult.

R. Whitcomb on being healed of cerebral palsy

I have been invited to come here this morning to tell you what it is like to receive a healing on this side of life. I was a victim. No, I made myself a victim of cerebral palsy, a neurological disorder or functional handicap that mainly affects motor performance. I had chosen that as a way of working off karma. I had been an English schoolmistress in a private boarding school and I was very cruel to the children. I had no patience with them. I did not know how to make a living otherwise. I had been widowed and had no children of my own, and because I was well educated, I chose something that I could do.

I had no regard for the children. To me, they were just little monsters. If they never opened their mouth, except when I was giving them lessons, that was fine for me. With lessons, they had better open their mouths and they had better give me the correct answers. As far as any sympathy for them when they were lonely and missed their family, there was none. In that day and age there was such a coldness. There wasn't the warmth shown, especially by the fathers in those days (approximately 250 years ago). They were just very stern, cold people. They sent their kids off to let somebody discipline them, and discipline them we did! We never spared the rod. Many of them grew up to hate us. I had one come back and tell me how much he hated me, and by that time, I felt terrible about it. But I did really make life miserable for those children. I was not sensitive to their delicate feelings, and that is an understatement.

And so when I went to Spirit after that incarnation, I thought I had done the right thing because it just never occurred to me that this was not the way you treated children—every one in the school, from the schoolmaster on down. There was one teacher there who was kind and the kids loved her. She showed some warmth, especially when she was not being observed by elders. She tried not to be so stern.

When I came to Spirit, I had to face that, and it took me a long time. When the students I had came over, they were the most helpful to me because they told me how much they had suffered at my hands, and how much they had really wanted me to show them just a little bit of warmth and empathy and real caring for them. They just felt there was no regard or understanding, and there wasn't. They helped me most to really face what I had done to them and to the other children. And as I grew spiritually, I had more of a conscience about what I had done, and it really bothered me very much. So when the time came to reincarnate, I chose cerebral palsy so that I could be a child dependent on someone, as those children in boarding school were dependent upon me when I was a school teacher. And I chose to be really dependent to know what it was like, and I chose a family that really did not want to cope with me. They were wealthy, and so they sent me off to be institutionalized. There, I received minimal attention. The staff did what they had to do, but it was like being warehoused. There was a lack of warmth. In my school, we fed the children, we clothed them, gave them a place to sleep and an education. In the institution that I went to in my wheelchair, they fed me, clothed me, and housed me but there was very little stimulation.

And so when I came to this side of life, I had not been given any love, which is what I deserved. When I was told that I no longer needed to be in a wheelchair, that my etheric body was perfect, it took me some time to really accept that. It took me time to believe that when people were showing me love and kindness that they really meant it. It was so touching to me I did not think anybody would care enough about me to do this. And so it is painful when I even think about it. They did show me love, real love.

I have been on this side now, probably 50 or 60 years of your earth time. I am now trying to help cerebral palsy patients on earth. I try to impress them but it is so hard to get through. When they come to this side, I work with them. I explain to them that I, too, had this condition when on earth, and if they would like, when they are ready and their guides and teachers are ready for them to go through the Akashic records, that I would be willing to go with them, if they choose, and really see what they went through and how it compares with what I went through and to really give them support. And so this is what I have been doing. I have worked off my karma from that incarnation. And maybe someday I will come back and work on elevating myself more. I wanted to share this with you. It is an awful thing that we do to ourselves, and we think we can get by with what we do! And we can't! It is all recorded; we all have to face personal responsibility in the end. I hope others will take the essence of the story, though the details may not apply to them—they will take the principle and apply it while they are on earth, or they will help someone else apply it while they are on earth where it will do some good.

I did want to say that I did go back, and I am now in the etheric body of that English school teacher. I have gone back to that life. I am also trying to impress people about how to treat children. I am working from that body and lifetime, and it is interesting that this body has so much more light in it, and my facial features are so much softer than they were. ✦

13.

MUSCULOSKELETAL SYSTEM

Function of the Musculoskeletal System

The skeleton provides an anchor point against which muscles, attached via tendons, can exert force. There are a number of diseases that are caused by defects in genes important for the formation and function of muscles and connective tissues. (Connective tissue is a broad term that includes bones, cartilage and tendons.) Conditions other than genetic will also be included in this chapter.

Diseases and Karma Association with the Musculoskeletal System

In the history of mankind on earth, many atrocities have been recorded. There were hideous punishments meted out in the horror chambers of the Inquisition, and sadly the perpetration of such cruelties did not begin nor end with that period. As a result of having participated in unspeakable tortures, cruel individuals have returned to earth, taking on a deformed body to work off their karma. Murderers and very, very mean individuals may also pay restitution through living in a deformed body. When they go to Spirit, however, their etheric body will be perfectly formed.

An abuse of mental powers can react as physical disabilities, and physical abuses as mental weaknesses. Through suffering, the spirit comes to realize that the body is the pure temple of God and that this temple must be kept inviolate for the development of its own individual spirit.

Symbolically, the arms and the hands represent a person's ability to grasp ideas. When they do receive new ideas, they need to stand up for their convictions. A person may read a number of books and get ideas which they take inside themselves. They may really believe these new thoughts, but then they do not stand up for them. They may be easily swayed by the ideas of friends and others. When we can read something and have the inner knowing that it is right, and apply the ideas to ourselves, then the book will be beneficial. Many people are not looking for anything beyond what they have been taught in the past. People may go to one church all their life and yet not totally believe in that religion. Their parents taught them that was right and they feel they have to believe it.

What we are supposed to be grasping is truth, not just because it comes out of a book, or from what parents, teachers or ministers have told us. Those significant individuals in our life are filling us with their ways of thinking and we are not exercising the ability to think for ourselves. We have to be open and willing to stand up for our convictions regardless of what the other person down the street thinks.

If over a long period of time we are not standing up for what we believe, we may well have problems with our hands and our arms. Our hands and arms need to grasp all new things. That is one of the reasons why people get arthritis and are crippled in their hands. They have been too set in their ways. The spirit teachers believe that we can clear up many problems with our hands and our arms if only we will grasp spirituality. We are talking about the true spirituality that comes from within ourselves, not religious dogma. It is a matter of reaching the point where we truly realize that God is within, that we are spirit here and now. And how many people truly believe that? This cannot be just an intellectual knowing. We have to be able to feel it deep within our being. We can help ourselves in so many ways if we just think more spiritually.

We have to learn not only to reach out but reach for the right things. This also entails helping other people as well. If we are willing to help, if we are willing to give of ourselves, then we are not going to have the problems in our arms and hands. If we once get problems in this area, then we can change our thinking. Many people are reluctant to believe that thoughts are things. Understandably, while in the physical body, they cannot follow through as easily as one can in Spirit to see how thoughts manifest. It does take more faith, but if we just accept how spiritual laws operate, we could help ourselves so much more.

This does not apply to an amputation of an arm or hand. We are talking about conditions like arthritis or bursitis and that kind of thing. If it came to an amputation, then this probably would be related to karma carried over from a past life. For example, the loss of fingers through an accident or surgical amputation could be the result of unfair and or dishonest practices in a past life. The loss of a hand or hands could be as a result of committing wanton destruction as during a war. The loss of feet could result from walking in paths of wrong doing or leading others to do the same.

It is usually a karmic situation when a person is born with a missing arm, leg, finger, or toe. They probably were very mean or did something in a past life that they wanted to work out by handicapping themselves. They may have misused a hand by stealing or engaging in dishonest dealings. The limb chosen would indicate the degree to which they wanted to be handicapped. If they lost, as in an accident, or were born without an arm, that would be more of a handicap than a leg. A right arm would be more of a handicap than the absence of a left arm since we are a right arm society. Some people are born with extra fingers or toes. This is an inherited condition but is not karmic specifically. Also having abnormal length fingers or toes is congenital but not karmic. It is not the person's karma, rather it is a matter of coming back to a family because of situations that had to be experienced and the person simply inherited that anatomical feature. It is important to understand that when they make their transition to spirit, they will bring an etheric arm or leg with them if one is missing. The etheric body is whole and complete.

In the case of a midget, it is usually caused by something that is missing in their system. It could be an endocrine problem with the pituitary gland. They have chosen a family capable of producing that type body. It is not necessarily karmic. In other words, they may need to work out something with these parents, and they just happened to pick up the gene.

Usually dwarfism is a karmic condition for having abused one's soul to a great extent, like being mean, showing no love, being critical and arrogant and that type of thing. They have chosen to come back as a dwarf to call attention to themselves so they will receive ridicule and criticism in return. They will just get back what they dished out, so to speak. They have to learn to accept it in a spirit of humility.

Twins definitely have a need to work out karma through a close relationship. Conjoined twins have been together before. No doubt there was a lot of cruelty and meanness expressed toward each other in a former life. They come back physically joined so they cannot get away from each other. They have to face their past, literally head on in some cases.

Spinal problems can stem from not standing up for what was right in a past life. They can also be caused by using spiritual forces for purposes of black magic and the like.

The extremely rare disorder called fibrodysplasic ossificans progressiva is a genetic disease that causes muscle to be turned into bone. The condition was first reported in the 17th century by Patin, a French physician, who described a woman who "turned into wood". The wood he described was actually the formation of new bone. The afflicted have a genetic fault, which means that their bodies cannot switch off the mechanism that grows the skeleton in the womb. Any small injury to connective tissue (muscles, ligaments, and tendons) can result in the formation of hard bone around the damaged site. Children are born with a characteristic malformation of the big toes and begin to develop extra bone formation during early childhood. Eventually, a second skeleton begins to form that severely restricts mobility. It occurs about 1 or 2 times in a million people. With a karmic condition so severe, it indicates the individual has a very heavy debt to pay for wrongs of an extremely serious nature. It could relate to past life activities in a horror chamber, inflicting torture on others. It is unlikely the individual would have consciously chosen to work off his/her karma in this manner. Divine justice always demands the scales be balanced at some point in our many lives.

Congenital dislocation of the hip seen in children is karmic, however, it really is not caused by any specific thing in a past life. It is just a combination of things. Many people feel a sense of loss and grief when they lose a body part. Others are bothered by phantom limb syndrome, where they feel as if the amputated part is still in place. They may even feel pain in this limb that does not exist physically. This is because that limb still exists on the etheric body and they are feeling the sensation.

The feet and legs enable to walk upright. If we are led by that inner mind, then we are guided into truth and we are not going to have problems with our feet and our legs. On the other hand, if a person is truly materialistic and does not follow any kind of inner conscience, they probably can expect to have some problems with their feet and their legs. They could have diabetes or arthritis or some other uncomfortable condition.

A person has to stand upright to follow their own conscience. When the feet and legs hurt us quite a bit, it is actually worse than the arms and hands because we have to walk. We could have swollen ankles. Malformed feet comes from a past life. Here, we are talking about people with good legs and feet who develop a problem. We have to listen and abide by our conscience. We may hear people say, "Oh, she doesn't have a conscience." We all have a conscience. It is simply that we do not listen to it. It is not active. If one is anywhere on the spiritual pathway, he/she does have that inner feeling of what is right or wrong and does not have to be told the difference. Some say a child really does not have a conscience until he/she gets to be about 12 years of age. His/her sense of right and wrong is coming from what the parents teach him/her and at school. Or, learning the Ten Commandments in church will help to bring about the activation of the conscience. When the chakras (spiritual centers) are open, then one's conscience becomes much more active.

Certain diseases, such as osteoporosis, run in families. A person comes into a particular family in order to work out whatever karma they have brought with them, and the predisposition for developing osteoporosis is there. With that kind of disease, it would actually limit one's ability to work and walk in time. The bones become so porous that they start compacting and it shortens the person, crushes their organs and can cause death. We have a contract when we come to earth, and if a person is working toward fulfilling the soul's goal, the soul will want to stay and will do much to stall the progress of any disease. If, however, effort is not being made to fulfill the contract, the soul uses any avenues that it can when it is ready to leave the body. On the other hand, if the karma has been satisfied through right living and good deeds prior to the proposed onset of the disease, one will not develop the condition at all, even though the genes are present.

Following is a chart showing conditions affecting the musculoskeletal system.

Chart of Conditions of the Musculoskeletal System

Note: In the chart below are listed diseases which can be inherited, but some are only karmic "to a point." In other words, in keeping with our soul contract, we may have specifically and intentionally chosen a family who could provide the gene to develop a particular "karmic" disease or condition as our way of balancing our karma, but the predisposition also existed in that family for one of the "karmic to a point" diseases, and we simply picked up that gene as well. Depending on how we live our life prior to the proposed onset of a disorder, we may not develop a "karmic" or a "karmic to a point" disease at all, having already worked off our karma in another way. Or, the case may be mild and very responsive to treatment.

Disease	Description	Genetic	Karmic
Achondroplasia	Congenital dwarfism characterized by typical skeletal dysplasias, a large head, and neurological manifestations.	yes	yes
Amyotrophic Lateral Sclerosis	Characterized by progressive degeneration of motor neuron cells in the spinal cord and brain, which ultimately results in paralysis and death. Known as Lou Gehrig disease.	yes	Karmic to a point
Arachnodactyly	Abnormal length and slenderness of the fingers and toes.	yes	no
Charcot-Marie-Tooth Syndrome	Most common inherited peripheral neuropathy in the world, characterized by a slowly progressive degeneration of the muscles in the foot, lower leg, hand, and forearm and a mild loss of sensation in the limbs, fingers, and toes.	yes	Karmic to a point

Disease	Description	Genetic	Karmic
Cockayne Syndrome	Rare inherited disorder in which patient is sensitive to sunlight, has short stature, and has the appearance of premature aging. Progressive and apparent in infancy.	yes	yes
Diastrophic Dysplasia	A rare growth disorder in which patients are usually short, have club feet, and malformed hands and joints. Particularly prevalent in Finland.	yes	yes
Duchenne Muscular Dystrophy	Most common form of muscular dystrophy to present in children. Often takes their life in young adulthood.	yes	yes
Ellis-van Creveld	A rare genetic disorder characterized by short-limb dwarfism, polydactyly (additional fingers or toes), malformation of the bones of the wrist, dystrophy of the fingernails, partial hare-lip, cardiac malformation, and often prenatal eruption of the teeth. Often seen among the Old Order Amish community in Lancaster County, Pennsylvania.	yes	yes
Fibrodysplasia Ossificans Progressiva	Causes muscles to be turned into bones.	yes	yes

Disease	Description	Genetic	Karmic
Friedreich's Ataxia	A rare inherited disease characterized by the progressive loss of voluntary muscular coordination (ataxia) and heart enlargement. Generally diagnosed in childhood and affects both males and females.	yes	yes
Homocystinuria	Inherited disorder of the metabolism of the amino acid methionine. Characterized by nearsightedness, blood clots in veins and arteries, mental retardation may be seen, tall, thin build with long limbs spidery fingers, knock-knees and curved spine.	yes	yes
Marfan Syndrome	Inherited connective tissue disorder affecting many structures, including the skeleton, lungs, eyes, heart and blood vessels. Characterized by unusually long limbs, and is believed to have affected Abraham Lincoln.	yes	Karmic to a point
Missing Limbs		no	yes
Midget	Perfectly formed little individual.	yes	Karmic to a point
Morquio Disease	Progressive skeletal deformity leading to cervical cord compression.	yes	yes
Muscular Dystrophy	A group of congenital disorders characterized by progressive wasting of skeletal muscles.	yes	yes

Disease	Description	Genetic	Karmic
Myotonic Dystrophy	Inherited disorder in which muscles contract but have decreasing power to relax. Muscles become weak and waste away.	yes	Karmic to a point
Osteoporosis	Characterized by a reduction in bone mass. "Porous bones" become so weak and brittle that even mild stresses can cause a fracture, loss of height.	yes	Karmic to a point
Paget's Disease	Abnormal formation of bone tissue that results in weakened and deformed bones.	no	yes
Polydactyly	The presence of extra digits on the hand or foot.	yes	no
Sciatica	Due to herniated disk.	yes	yes
Scoliosis	Progressive lateral curvature of the spine.	no	yes
Werner Syndrome	Premature aging disease that begins in adolescence or early adulthood and results in the appearance of old age by 30-40 years of age. Characteristics include: short stature (common from childhood on), wrinkled skin, baldness, cataracts, muscular atrophy and a tendency to diabetes mellitus.	yes	yes

Enlightening Voices from the Other Side

Dr. Waltham on amputations and physical deformities

Spirits who have had amputations on their physical body now look down at their etheric body and see that they are whole. Amputations only affect the physical body on earth. The etheric body remains intact. That is why many amputees will say they feel sensation or pain in the area of the lost arm or leg although that limb has been physically removed. We explain to them this probably was a karmic thing, and when they are strong enough their spirit teacher will help them to understand why that happened.

As far as someone continuing to use crutches, we firmly discourage that. If you see that, or see a spirit insisting upon keeping his peg leg, we want them to get over those remnants of disability carried over from the earth plane. They cannot move on spiritually as long as they retain such close ties of that sort with the earth realm which is lower. So we encourage them to let the past go, that this is a new life and to get on the "road to recovery." It is an important step to take.

The same applies to one who was born without a limb. The physical body was imperfect but that was the form of the etheric body which is the pattern for the physical. Parents should not feel a sense of guilt in having a physically deformed child. Their function was to provide the incoming soul with a body that would enable that soul to work off a karmic debt. Usually, however, there is a karmic tie with the parents or caregiver which affords them the opportunity to erase karma as well.

Dr. Canaan on amputation of a limb due to cancer

I have actually come here to talk to you about cancer today. I know that others have come in, but I wanted to talk to you about cancer of the bone. This is not as common as some other types of cancer, but it is just as devastating. When a person has to have an amputation, it is very, very hard psychologically because they feel they are no longer whole. And the same thing is true with many women who lose a breast to cancer. It depends on the person. But when you have an amputation of a limb, it does interfere greatly with your ability to use your body. It limits to some extent what you can do, depending on which hand or arm or leg is removed.

A prostheses can be devised which works quite nicely, but it is a constant reminder that a person is not whole and complete. Now, again that depends entirely on how the person has adjusted. If one can say, *I am so grateful that God has inspired doctors and technicians to make and fit prostheses that enable me to carry on my life in a reasonably intact manner*, then that person has made a good adjustment and does very well. And when that person comes to this side, there may not be as much of an attachment to the idea that they are not perfect. That person can be told that they no longer need a prostheses, they are now in their etheric body which is whole and perfect. They are more accepting, much more accepting of the perfect body, and they say, *Hallelujah!! Thank you, God. I am grateful not to need this any longer, but I was grateful on earth to be able to have a good prostheses.*

Now those who deeply resented having had part of their body taken away, and having had to use an instrument do not make as good of an adjustment here as you would think. You might think that the person would be so happy to know that they have a perfect body now and don't need an artificial limb, that they would be glad to get rid of the prostheses. But instead, their resentment is so strong that they are holding on to what they really want to get rid of. They are holding on to both the idea of wearing a prostheses and their resentment about their loss. You cannot have these attachments to your patterns of thinking because they hold you in bondage. If only we could get across to people on earth that a prostheses is just a temporary crutch—that is all that it is—and that when they pass to this side of life, they will no longer need it. If we could get that across, that would really help people greatly. Of course, they first of all have to know that there is an afterlife. And then they need to be told they will be perfect when they come over here. So instead of resenting it, just use it and be grateful that you have something that will help you to be functional and mobile while on earth.

It is very hard, especially for someone who is right-handed, to lose a right hand or arm. That is a very difficult adjustment, but again, it depends on what is in their head. You do not want to make an attachment to an adversity in consciousness. You might think this is an easy thing for us to help somebody on this side when there is that attachment to their adversity, but it takes time. It is so ingrained in their head, especially if they have had the condition for a long time. They want to keep their prostheses and use it over here. We have an awful time trying to convince them that they do not need it. The truth of the matter is that the etheric leg, for example, is right there, but they have covered it over with the prostheses and they cannot see it. We ask them, individually and in a group setting, if they won't just take it off for a minute and take a look and see what is there. You see, thoughts are things. Things are created very easily on this side by thinking them into existence. This is very, very strong on this side, but they see what they want to see—their own creation of an artificial limb.

Now I may have gotten away a bit from talking about cancer, but many of these spirits that I work with especially have had cancer, as opposed to someone losing a limb through an accident or in the war, or someone having been born without a limb. Most of the people I deal with have had cancer of the bone. I was an oncologist and surgeon, and I saw what happened to these people emotionally—the fear that rose when a diagnosis of cancer was given to them. So over here I am dealing with disease by helping them to go back and relive and reevaluate the whole experience, as well as, coping with the lose of an actual limb.

It is true that amputees can fall into categories, depending on the circumstances of the amputation. There are those over here who work with a mixed background in their groups. We do what we feel will be most helpful to the individual and we direct them to that group. We cover everything. There are amputees from the war, and they usually feel more comfortable with other amputees who have served in a war. There is a greater sense of comraderie. There is always some one available to help in each unique situation.

When I am able to get the information, with the spirit's permission and through the help of their guides and teachers, we find out what transpired in a previous life to bring on the cancer. It helps to know how to proceed in the healing process.

I had leprosy in one of my past lives. That was a very long time ago. There is some leprosy still around but it is phasing out. Leprosy has been replaced by cancer as they are about the same in terms of severity of karma that needs to be worked off. Any disease is simply a tool by which a person can work off their karma. Leprosy is fading and cancer is coming more to the fore. But there are better treatments for cancer, and as people elevate themselves, there will be less need someday for something as serious as cancer. There will always be something because something is needed as a tool. Many people do not reincarnate for a very long time. They should wait for about 200 years to work through their current life before they consider coming back, and they want to come back with others with whom they have karmic connections. So it is a very complicated and intricate plan that has to be worked out by those who really want to grow. Not all have a real plan. There are many on this side of life who have not grown. It will be some time yet before some are ready to reincarnate; so there must be some serious illnesses to meet the karmic needs of those who did pretty awful things.

I am so pleased you are doing this kind of book. It will help people to think about what they are doing to themselves right now, what they have done to themselves in the past, and what they can expect in the future.

Dr. Nielsen on working with crippled bodies

I am going to talk about cripples who have come over to this side for having been injured in the war, having been in horrible accidents, having been born with a serious condition of spina bifida, or have other problems such as cerebral palsy, multiple sclerosis, muscular dystrophy. All of these diseases progress to the point where the patient is really paralyzed, but their brain is functioning and they can speak, That is the difference between the stroke people that Dr. Barnes (see chapter on the Brain and Nervous System, page 117) works with and those with whom I work.

So when these people come over, what they go through is very sad indeed. They are functioning mentally and have the intensive frustration of not being able to carry on a productive life. They have a difficult time accepting that they no longer have that crippled physical body. They think they are dreaming, and we have to work to wake them up. They are not dreaming. You see, so many people come over, the majority of the people who come over, 95% of them, come not believing there is an afterlife. Some think there is but do not think they have a body to function in. They think they will be resting for the rest of eternity, and all that kind of foolishness.

So we have a lot of educational work to do to get these people to recognize they are alive in a perfect body. I take them from all different categories that have been crippled. We work in groups.

We do talk about what has happened with someone who has come back from the war who is severely crippled, the anger that they feel. I do not think that many of them feel very patriotic at that point. They may go into the war very brave and courageous, but when they come out, having sustained so many disabilities, they are not very pleased, especially when they understand that a war was not really necessary—that perhaps it could have been controlled in a very different way. There are some, of course, who are glad they could protect their country, but they are not the majority.

I have worked with some German soldiers who fought in World War II and they are not happy campers that their leaders allowed Hitler to rise and to create such a huge, huge war involving so many. One of these soldiers, especially, has made a point of going to some of the Jews who were in the Holocaust. He tells them this was a sorry state of affairs that this was allowed to happen, and that he was a part of that. He has really tried to purge himself of having any part in it.

Now, there are so many conditions that we work with. Some lost the use of their arms but learned to work with their feet. They were able to do wonderful things with their feet. We have some that were born with missing arms as a result of Thalidomide, and they do wonderful things with their feet. They learn to drive and become foot artists. We bring them into this group because they now have arms, and they need to learn to work with those arms. We have different ones here. The group sessions are fascinating. I try not to work with more than 10 or 12 at a time. I do like that mixture rather than keeping them all with the same condition. I like to make a mixture so they can see that there are other people, not just soldiers, or not just cerebral palsy patients. There are others who are suffering and they have come to this state of affairs or conditions for other reasons.

One of my present groups is ready to go through the akashic records. We have to work on this life first, so we work in groups and we work individually. That is why I do not want to have my group too large. I do have helpers, and we do work individually and we work with their guides and teachers so they go through their past lives and everything that has happened to them. If they us some reason why. So many of these things happen for karmic reasons. Even for some of the soldiers, it is for karmic conditions. We have to work through their frustrations and anger, and to help them to realize that they are working off karma. So where it is necessary, we do get enough information to give them so they can accept that this is karma that they have had to work through. Some of them are pretty skeptical about this, but in time we are usually able to convince them, and to get them to move on. They are so grateful they are now able to use their limbs. We usually have a good level of success because of their gratitude that they are now in surroundings where they can function as a whole being. I would say the success rate is about 90% which is very, very high. It is much higher than working strictly with people who have been more average, or have had less disabling health problems.

I don't know how much else I can say except they are so anxious to let their people on earth know that they are perfect again, and it is really rather pathetic at times when we take them back for a visit on earth with their loved ones. More often than not, they cannot make themselves known to their loved ones. But they do await their loved ones with a sense of joy that they can show they are no longer in a wheelchair or bedridden.

I did forget to tell you how I got into this. Actually, I was not crippled on earth. I was an orthopedic doctor, and I had been crippled in the previous life. In going through the akashic records, I did find that out. At that time, I was given very little help because it was many, many, many years ago, actually, a couple of centuries ago in that past life, and they did not have the knowledge. There was little hope of being as independent as patients are today given the various mechanical devices and treatment available. You were at the mercy of someone taking care of you in my time. So, I came back wanting to help people and I did choose orthopedics. When I came to this side, I still wanted to continue to work with that group because I had the understanding more of the karmic conditions that may have brought about the paralysis of those individuals. I wanted to do this work with them and to help them grow through it.

I am so pleased that conditions are changing on earth and that there is a great deal more hope given, especially when there is a paralysis from a spinal cord injury. There is definite hope with stem cell research. We are hoping that your leaders will be open enough to really progress in that area. There is so much that can be done. As people on earth progress spiritually, they will have less need to be so severely paralyzed, and they can work off their karma in a shorter time, if that is the condition that is chosen to satisfy the karmic debt. Or, something else will crop up so people can work off their karma. It may get to a point where they will not come back to undo the particular conditions that they experienced in a past life, but will be doing something else. It does not really have to reverse a situation. It does not matter what kind of karmic condition they select. It could be something else entirely. It depends on the availability of a parent who can bring forth the propensity, and if that cannot be easily found, they will come back to someone who has the propensity for something else. So there will also be an opportunity to work off karma, but it may evolve to be worked off a little differently than by the pattern we are seeing at the present time.

Comments by the Master Teacher
Research is going on and will make a tremendous difference in the future. But as we have talked before, something else will crop up so people can work off their karma. For example, a person who might have been very mean may not necessarily come back and have a disorder of the brain. It could be something else entirely.

Joan, Queen of France—why she chose to be a cripple
This is Joan, Queen of France a long, long time ago, at least 500 years ago. I have been in Spirit all of that time. I have not been back to earth. You wanted to know a bit about why I came into this incarnation crippled. Well, that was because I had not lived a very good life in one of my previous incarnations. I found this out when I went through the akashic records a very long time ago. I had been a very mean and very unkind person. I was poor and I had a mother who had broken her leg in an accident. It happened when she was run over by a horse drawn carriage. In those days, they didn't know how to do things as effectively as now. The leg was never properly set, so she really was crippled to some extent. She used a stick and got around as best she could, but I had no desire to really help her. I thought it was very foolish of her to have tried to run in front of the carriage rather than wait until it passed. I never felt her disability to the point of empathizing with her. This, of course, was wrong.

When I came back to this incarnation, I chose to come crippled from birth. I had a deformed leg and I really was not able to walk like other people. I did learn to walk but with a very severe limp. It was ugly. I was not able to carry myself as a stately person. I was born to a king, a gentleman that I had previous incarnations with. He had actually been my husband in a previous incarnation. He loved me very much and he wanted me to marry for political reasons, which was done in those days, so that he would have some connection with the man who became the King of France. He thought as the Queen of France I would have some influence over my husband and things would go very well between the two countries. Well, my husband was happy to marry me because he was given an opportunity to sit on the throne, but he did not love me. He had absolutely nothing to do with me. He totally and completely rejected me. He did not care if I attended any official functions or not. But I did do my duty because I had been raised in a family as a princess where you did your duty. Fortunately, my father was a kind man and he instilled in me the importance of helping your subjects, and doing for them as best you could. And so, as Queen of France, I busied myself serving the poor and the needy. I worked off my karma pretty well while I was on earth because I realized that although I had a great deal of wealth and many, many, many jewels, that the most important jewels were the jewels that were stored in one's soul. And these jewels became bright and sparkly as we applied or used them—love, trust, honor, understanding, kindness, truth and all of these things are really the only treasures that one should accumulate. They are the only ones that we can bring to Spirit with us, not the jewels of earth. Do not make them your gods. They have absolutely no meaning on this side of life.

I came to this side to continue my work. All over the world I go and wherever there is a medium who is open and receptive to my vibration, I come in and talk. I tell them my story. I try very hard to work with the leaders of the various countries to get them to consider improving the human rights of their subjects. I try hard to instill in them a sense of peace. Unfortunately, we were not able to avoid this war with Iraq. We did not approve of it from this side of life. We wanted more peaceful means used to get rid of dictators and forceful methods to get rid of the terrorists. These will go in time, but you are going through a very difficult chaotic period between now and the time when the new millennium really begins. We encourage everyone to hold on, to raise their consciousness and to contribute positive good thoughts and to send out love that this can be accelerated.

I am very happy to have been able to come in today. I am so pleased that you asked for me and delighted to have been able to say what I would like to say. We want people on earth to be more aware of what goes on in their individual lives and what goes on over here so they can come over knowledgeable and ready to participate and grow. ◆

13.

PARALYSIS

Karmic and Emotional Aspects of Paralysis

Although some forms of paralysis more logically would be discussed under the Brain and Nervous System, Dr. Blake, Spirit teacher, has chosen to consider them separately in the information he has shared with us here.

A great deal of paralysis is karmic in nature. It is the result of some form of fear—a deep and profound fear centered in the subconscious mind that may have been experienced for many lives. It impedes and slows down the life functions and eventually the physical body becomes inert. It is no longer responsive to the communications from the brain. A person may think, *I brought this with me from a past life. This is karmic. There is nothing I can do to help it.* But there is! Let us say a person is paralyzed, then he/she, by changing his/her thinking, can help the situation, maybe not cure it, but help it. If he/she feels restricted—paralysis comes from a feeling of restriction based on fear—that is the thinking that is the basis for the manifestation of paralysis. And usually, the person is of a very emotional nature. There is also a lot of stubbornness and much resistance to healing. That is what they brought from a past life and what they are still doing in this life. The goal is to get rid of that pattern of thinking and learn to accept, not resist healing. Many times with paralysis, individuals enjoy all the attention they can get. Often, they have had very little love or attention either in this life or in a past life. That is why some of them cling to their condition. A notable exception, of course, is someone like Christopher Reeve who did not feel restricted at all really—someone who wanted to help others, and was trying to heal himself because he was not stubborn or resisting the healing. Even those who are paralyzed can do a lot to help themselves and should try to do so. That is what is necessary in paralysis.

The Spirit teachers have repeatedly said if they could get one thing across to mankind today, they would be doing a great, great service to humanity. And that one thing is: **Thoughts are things**. We can bring so many things into our own life. Let us say a person is paralyzed because of a karmic condition from a past life and is constantly dwelling on it and feels very restricted and only wants attention, then that person is not going to be half-way cured.

With each thought, we direct energy to create a form in our aura. As the creator of the form, it can only serve the purpose for which we have designed and created it. If it has soul, it may serve us well. If it is soulless, it will constantly call (tempt) to receive the life force that it needs for its continuity. So the tool which we designed to serve us, we are serving instead. Each moment is our moment unless we make it the moment of the hollow form of the past.

All paralysis falls into a pattern. Usually there is a very emotional nature. The onset of a disease may occur later in life and could be avoided in many cases. The predisposition would be there, but they would not need for it to become full blown. So much depends on their thoughts and actions prior to the onset.

In the infantile paralysis epidemic sixty plus years ago, some of the cases were so mild, it passed in a very short time. That is because those infected were not accepting it. Or, perhaps they had worked off their karma in another way prior to that time. On the other hand, many were permanently paralyzed by the disease in order to balance their karma.

In the case of very young children, however, who are paralyzed, that is definitely karmic. They have not caused it in this life. It can also be a karmic condition for the family, and usually it is. In other words, there may be karma between the child and one or both of the parents. The soul chose to accept this condition to work out his/her karma from a previous life. If the parents help the child correctly, and if the child accepts it, then the child can help himself/

herself a great deal. The child may not get completely well, but can certainly help himself/herself.

Karma is important. We have to work out our karma, but on the other hand, we can help ourselves to work out that karma by the way we think. If we think negatively all the time, we are just attracting more and more to us. We have found in cases where there is a husband or a wife who is the caregiver, he/she sometimes begin to resent the burden they feel that has been put upon them. By believing that this is a burden they are having to carry, they are giving more power to the paralysis. In other words, when the spouse of the person who is paralyzed is saying, *what a burden I have been given! Why have I been given this burden?* and is constantly dwelling on it, feeling sorry for himself or herself, they are bringing a great degree of paralysis to the person supposedly being helped, and the spouse or caregiver is also attracting it to himself or herself. If someone is constantly saying to the paralyzed person, "Oh, you can't move, you can't do anything," and tells the patient what a burden he or she is, they are making the patient worse by seeing that person more helpless than that person really may be. Energy follows attention, so constantly dwelling on that situation directs more and more energy to make things worse. Instead of trying to lift their spirits and help them, the caretaker is actually doing the opposite. And after awhile, the paralyzed individuals do not even want to help themselves at all. In some cases where finances are limited and there is no way to pay for outside help to relieve the care giver, the situation is worse.

In John 5: 1-14 of the *New Testament*, Jesus healed the paralyzed man at Bethesda. He made him whole in consciousness first. In other words, he changed his thinking, and then he injected into the man's thoughts that God's power was within him. He asked him if he wanted to be healed. Then, he said, take up your bed and walk. First of all, he tried to infuse within him (probably did this silently) that God was within him. And the man, by asking that he be healed, knew that there was a power that could reach him. This is what has to be in all kinds of healing. We have to know that there is a power within us that will heal us, if we want it, but some people do not believe this. We would be surprised at how many people actually enjoy being cared for and babied. A lot of that comes from a lack of love in their life and a lack of attention. This is a very negative way to get attention.

John 5:1 After this there was a feast of the Jews; and Jesus went up to Jerusalem.

2 Now there is at Jerusalem by the sheep market a pool, which is called in the Hebrew tongue Bethesda, having five porches.

3 In these lay a great multitude of impotent folk, of blind, halt, withered, waiting for the moving of the water.

4 For an angel went down at a certain season into the pool, and troubled the water: whosoever then first after the troubling of the water stepped in was made whole of whatsoever disease he had.

5 And a certain man was there, which had an infirmity thirty and eight years.

6 When Jesus saw him lie, and knew that he had been now a long time in that case, he saith unto him, Wilt thou be made whole?

7 The impotent man answered him, Sir, I have no man, when the water is troubled, to put me into the pool: but while I am coming, another steppeth down before me.

8 Jesus saith unto him, Rise, take up thy bed, and walk.

9 And immediately the man was made whole, and took up his bed, and walked: and on the same day was the sabbath.

What convinced the man to follow the command of Jesus and pick up his sleeping mat and walk when he had been an invalid for so many years? This was a karmic condition that had been satisfied and the man now merited being healed. Jesus was aware of this and was impressed by Spirit to heal the man. He concentrated on seeing the man as whole, complete, and perfect, and instantly the healing took place.

John 5:10 The Jews therefore said unto him that was cured, It is the sabbath day: it is not lawful for thee to carry thy bed.

11 He answered them, He that made me whole, the same said unto me, Take up thy bed, and walk.

12   Then asked they him, What man is that which said unto thee, Take up thy bed, and walk?

13   And he that was healed wist not who it was: for Jesus had conveyed himself away, a multitude being in that place.

14   Afterward Jesus findeth him in the temple, and said unto him, Behold, thou art made whole: sin no more, lest a worse thing come unto thee.

Jesus was trying to get the man to change his ways. And this applies to healing of all types. A person can be healed by a spiritual healer and then get home and let doubt creep in, only to find the condition has returned. During the healing, they are raised to a higher level and get all caught up in their emotions, but they must have faith to sustain it.

Jesus said to the man "sin no more." He recognized that in order to sustain a healing, one must have sufficient faith and remove all doubt. By cautioning the man that now that he was well, he must stop sinning (refraining from all negativity) or a worse condition could result. Jesus was really telling him to stop doubting. The mind can affect the physical body, and when we doubt that a healing has taken place, it can return and frequently does.

The same power that Jesus used when he told the man to take up his bed and walk is the same power that can be used to revitalize our legs and arms today. The power is within each individual if they would just learn how to use it and to work with it. It is what people are doing now to cause disease and cause these things to happen in their body that must be acknowledged. But we have to have the belief that there is the Christ within, and that the Christ Spirit, the Buddha Nature, Jehovah, the Great White Spirit, or whatever you choose to call it, can do all things if we just let it. The Light which flows within each individual is perfect, and if we can accept that thought in our conscious mind, then we realize that it is perfect life.

Chart of Diseases Involving Paralysis

Note: In the following chart are listed diseases which can be inherited, but some are only karmic "to a point." In other words, in keeping with our soul contract, we may have specifically and intentionally chosen a family who could provide the gene to develop a particular "karmic" disease or condition. This is our way of balancing our karma. The predisposition also existed in that family for one of the "karmic to a point" diseases, and we simply picked up that gene as well. Depending on how we live our life prior to the proposed onset of a disorder, we may not develop a "karmic" or a "karmic to a point" disease at all, having already worked off our karma in another way. Or, the disease may be mild and very responsive to treatment.

Disease	Description	Genetic	Karmic
Amyotrophic Lateral Sclerosis	Characterized by progressive degeneration of motor neuron cells in the spinal cord and brain, which ultimately results in paralysis and death. Known as Lou Gehrig disease.	yes	Karmic to a point
Cerebral Palsy	A group of motor problems and physical disorders that result from a brain injury or abnormal brain development that may occur during fetal growth, at the time of birth, or within the first 2 or 3 years of a child s life. Although permanent, the brain abnormality does not get worse over time. It is the most common cause of neuromuscular scoliosis. Cerebral palsy may cause complications that result in an early death.	no	Karmic to a point
Multiple Sclerosis	Degenerative and progressive disease which attacks the brain, spinal cord and nerves. It destroys myelin, an insulating material that covers nerve fibers and is necessary for normal electrical function of nervous system. Sudden paralysis of a leg, half of body, or sudden loss of vision in one eye.	no	Karmic

Disease	Description	Genetic	Karmic
Muscular Dystrophy	Umbrella term used to indicate several inherited diseases of muscle that cause progressive weakness and disability. Symptoms usually appear before age 3. Affects males.	yes	Karmic
Poliomyelitis Infantile Paralysis	Acute infectious disease of central nervous system. Virus invades bloodstream, affects spinal cord and brain, paralysis can ensue in 25% of cases.	no	Karmic to a point
Spina Bifida	Baby is born with opening in the back where tube and spine don t close. Degree of paralysis depends on where opening is on baby s back.	Uncertain	Karmic
Spinal Muscular Atrophy	Death of spinal motor neurons and subsequent muscle paralysis. Infantile onset form causes early death from respiratory failure. Rare if begins in adulthood. Then usually milder in form and due to what is going on in life at that particular time which may cause changes in spine.	yes	Definitely if occurs in child-hood.
Spinocerebellar Ataxia	Degeneration of spinal cord and a wasting away of cerebellum resulting in loss of muscle coordination-paralysis	yes	no
Stroke	Sudden neurological disorder due to interruption of the blood supply to part of the brain.	yes	Karmic to a point

Enlightening Voices from the Other Side

Dr. Whitaker on Infantile Paralysis

You have about controlled infantile paralysis through the shots that are given. It was a very, very sweeping and very bad thing that occurred with an epidemic some years ago. We are still receiving people on this side who suffered from it. It was spread by a virus, but it was karmic in nature.

Your President Roosevelt was stricken and yet he was able to carry on for many years. He realized when he got to this side and reviewed the akashic records that it was karmic for what he had done in a previous life, and that he had wiped the slate clean. Then he was able to move on. At first, he came to us believing that he could not move his lower limbs. And so, we found it helpful in his case, and with others who had infantile paralysis, or actually any form of paralysis of the legs, to do water therapy with them, and get them to move in the water. From there, we can graduate to standing on their own and walking—our walk is more of a glide—and to know that those limbs are perfectly straight. No braces are needed, although many times they come over still wanting their braces. When they come to earth to visit, as in a materialization seance, they probably would put on their braces for identification.

I thought you might like to know how we did this. It is a combination of changing the attitude—attitudinal healing—as well as the water therapy. It works very well. And so President Roosevelt is very spry, to say the least, and he has chosen to go back to an earlier age in his life when he was functioning very well. So there are three steps in his treatment and in the treatment of others. Usually, they do prefer to go back to before the onset of paralysis.

We use water therapy actually for other forms of paralysis and deformities. It helps them so much because the water buoys the body and they are in deep enough that they think they will drown if they don't use their limbs, and so they find they can use them. They can look down at their body and see that it is not twisted or wasted away, yet that old mind insists so much upon believing that it is incapacitated. We have a remedy for everything, if only our patients will permit us to help them.

President Franklin Delano Roosevelt on having polio

Well, I am very pleased that you asked for me. This is Franklin Roosevelt and I am really delighted to have an opportunity to speak to someone on earth. I have tried to get through a few mediums and they will recognize that I am present, but I am not really able to say very much. So I understand that I can talk as much as I would like through you. You know, I was always a great talker. I loved to have my fireside chats, believe me, so that I could talk to the people. Talking was always something that I liked to do. And so I do want to tell you a little bit about myself since you are doing a very unusual book. We want it to be successful. Master Joseph has told me a bit about some of the different doctors who have come in, and that you have received information from a very wide gamut of sources. Now, I understand that you are going to concentrate on physical and mental problems in this first book, so this is very timely for me to come in and tell you a bit.

When I was on earth, I could not believe at first what was happening to my limbs. There was an epidemic of infantile paralysis (poliomyelitis) and many people recovered, and many people only had very mild cases. So I had every expectation that I would be cured, for certainly I had the very best doctors and very best medical care. I was very certain, but that did not come to be. And I wondered why me? I had not been a perfect person on earth and I felt that I was being punished. I had some talks with God. I wanted to do my work politically because I was politically ambitious despite my physical condition. I prayed that I would be able to do it.

As you know, in those days the news media was very kind to us and very protective. They did not want to show or talk about my disability. And we worked it so that I could be lifted and I could even be helped to stand in braces so the public would not be aware of how wasted my lower body really was. I was very grateful to them. I don't think in this day and age they would be that kind. I don't know what has happened to people. They seem to want to find all of the defects, all of the worst about a person, and to emphasize that. When the public knows about physical weaknesses especially, they question whether you can really do the job. And so, I am grateful that I was protected in that respect.

I enjoyed serving as your President. I truly did. But when I reached my fourth and last term, I was very tired. I was ready to come to this side of life. And what a shock it was to me! I had no idea what to expect. At first, I was taken to a kind of hospital-like setting to rest. When I was ready to get up, I was told that I could walk. And I said yes, perhaps I can with my braces. And the doctors said no, you do not need braces. Your legs are in perfect condition. And you know, I did not believe them. I truly did not believe them. After the many years that I had suffered, it was so ingrained in my mind, I simply could not accept that I had a perfect body. I did realize that I had a new and different body because it did look a little different. It was more translucent. But I could not accept that it was perfect. So they used water therapy with me. I would be taken to a beautiful pool and put in deep enough water that I guess self-preservation rose and I began to swim. It did not happen over night because then I said, *All right I can use my limbs in water, but I can't use them on the ground.* We kind of shuffle over here more than walk as you do on earth. And it took a number of times of going to the pool. Finally, finally, it got through to me, yes, I really am able to use my limbs.

And they asked me if I would feel more comfortable going back to an earlier period of my life. I thought, my goodness, we can do that? And so I chose to go back to the time before I had infantile paralysis when I was a very healthy, strong individual. That is how I appear today. Now I suppose if I were coming through a materialization medium, I would need to come in a wheelchair or something for identification purposes only. But, otherwise, I am very, very strong and I enjoy my life here.

I work a great deal with helping people to be politically honest. This is my main work. I want people to tell the population the truth. Politicians have a way of telling you what they want you to know. I don't always get through by any means, I don't. And it is frustrating, but I do work with both Democrats and Republicans. It makes no difference to me what party—just tell the truth.

I also would like to see the Democratic party back in power. I think that we need the change as much for the country as for the world to regain creditability as being a peaceful nation. From this side, we recognized that a dictator of such great butchering tendencies had to be eliminated. We don't like to see dictators operate at all. If they were benevolent despots, that would be one thing, but that is not how it goes. We would like to see them all removed from office, but done in more peaceful ways. We do not want to see wars, and we feel this war with Iraq was wrong. It could have been done differently, but it is now done and we have to rebuild the pieces and rebuild our image as a nation. This will take some time, but it can be done. And I do feel that a change of administration will speed up the process. Your President has done some good things and he is to be commended for those, but there will be a dear price to pay for the war.

I also help in working with patients who had suffered from polio. When I am invited, I will go to groups that are held. I am always willing to answer the call. I tell them my experience, and the fact that it did not hold me back from holding the highest office in the most powerful nation of the world for into the beginning of four terms. I do feel that it is good that the terms have been limited to two, but I am glad that I had that opportunity.

And yes, I know Dr. Whittaker who has come to you. He has been very helpful to me. I did have to go through a review of my life, and then later went through the akashic records. When I went through the akashic records, I learned that in a previous life, I had been a very restricted person in many ways. I did not allow myself to really work on truth. I walked away from it. And so, I had to come back in this life and to suffer for what I had done before. I had been given some spiritual teachings in that previous life and I literally walked away from them. I had been born into a family of privilege and I had no compassion for those who were needy, and especially for those who were paralyzed. I thought that they were just taking up space. I had no compassion whatsoever. My attitude was, let somebody else take care of them.

When I came to this life, I was again born into a family of privilege that I might show compassion for those who were in need. My family was a family that believed very much in philanthropy. We did care about the underprivileged. So for that part, I did compensate for the karma I had acquired in the past life. I did truly care about what was happening to those in need. I cared very much when the stock market collapsed and there were so many people begging for food. So when I came to office, it was a true blessing to me that I was in a position to bring about changes in the law to help people who were not employed to receive some financial aid and jobs. We developed jobs to put them to work. The New Deal program achieved some measure of recovery for business and agriculture. And my wife supported very much what I was doing, and while we had grown apart in some ways, she was a very trusted ally in going around the country and reporting back to me. I knew that I could depend on her to tell me the absolute truth, and I trusted her assessment of conditions. On this side of life, she has forgiven me because she is a spiritually evolved lady. She does her work with the underprivileged.

And so, as I look back on my life, I did accomplish many things that I came to do. I did work off most of my karma. In fact, all of it from the previous life, but I did accumulate more on earth. There were many difficult problems to be solved. Because I was in office so long, I helped economically in the beginning of my administration, and then went into World War II. We did the best that we could, and I think we did a fine job. I have spoken to many of the men and women who served our country and they felt that it was a noble job that they did. They felt it was a war that we really had to become involved in. Of course, with Japan we had no choice. But with the European front, we were needed. We could not have Hitler spread any further. I have regrets about Russia, then the Soviet Union, truly I do. I do wish we could have somehow curtailed the activities of Stalin. He was a mighty force to deal with, but I do feel we should have insisted upon a better settlement because many people suffered behind that Iron Curtain. We should not have divided Germany. And I am very pleased that the cold war is over and that there are better relationships with all of the countries that were once a part of the Soviet Union.

From this side, we naturally want to see terrorism obliterated from the face of the earth. It will come about but it will take time. We are working from this side to help with that process. We cannot get through to the terrorists themselves for their minds are so filled with evil there is no possible way. But we do try to work with those who are trying to track down the terrorists and to help them and to guide them. If we had people who were more mediumistic serving in the armed forces, that would help, or, who are serving in the CIA or FBI or whatever. It would truly help because they would get hunches, and many of them are able to receive our impressions. This helps them to do their work.

So I stay very busy on this side and I truly hope that the day will come when the consciousness of the whole world is raised so that you have peace, peace everywhere. The spirit teachers do tell us this will come about.

I hope that I have given you enough to put a little something in your book. I would like to leave with some parting thoughts— no matter what your physical condition, you can rise above it, and that you should get as much help as is available. And to know that it is not God that is punishing you. You are simply reaping the rewards, good or bad, of what you have sown. Karma has to be worked off in one lifetime or another. We cannot escape its consequences. I am very pleased that I have been able to come in this morning and to share a little of my story.

R. Benito on having infantile paralysis to pay off karma

In the incarnation prior to the last one, I was a schoolmaster in the 18th century and I was really a very difficult, unbending, harsh man. My father had been this way with me and I suppose through his example, I was the same with those who were under my care. I learned this in reviewing the akashic records. I do want to tell you that because I was so unloving, so unbending, I frightened the children and I enjoyed the power and determined to keep those little monsters in total submission to me.

I came back into incarnation and I suffered greatly when I was on earth. I had so many physical restrictions. My health was terrible from day one. I suffered infantile paralysis at a very, very early age. I could watch children all around me laughing and playing since our home was near a school ground, and I could be there at the window looking out. I was home-schooled. I developed a heart condition, and I went to Spirit when I was about 36, I guess. When I got to this side, I was very surprised to know there was a life here that could be beautiful. I had to elevate myself in these few years that I have been here so that I could help others with their afflictions, because we are receiving many with infantile paralysis who developed it at about the same time that I did. We have not cured infantile paralysis in all parts of the world. It is still going on in a few places.

There are so many things that we can do over here to help others but we first have to face what we have done. I think that the point I want to make is that although I had infantile paralysis and I had a heart condition, I did not totally work off all my karma from the previous life. There was some residue. I refused to get treatment for the heart condition because I wanted to die. I did not want to live in a wheel chair any longer. And so I did not get the help that would have been available to me. In looking back, I wish that I had, for then I would have stayed and completed my karma. I should point out that it is a little unusual not to work off karma when there is a definite physical condition, but that is certainly possible. We always have free choice and I want to emphasize that. We do have free choice and if we choose not to work on something, then boom, boom boom, it is going to come back and face us again. My choice was to come to this side and I still have some residue, so I know that when I go back again I will elect to work the rest of it out in some way. I am working over here to try to help those who lack understanding. I hope that has helped you. We cannot escape our past, but we certainly can lay down the steps for a better future.

Comments by the Master Teacher

You can see the enormous variety of problems that we deal with on this side. And I am so glad that we have found so many workers who are willing to share their interest and their work so that anyone reading your book may find a little help in the area of their own interest. Or, they may know someone who has been in a particular situation and they will be comforted knowing that we are equipped, we are qualified to address every problem situation presented. They have to want to be helped, and then we can step in and help them. We try to get them ready for wanting help, and we do it in different ways.

Trixie tells what it is like to become a quadriplegic

My name is Trixie. I have come this morning because I was asked to share my experiences as a quadriplegic. I had played in sports and I was very athletic. Then in my early twenties, I was in a very serious automobile accident, and I wound up without the use of my arms and legs. I was paralyzed from the neck down. There was no movement. I could not even turn my head. I could talk in a very limited way because I did not have the energy to say too much without getting tired.

I was very, very, very bitter, very, very angry because my car was hit by a drunk driver. He had been in other accidents because of his intoxication. He was not supposed to be driving. His license had been taken away, but he came out to finish me off, I felt. It was a miserable existence from that time on. I was totally and completely helpless. I did not want to live, but I had such a healthy body before this happened, that I had a strong constitution. I did not want to eat or live. I tried to refuse food, to spit it out. I wanted just to die.

The minister of my mother's church came and talked to me until he was blue in the face, telling me that it was God's will that

I stay, that I could not question what had happened to me, and all that stuff. I hated to see him coming. I did not want him to come. I told him to leave me alone. I felt very guilty that my poor mother had to take care of me. And my father when he was at home, and a brother when he was around. I was embarrassed that I was a grown woman that needed this care. It was awful.

Television was just coming in, and it was a very expensive thing, but the church group—that's one good thing the minister did, at least I felt at the time—they raised money so that I could have a television set and have some contact with the outside world and not just have to look at four walls. We could not afford to keep me in a hospital too long. The insurance settlement was not that big. It was not like the settlements of today. It ran out pretty quickly. There was a little reserve to have a physiotherapist come in, I believe, on a weekly basis.

I prayed and prayed and prayed to die. Others, especially, in that church, prayed and prayed and prayed that I would get well. Now, I am glad that I have had this opportunity to come and talk to you because people must understand that when they pray for a person to get well, they may be praying for that person to stay on earth longer than the person needs to be. It should always be that God's will be done, not what someone else wants. And then the soul of that person can make the decision as to when the soul should depart. I believe that I was given so much energy from these wellmeaning people that it kept me going. They really thought they were doing the right thing. And my mother thought they were doing the right thing, for she thought there would be a miracle. But I was too paralyzed for a miracle to take place unless Jesus himself came down and healed me. Truly, they did me a disservice though their hearts were in the right place.

I begged and begged and begged to die. And I continued to refuse food so that I did get myself in a bad state, and they promised to put a feeding tube in me to keep me going. I cried and cried and cried not to do it. I stayed in that condition, I believe it was about twelve years, and I finally was released from my body because I had a stroke. Actually, I had so much anger that I had a stroke. They knew I had high blood pressure from my anger, and I refused to take the medication to lower it. If they tried to dissolve pills in my liquids, I knew it and refused it. But the good Lord did release me.

When I got to this side, I thought I was dreaming. I really did because I saw myself as I once was in a whole body that could move. The only difference was my body looked a little different, but it was all complete. And I thought, *Oh boy, if I could just remain in a dream state all the time.* I remembered going through that tunnel of light and seeing grandparents waiting for me. I thought, *Man, this is really wonderful.* They had to do a lot of convincing that I was actually in the Spirit World, and that this was the real world. They told me I was going to have a new life because I was free.

Well, I had to go back and I had to review my life in great detail. And I had to put up with listening to myself complaining, *Why did God do this to me, why did that drunken driver do it to me, why did society let him out, why didn't they keep him in jail,* and I had to go through all of that all over again and really come to grips with it. I just was so tormented that my spirit guides did tell me that this was karma that I had to go through, being paralyzed because I had done some very mean things to others in a previous life. And I listened to them, and I thought, *Well, that is an easy excuse to give me.* And so they took me to a group where there were other people who were paralyzed. In fact, it was with Dr. Neilsen, who has already come in and talked to you about his group. It was in his group that it finally got through my dense skull that maybe there was something to this business of retribution, and that I should look at it in a positive way. I had freed myself through what I had suffered as a quadriplegic. And they told me the drunk driver will suffer for what he has done, but that was not my problem. He simply was the instrument to get me where I was. And possibly he might have been one that I had inflicted some torture on. I was not to learn this until I did eventually go through the akashic records, and to learn that literally the drunken driver was getting back at me for the horrible things that I had done, actually centuries ago. I did not pay for those deeds in one lifetime. It took two lifetimes of suffering for me to finally be free. It goes back to the days of the Roman Empire when I did gladly the dirty work for the Emperor. I was well paid for my willingness to torture other human beings. And so, after going through the akashic records, it made me feel sick to my stomach to know what I had done, but it also was a freeing experience. No question about it, I could see that the divine scales of justice worked perfectly. They are never out of kilter.

There is divine justice, if people would only realize, there is divine justice. If you don't get it now, you will get it later. We don't get away with one single, solitary thing we do because we have to review every thought, every deed and every action we have taken. There is no getting away. It is all recorded perfectly. We cannot in any way change it. That little recorder inside that they call the heart seed atom is the most perfect recorder. There is none on earth that will ever match the technology of that internal recorder. I wish that I could come back and speak in some of your Spiritualist churches and others, in all of the places, and let people know what I have gone through because of what I have done. I want to save them from having to make other people suffer and from them suffering as well. Whatever you can do to make up for your wrongdoing while you are on earth, do it, don't save, but do it. Do what you can. Make your amends.

The drunk driver, of course, eventually came to this side. He was put in prison for awhile, and there he worked off his karma. And when he came over here, he had to go through the same experience as I did in reviewing his life. I believe I was helpful to him. We became friends. I helped him to get through his life review, and he went through the akashic records also, and saw what I had done to him. I told him how I had suffered on earth, not once, but in two lifetimes to try to make up, and that it was pretty much even now. We could continue on in life helping each other to grow. He works with those who have come over as alcoholics, because you know, the alcoholic still wants the drink. He works with them and tries to help them. And I try to help with what I can do as Dr. Neilsen's assistant.

And so I think that I have given you as much as I can describe. It is just a horrible thing to be totally dependent on others. You feel like a baby again, except you are an adult. But when I tortured people, they were dependent on me and they begged and pleaded, and I showed them no mercy. And so I had to be in a position where I was totally dependent, begging and pleading to let me die. God bless you for listening and may my experience help at least one person to think. I don't expect that it will reach someone who is torturing someone, but it may reach someone who is mean or has done nasty little things. Hopefully, it will shake them up to ask for forgiveness. God forgives, but God's laws are unchangeable. They are ever fair. You either use them or you abuse them. And that little inner recorder catches all the action, and then you review it like a movie when you get to this side. It is a torturous horrible film, if you have not done your best to be a good person.

Comments by the Master Teacher

Well, you certainly had a very detailed feeling description of what a spirit can go through on this side. What Trixie did not tell you was that she was a he in the Roman Empire, and has wanted, and has gone back to every single person that was tortured when she was a Roman soldier. And she has tried very sincerely to make amends, and to help those who are stuck to elevate themselves. ✦

14.

RESPIRATORY SYSTEM

Function of the Respiratory System

The respiratory system plays a vital role in delivering oxygen to the body—fuel for all the body's functions. It also removes carbon dioxide waste, eliminates toxic waste, regulates temperature, and stabilizes blood acidalkaline balance (pH). The lungs are the largest part of this system.

Diseases and Karmic Conditions
Associated with the Respiratory System

Again, Dr. Blake has contributed to this section. Lungs are the organs causing the most problems in newborns, infants, and young children. Every part of our body is perfect unless the soul, because of karmic conditions, has chosen some problem that will help the soul to remove the karma. So human life is really an incarnation of God in mankind. With every indrawn breath, we breathe in life, and with every outgoing breath, we are giving it out. If we live our life in faith and good deeds, then we are expressing God. We are letting the Christ Spirit, Jehovah, the Buddha Nature, the Great White Spirit, etc. come forth.

We know that smoking, second hand smoke, asbestos, pollution in the atmosphere and such things do affect our lungs. Stay away from the things that we feel are not good for us and do not dwell upon them because the more we dwell upon them, the more we are going to attract them. We have to remember just how important it is that thoughts are things. Thoughts bring into our life that which we are thinking.

Tears, colds, and similar physical conditions belong to the water element and may be traced to the lack of control in the emotional nature. Lung trouble is connected to the emotions—a very strong desire that has never been realized. We have to learn to breathe in life, and as we let that breath out, we are sending that life on. We are using that life. It is very important to get our emotions under control and not have so much fear, and not want something that we cannot possibly have, for these things result in lung problems. For example, a love problem not only affects the heart but also the lungs because it is in the lungs where we are taking in life all the time. People who have emphysema have a difficult time breathing, as well as those with asthma—they are not actually taking in life.

Many individuals think that they are very susceptible to weather. Colds and flu really has nothing to do with it, but it does only because they are thinking that it does. They are bringing it to them. You have heard people say, *if I go out there in the rain I am going to get a cold. If I sit in a draft, I am going to get pneumonia.* It is not the weather, it is the thinking.

You hear people say that a cold will last a week. And then they will talk about the symptoms of a cold, and how often they get a cold. This creates an actual pattern. If we no longer wish to use that pattern, we have to get rid of the pattern. More colds result from damp spirits than from wet feet. So get rid of the fear of the weather and do not resist it. If it is a very cold and windy day, and we have to go out in the cold, dress for the cold. We do not have to chill. We are thinking that this is what is going to happen. *I am going to be so cold, I am going to get a cold. I am going to come down with the flu.* Many people do that with the flu. We go to someone's house and someone there has the flu, so we think we are going to catch it. When we realize that we are spirit here and now, spirit is not subject to either cold or heat. If it is the spirit that is working in us, then we do not have to worry about it.

Nervous people, people constantly thinking about conditions that they do not feel that they can prevent, often, if their work is largely mental, do attract asthma, hayfever and allergies. This is the result of being overly sensitive. They have to realize that they should have no fear because the breath of God is in each one of us. If we can believe that, and if we are expressing only good, then we have no time to express things that are not good. We have to know that our body is the temple of God and we are the doorkeeper. We can let in what we want, and we can let out what we do not want. It is sad that more churches or religious institutions do not actually teach that we are the doorkeeper to our own body and we have the right to let in what we want and to let out what we do not want. Let in the good and realize that it is the breath of God that animates every creation.

Tuberculosis can be caused by karmic and environmental conditions. If karmic, it results from materialistic thinking and living. Smoking, which affects the lungs, has nothing to do with karma. That is a physical thing. SIDS or sudden infant death syndrome is karmic. The soul only needs to come in for just a short time, perhaps to teach the family something. Usually, when this occurs, it is part of the preincarnation plan.

Cystic fibrosis affects the function of mucous and sweat glands and usually results in death during young adulthood. Generally, when we come into a family, it is to work out the karma with the family. In other words, a person may come to help the family, as well as to work out karma with the family. We generally come back to people we have been with in a past life, not always, but most of the time. Generally we have had problems in past lives with these people and are trying to work it out with them.

Asthma is a karmic condition, but asthmatics can help themselves by realizing that it is God life that flows in and through us. If there is anxiety, strain, indecision, deep-seated worry and concern, these aggravate asthma and hayfever. Some feel that asthma is symbolically the cry for the mother. It could be because they are very anxious people and very indecisive. That is what actually causes asthma and deep-seated fear. Their fear is not centered on particular things for they can be afraid of almost anything. And if we cannot catch our breath, that only compounds the fear. The things that really cause breathing problems are worry and concern and anxiety and indecision. It can come from a past life or it can come from this life. If asthmatics would learn to take long, deep breaths, hold them a little bit and then exhale very slowly, they could calm themselves and relieve themselves of their anxiety. So many times they worry about things that are not even going to happen. Of course, we all do that to some extent.

It is a very good practice to take time out during the day to take several deep breaths. The correct way to breathe is very important. Breathe through the nostrils to the count of 4, hold each breath to the count of 7, exhale slowly through the mouth to the count of 8. Do this three or four times. If we are really worried or anxious about something, sit down, be calm and take deep breaths. It works!

If we are working for spiritual development, remember to take deep breaths, especially before starting to work. By doing so, we can receive a great deal more from spirit. Our breathing calms and relaxes us, opening the door to spirit. We will find that when we become very calm, we will open ourselves to spirit much easier. Calmness puts us on a totally different level of consciousness and gets rid of the worries and concerns of the day. It is harder to tune into spirit when we have mundane things on our mind that we are worried about.

Chart Showing Respiratory Conditions
Note: On the following chart are listed diseases which can be inherited, but some are only karmic "to a point." In other words, in keeping with our soul contract, we may have specifically and intentionally chosen a family who could provide the gene to develop a particular "karmic" disease or condition. This is our way of balancing our karma. The predisposition also existed in that family for one of the "karmic to a point" diseases, and we simply picked up that gene as well. Depending on how we live our life prior to the proposed onset of a disorder, we may not develop a "karmic" or a "karmic to a point" disease at all, having already worked off our karma in another way. Or, the disease may be mild and very responsive to treatment.

Chart Showing Respiratory Conditions

Disease	Description	Genetic	Karmic
Alpha-1-antitrypsin Deficiency	Deficiency of this protein, which protects the body from damage by its immune cells, leaves the lung, and occasionally the liver, vulnerable to injury.	yes	yes
Asthma	A chronic inflammatory disorder of the airways characterized by coughing, shortness of breath, and chest tightness. Affects more than 5% of our population, including children. Trying to work out karma with the family.	yes	yes
Chronic Sinusitis	Due to anatomical malformation.	yes	yes
Cystic Fibrosis	Most common fatal genetic disease in the U.S. Today. It causes the body to produce a thick, sticky mucus that clogs the lungs, leading to infection, and blocks the pancreas, stopping digestive enzymes from reaching the intestines where they are required to digest food. Sweat is very salty.	yes	yes

Disease	Description	Genetic	Karmic
Emphysema	Characterized by loss of the normal elasticity of the lung that helps to hold the airways open. With progressive inelasticity of the lungs, the small airways collapse on expiration, making it impossible to fully exhale stale air.	no	yes
Lung Carcinoma, Small Cell	Lung cancer is the most frequent cause of cancer deaths. Smoking and inhaling industrial substances, such as asbestos, and environmental factors can contribute.	yes	yes
Sudden Infant Death Syndrome (SIDS)	Seemingly healthy infants, usually between 2 to 4 months old, are put to bed and are later found dead. Rarely seen after age 6 months.	no	yes
Tuberculosis	Contagious lung disease which can spread to the kidneys and bones. Cause can be either karmic or environmental.	no	yes

Enlightening Voices from the Other Side

Dr. Parkinson on working with lung diseases

I have come today at the request of Master Joseph to tell you how I work with people who have had various physical problems with their lungs: asthma, emphysema, and tuberculosis. You probably have heard that asthma is caused by a cry for the mother, or it could be a smothering kind of condition. Truly it is, yes. Let us say a baby comes into this world and the mother is not really the type of person that she should be, but the child attracts that mother in order to have that disease. There has to be something about the mother that the child has to go through in order to progress. Now as the child does progress and gets older and realizes some of the things that they should not do, or should do and do not do, and they work at those things and get them behind them, then they do not have to have that problem any longer. It has been 333worked out.

The mother might also smother her child. Yes, that will cause it, too. The mother that smothers her child is not a good parent actually, because we should not be overly protective. But as that changes, the child does not need the asthma any longer. Many people do have it in adulthood, but asthma is the thing that usually starts out with very young children. In some cases, it never gets better, but in other cases yes, by the time of 12 or 15, they have very few attacks. When they get to the other side, then they have to work on the basis for it.

Emphysema has long been associated with smoking and Tuberculosis with problems around material desires. All three of these conditions are really karmic in nature. Although the predisposition may be present, a condition may not necessarily develop. This depends on how a person has lived his or her early life, that is, the life that the karma is to be worked out. This is possible with anything that is karmic. If they have made some radical changes in other ways, in the ways that brought about the karma in the first place, then that condition may not develop, or could take a very mild form. Actually, it could be mild or very advanced, depending on the degree of the karma. It has been my experience that some of this can be warded off by the way a person lives in his or her early life, although it may be a part of the preincarnation plan or contract. Many young kids have asthma and they outgrow it by the time they are 12 or 15 years old. That is because they have a greater understanding and they are working out their karma. They do not have to have the asthma, more so than the other two conditions—emphysema and tuberculosis.

Emphysema generally affects an older person who has not worked at any kind of soul growth, or much of it, affecting them around 40 or 50 or on. When they get to this side they may still think they have lung problems. We tell them their body is perfect. They no longer have that condition. They must not think that they have to suffer in any way. Tuberculosis takes its toll on the lungs and the whole body is affected. It is a matter of convincing them that their karma has been served, and that they can go on with their life in the Spirit World. TB is not always a karmic condition. It is a communicable disease. And usually we are with people who are going to produce that. If it is karmic, that is what is going to happen. But if it is not karmic, maybe some other problem has caused the lungs to be weak. Everything in your physical body does affect other parts. We could have a situation where the lung is weak and because of that we did develop TB.

As we go through and consider diseases, we can see as we evolve and as we grow older, some diseases go. We don't have a great deal of TB any longer, not like we used to have. Now we have cancer, we have Aids. These things actually appear because of the environment, attitudes of the people on earth, and the way they have given up their moral structure. Although these are different diseases, it is almost like the same thing, but different. Certain diseases seem to be prevalent at a particular time only to be replaced by other diseases capable of similar effects on the physical body. With TB it could have its basis in desire for material things in the past life. It, of course, has to do with breathing. On the whole, we choose the diseases that will help us to grow the most. If we had cancer, it could affect the lungs or anywhere else in the body. Yet there are people who have recovered from cancer in the body because they have learned that whatever they have had in the past that caused this is over. They have worked it out.

When one has had a condition for a long time, it becomes rather habit forming to expect symptoms even when they come to this side of life. And so, they do get over it, but it takes a little while to be assured that it is not going to come back, etc. We work by getting to the cause and trying to help them to recognize that the only thing that really and truly matters is the spiritual. There are people who come over here who have not earned a big house, but want a big house, beautiful furnishings, and these are simply not available to them. Their vibrations must radically change in order for them to gravitate to more refined treasures.

Dr. Lange emphasizes the importance of the chakras

I was a lung specialist. I dealt with many aspects of lung disease. As you know, the lungs are very, very important. A person can, however, survive with one lung if they do not push it too far. I know that you have been given some awareness of some of the problems and what causes them. I have seen many cases of tuberculosis. Some of that is a karmic thing, carried over from a past life, being born with a certain weakness. Some cases are really from karma in this life in the sense people have not lived right, and so when they are exposed to tuberculosis, they pick it up. So that works in both ways.

We do feel that emphysema has its roots more in this life experience. And there is cancer which is very, very bad because the lungs are really very vulnerable. When there is cancer of the lungs, which is karmic, there is not a lot we can do if it has spread over a large area. We do wish people would not smoke, but it is not entirely due to smoking. Smoking just aggravates the underlying problem. When people breathe in and breathe out negativity, it definitely affects the lungs. And, of course, there are many carcinogenics in your environment.

I treated people with asthma which is certainly karmic. It was sad to see people wheezing. And frequently, in some conditions, holding on to their last breath. It is very frightening when there is a lung problem, because I think most people are educated to the fact that they must be able to breathe to stay alive. I do believe, of all the physical automatic processes that go on, not being able to breathe is one of the most frightening. It is terrifying. You can tell with animals when something is put over an animal's head how they fight and claw to be free, and humans the same way. The instinct of preservation is fighting for breath. I truly believe that it is the most frightening. And when a person is drowning, of course, they are not getting breath. What does this do? We put them on ventilators and do all sorts of things when they are on earth.

But what does this do to a person who comes to this side? They don't really have to breathe here because there are no functional lungs in the etheric body. The chakras, those spiritual energy centers, take care of our needs on this side. They perform the same function as they do on earth. We don't have to worry about breathing because we have no lungs, but we are concerned that the energies that come in through the chakras, come in freely. When on earth, the people have frequently shut off the heart and throat chakras, so they are not functioning as they should. We work with those on this side to get them to understand initially that while the body looks like the physical body in many respects, it functions differently internally. Our lungs do not function because we do not need them. The etheric body is just made up in a way so that it would be a form, template, or pattern by which the physical body could be duplicated. So it has dummy organs. Our main functioning is through the chakras. They are extremely important to our growth on this side. The same is true on earth. The more light we let in, the more light that is going to shine forth from our aura. We have to take it in for it to shine out. It is like an automobile, no gas, the engine does not turn over. Or, if the car has become electrified, you have to charge the battery in order for the car to go. And so that is the way that it works here.

We raise our consciousness and let more light in. The chakra study is very, very, very important for those who are working in any kind of health field. It is important for ministers, all the clergy to understand how the chakras function. It is absolutely important for anyone on a spiritual path to understand. In fact, for everyone to understand the importance of the chakras. This was a wonderful contribution that the Hindus taught us. I do wish that everyone would understand that while Jesus did not mention the chakras when he was on earth, he certainly was able to see how they were functioning and that played a tremendous part in the healings that he did. But Jesus did not leave us in darkness because he came to St. John and he explained how each of these chakras can be opened. Recorded in the *Book of Revelation*, he used the analogy of the seven churches, each one representing a chakra. The writing is very, very difficult to understand, we realize that, but you have, with the help of your teachers and with the help of Edgar Cayce's work, done a wonderful job in your manuscript which we definitely want to see published when the time is right. (*The Empowered Soul: Revelation for the New Millennium*). It is very important for people to understand how the chakras open.

I got into working with the lungs because both my parents had problems, and I saw how they suffered and I wanted to alleviate the pain of others. They did not live long enough for me to help them personally, but my love for them really inspired me to try to do my best while I was on earth. In a previous life, I had problems. I had asthma which was very, very bad; so I was attracted to a family where I could see what lung problems do to people. Between my previous life and this last one, I had grown a great deal while in the Spirit World during that intervening period. And so I did not really need to suffer lung problems again. I had simply to come and observe how difficult and frightening they can be. I worked off karma for other reasons by dedicating myself on earth to helping others. I do hope this gives you a better understanding of the importance of the chakras.

Comments by the Master Teacher

I am glad that Dr. Lange did emphasize the importance of the chakras. It is very helpful to those working on earth if they have a good understanding of how the chakras function, and to know that this is a part of earth functioning that becomes an even more important function in the afterlife. We spend a great deal of time over here in our more advanced classes helping spirits to gain a better understanding of the chakras and how their thinking directly affects the opening of them. I am happy that he brought out the importance of this and related it to the teachings of Jesus.

Lucy K. on attracting cystic fibrosis to work out karma

I have come this morning to talk to you about cystic fibrosis. I came into this world to really work off my karma from a previous life by having cystic fibrosis. It was a miserable disease, and as you probably know, people who are afflicted do not live to a ripe old age. The nature of the disease causes all kinds of problems that really shut down your healthy functioning of the body. There are many problems. It affects the mucus. It affects the functioning of the pancreas. It affects many things. It is frightening because you know that people don't live long. I lived until I was almost 19.

I did have a karmic relationship with my mother. My mother and father were both carriers of it. I had had a very, very poor relationship with my mother in past incarnations. We were just at each other's throats constantly. I know this because I reviewed the akashic records and it was a bad relationship carried over from a prior lifetime long, long ago. We came back to try to work it out. We were at each other's throats. We didn't work it out. Then we came back into this last life to try again to make some amends. I just did not like my mother because she was very distant. That probably was her way of not verbally fighting with me, but she just was not a warm person. I needed comfort. And so what is going to happen? We are going to have to come back and do it all over again. I have forgiven her for her coldness and aloofness toward me. She has not yet come over to this side. I think that she regrets not having been a better mother because I do believe we could have worked it out. We could have settled the karma this time, but unfortunately we didn't.

Once I reviewed my life, went through the akashic records, and really accepted why I suffered cystic fibrosis, I understood that I did not need a long time on earth. If I had something that would cause me great distress, I could work off that karma from the past. But because I resented my mother's aloofness, I accumulated more. When I got the whole picture and understood it, then I have tried to help others coming to this side having suffered cystic fibrosis. I mainly work with this group. It is very interesting because we have all had some of the same problems of wanting to know why in the majority of the cases, but not always, it is the result of a problem with one or both parents in past lives. So we come back with something that really requires a lot of nurturing, and we don't always get it. There are national associations on earth that have tried to bring awareness to this disease, and to help in the treatment while on earth. But there are emotional dynamics that I don't think are really being addressed. We are doing our best on this side to try to impress people.

People suffering from cystic fibrosis usually come to this side much in advance of their parents, so we have a chance to work on ourselves and to find forgiveness. Then when the parent comes over with whom we have had the problem, we can be much more helpful to them because we have already forgiven them, that is, if we work on ourselves prior to their coming over. The parent usually has a lot of guilt that they have to work through, but our forgiveness does help them. They have to have that remorse in order to really want to ask and receive forgiveness. It all works out most of the time.

333I think you will probably be seeing more and more cases of cystic fibrosis because some of the other problems are being taken care of through medical advances, like heart problems being treated earlier. People have to have a way to work out karma, so there will always be ways.

Dr. L. Milton on helping newcomers adjust to their new bodies

As Lucy told you, cystic fibrosis is becoming more prevalent and people are gaining a greater awareness of this disease. It is, of course, genetic and it is very definitely a karmic disorder because it does affect children and the life span is relatively short. It is rare for some one at the present time to go much beyond their 20's or early 30's.

I was a doctor on earth and I treated a number of patients who had this problem, and it was very discouraging that we could do so little about it. Scientists will figure out how to prolong life for these patients, but I do not believe it will come to actually curing it. If we had on earth fabulous spiritual healers, then it might be possible. But medical science alone is not going to find the answer, at least not any time soon, as far as I can see. I think that almost anything, except deformities perhaps, can be cured through intensive and radical change in attitude.

When they get to this side, we have to really teach most of them some very basis things about their new body and the lack of restrictions, and that they are totally and completely healed if they get it out of their head that they are still sick. We work in groups. We work with individuals. We find that the group sessions are the most beneficial. We give them an opportunity to share what it was like for them on earth. And if there were problems with their parents or any significant person in a previous life, then we do ask their permission for the guides to go into the akashic records and confirm what the problem was. It takes intensive work to help them accept that they had a role in what happened. Many of them come over blaming their parents for being carriers of the gene, blaming God, blaming medical science for not finding a cure, and so forth. We work very gradually with them to get them to accept, to forgive, and to move on. And some do, and a few don't. A few will remain just where they are in consciousness, but we do offer them the opportunity to return at any time to the group if they would like. ◆

15.

DIGESTIVE SYSTEM

Function of the Digestive System

The major function of the digestive tract is to break down food into forms that can be absorbed and utilized by the body and to eliminate the waste. Digestion is a complex process that involves a number of finely coordinated chemical and mechanical functions. These are controlled by intricate feedback systems involving the nervous and endocrine systems. The digestive tract is a series of hollow organs joined in a long, twisting tube from mouth to the anus. Inside this tube is a lining called the mucosa. In the mouth, stomach, and small intestine, the mucosa contains tiny glands that produce enzymes to help digest food. There are also two solid digestive organs, the liver and the pancreas, which produce enzymes that reach the intestine through small tubes.

During the digestive process, food passes down the throat, through the esophagus, and into the stomach, where food continues to be broken down. The partially digested food passes into a short tube called the duodenum—the first part of the small intestine. The jejunum and ileum are also part of the small intestine. The liver, the gallbladder, and the pancreas produce enzymes and substances to help with digestion in the small intestine. After the digestive process is complete, the resulting waste travels downstream to the colon. The colon and rectum are parts of the body's digestive system which remove nutrients from food and store waste until it passes out of the body. Together, the colon and rectum form a long, muscular tube called the large intestine. The colon is involved in processes that solidify the waste products so that they may be excreted. The food we eat, the amount of exercise we get, and the pace and stress level of our day all affect the health of our digestive system.

Diseases and Karma Associated with the Digestive System

Crohn's disease is an inflammatory bowel disease that is generally karmic because the patients have not been able in past lives to get over things. They have held on. Now, there is no control.

It is a narrow way of thinking that can not only cause problems with the arteries and the blood vessels, but can cause problems in the colon with hemorrhoids where the elimination process is not working smoothly. In a very withholding person, the walls of the colon simply become perforated from the irritation of not eliminating in a normal fashion and there is bleeding.

With ulcerative colitis there is a family history. It is generally caused by a nerve problem because it usually occurs in people who are always worked up, always negative, which affects the nerves. The nerves, in turn, affect the body.

Pancreatic cancer is karmic, but it still can be avoided if we live right. We can come in with that as our karma, but if we are very diligently working out our karma, and getting ourselves on a spiritual path, we may not have to go through the disease, or we can go through the disease and respond well to treatment.

A gluttonous and debauched appetite in a past life may contribute to stomach and digestive troubles. Such problems in this life may have a mental basis. We can trace just about everything back to the mind and how we think. Maybe we could not digest or accept certain teachings.

With constipation, we cannot rid ourselves of certain thoughts and this results in our body not eliminating. For example, we are always thinking that something bad is going to happen. We cannot get over that. Or, you live in lack and limitation, thinking that is the only way it is going to be. That can result in constipation because we are not letting go and our body is not letting go. If it goes on for a long time, it definitely is going to affect the body.

Stomach troubles do respond to love and joy. If we eat when we are very upset, what happens? We will say, that really upset my stomach. It is our thoughts and emotions that are causing it. So when we are worried, or very anxious, it is better to just take in liquids rather than a lot of solid food until we can regain control of our emotions.

The liver, which is one of the most complex organs in the body, carries on many essential metabolic and chemical functions. In view of the variety of functions performed by the liver, and its susceptibility to a number of disorders, it has an amazing ability to regenerate, so that liver disease is not as common as might be expected. A baby is rarely born with liver problems. The organ usually works efficiently until viruses, alcohol, drugs, bacteria, fungal or parasitic infections cause damage. Karma can also play a role in making one susceptible to liver problems. If a person in a past life has caused a great deal of turmoil in other people's lives, and placed them into positions where there is constant tension at home or on the job, these people come back and have the same type of problems. This upset will affect the liver and/or the kidneys.

Chart of Diseases of the Digestive System

Note: On the following chart are listed diseases which can be inherited, but some are only karmic "to a point." In other words, in keeping with our soul contract, we may have specifically and intentionally chosen a family who could provide the gene to develop a particular "karmic" disease or condition. This is our way of balancing our karma. The predisposition also existed in that family for one of the "karmic to a point" diseases, and we simply picked up that gene as well. Depending on how we live our life prior to the proposed onset of a disorder, we may not develop a "karmic" or a "karmic to a point" disease at all, having already worked off our karma in another way. Or, the disease may be mild and very responsive to treatment.

Disease	Description	Genetic	Karmic
Celiac Disease	Intolerance to gluten, a protein found in wheat, rye, and barley flours. Weight loss and nutritional deficiencies are common to the disease. Usually appears in childhood.	yes	Karmic to a point
Cleft Lip and Palate	If untreated, may cause disfigurement to a greater or lesser degree, and cause swallowing problems and speech difficulties.	yes	Yes
Colorectal Cancer	Cancer that begins in the colon is called colon cancer, and cancer that begins in the rectum is called rectal cancer. Cancers affecting either of these organs also may be called colorectal cancer.

Colorectal cancer occurs when the cells that line the colon or the rectum become abnormal and grow out of control. The abnormal growing cells create a tumor, which is the cancer. | yes | Karmic to a point |
| Crohn's Disease | A chronic inflammatory condition of the gastro-intestinal tract from unknown origin similar to ulcerative colitis. There is a strong cultural factor as it occurs especially among Jewish people. | yes | yes |

Disease	Description	Genetic	Karmic
Cystic Fibrosis	The most common fatal genetic disease in the U. S. Today. It causes the body to produce a thick, sticky mucus that clogs the lungs, leading to infection, and blocks the pancreas, stopping digestive enzymes from reaching the intestines where they are required to digest food.	yes	yes
Diabetes, Type 1	Chronic metabolic disorder that adversely affects the body's ability to manufacture and use insulin, a hormone necessary for the conversion of food into energy. May appear in childhood or adolescence. Affects many organs and body functions eyes, feet, etc.	yes	yes
Gallstones	The most common manifestation of gallbladder disease.	yes	Karmic to a point
GERD (Gastro-esophageal Reflux Disease)	Acid reflux, stomach acid washing back into the esophagus can cause pain, irritation, and bleeding. Too much acid in system.	no	Due to conditions in this life

Disease	Description	Genetic	Karmic
Glucose Galactose Malabsorption	A rare metabolic disorder caused by a defect in glucose and galactose transport across the intestinal lining. Characterized by severe diarrhea and dehydration as early as the first day of life and can result in rapid death if lactose (milk sugar) sucrose (table sugar), glucose, and galactose are not removed from the diet.	yes	yes
Lactose Intolerance	A common disorder caused by a lack of lactase, an enzyme secreted in the walls of the small intestine that is needed to break down lactose, the sugar in cow's milk. Most common among blacks and people of Asian origin.	yes	Karmic to a point
Mechel s Diverticulum	Diverticula that form in the lower part of the ileum.	yes	Karmic to a point
Pancreatic Cancer	Usually occurs during middle age and is slightly more common in men than women.	yes	yes

Disease	Description	Genetic	Karmic
Ulcerative Colitis	Ulcerative colitis is a chronic (ongoing) disease of the colon, or large intestine. The disease is marked by inflammation and ulceration of the colon mucosa', or innermost lining. Tiny open sores, or ulcers, form on the surface of the lining, where they bleed and produce pus and mucus. Because the inflammation makes the colon empty frequently, symptoms typically include diarrhea (sometimes bloody) and often crampy abdominal pain. The inflammation usually begins in the rectum and lower colon, but it may also involve the entire colon.	yes	no
Wilson's Disease	A rare disorder of copper transport, resulting in copper accumulation and toxicity to the liver and brain. Liver disease is the most common symptom in children; neurological disease is most common in young adults. Cornea of the eye can also be affected.	yes	yes
Zellweger Syndrome	A rare hereditary disorder affecting infants, usually resulting in death. Unusual problems in prenatal development, an enlarged liver, high levels of iron and copper in the blood, and vision disturbances are among the major manifestations.	yes	yes

16.

THE ENDOCRINE SYSTEM

The Function of the Endocrine System

The endocrine system is a complex collection of hormone-producing glands that control basic body functions such as metabolism, growth and sexual development. The endocrine glands consist of: pineal, pituitary, thyroid and parathyroids, thymus, hypothalamus, adrenals, pancreas, ovaries (female), and testes (male).

The endocrine system plays a very important role spiritually. It is closely tied to the ethers and the energy that we bring into the body. When the chakras—those spiritual energy centers of the etheric body which plug into the various glands—are closed, they are not bringing the energy into our body. That is our spiritual energy. The chakras have to be open to get that energy into the body.

Diseases and Karma Associated with the Endocrine System

The chakras open ever in keeping with the degree that we raise our consciousness. The higher the consciousness, the more energy that is going to come in. If they are closed off, we are going to attract all kinds of diseases. It is only our own thoughts that hold us back from pulling in the etheric energy. So, in order to have the endocrine system working properly, we have to get on a spiritual path, however, only a very, very small percentage of the population is on a spiritual path. Most problems with the endocrine system are karmic.

People who are trying to develop spiritually are opening their chakras. They are indrawing the energy from the solar system. They are pulling it down all through their body. This is spiritual energy that is going to make the body much stronger, or make the person much stronger and better able to control himself or herself. Most of those on a spiritual path have had many lives when they were relatively strong and developed, so they are bringing back the ability to tap again into that energy. If they are new souls, they are going to have to work through two or three or four lives before they actually are bringing in the energy from spirit. So it is these souls who would be more likely to have a problem with the endocrine system.

Diabetes is definitely a karmic condition. It runs in families and is affecting the younger and younger. The implications are frightening and lead to a host of problems. It can affect the feet, resulting in the need for amputations. It can affect the eyes and cause blindness. Kidney failure and heart disease are of great concern. Obesity and lack of exercise play a role in the disease. From the mid-1960s to the present, the number of cases has tripled. Although it is a karmic condition, it can be helped by diet, exercise and proper treatment. There must be control of sugar intake.

Being born a midget usually stems from something that is missing in the endocrine system, probably with the pituitary gland. It is not necessarily karmic, but the soul did chose a family which could produce that possibility. The soul may need to work out something with those particular parents, or may have come to them for other reasons and just happened to pick up the gene. We should not think of karma as something that we absolutely have to go through no matter what it does to the body. Yes, we have to go through it, but we can do whatever will help us to control the condition. And in that way, we are working out the karma, too, because we are getting ourselves on a higher vibration.

Chart of Diseases of the Endocrine System

Note: On the following chart are listed diseases which can be inherited, but some are only karmic "to a point." In other words, in keeping with our soul contract, we may have specifically and intentionally chosen a family who could provide the gene to develop a particular "karmic" disease or condition. This is our way of balancing our karma. The predisposition also existed in that family for one of the "karmic to a point" diseases, and we simply picked up that gene as well. Depending on how we live our life prior to the proposed onset of a disorder, we may not develop a "karmic" or a "karmic to a point" disease at all, having already worked off our karma in another way. Or, the disease may be mild and

Disease	Description	Genetic	Karmic
Adrenoleuko-dystrophy	The fatty covering (myelin sheath) on nerve fibers in the brain is lost, and the adrenal gland degenerates, leading to progressive neurological disability and death. (1993 film "Lorenzo's Oil")	yes	yes
Addison's Disease	An endocrine disorder caused by destruction of the adrenal cortex.	no	yes
Autoimmune Polyglandular Syndrome	Depression of an endocrine organ as a result of an autoimmune reaction that ultimately results in partial or complete destruction of the gland. Disease affecting one organ is frequently followed by impairment of other glands, resulting in multiple endocrine failure.	yes	yes
Breast and Ovarian Cancer	A major cause of cancer death in American women.	yes	yes
Cockayne Syndrome	Rare inherited disorder in which patient is sensitive to sunlight, has short stature, and has the appearance of premature aging. Progressive and apparent in infancy.	yes	yes

Disease	Description	Genetic	Karmic
Congenital Adrenal Hyperplasia	A genetic disease that affects the adrenal glands.	yes	Karmic to a point
Cushing's Syndrome	Malignant tumors of pituitary, adrenal and/or other glands.	no	Karmic to a point
Diabetes	Chronic metabolic disorder that adversely affects the body's ability to manufacture and use insulin, a hormone necessary for the conversion of food into energy. May appear in childhood or adolescence. Affects many organs and body functions, eyes, feet, etc.	yes	yes
Diastrophic Dysplasia	Rate growth disorder in which patients are usually short, have club feet, and malformed hands and joints. Particularly prevalent in Finland.	yes	yes

Disease	Description	Genetic	Karmic
Dwarfism	Restricted growth. May be caused by failure of pituitary to secrete adequate growth hormone, or by thyroid disorders, malnutrition, and other illnesses. If hormonal deficiency is cause, hormone therapy can stimulate normal growth.	yes	yes
Goiter	Swelling or overgrowth of the thyroid gland	no	Yes, in some cases
Graves' Disease	Overactive thyroid. Eyes may bulge and take on a staring appearance, goiter may develop.	yes	yes
Homocystinuria	Inherited disorder of the metabolism of the amino acid methionine. Characterized by nearsightedness, blood clots in veins and arteries, mental retardation may be seen, a tall, thin build with long limbs spidery fingers, knock-knees and curved spine.	yes	yes
Infantile Hypothyroidism	A congenital defect in which a baby is born with no thyroid or one that does not produce enough hormone. Untreated, results in cretinism.	yes	yes

Disease	Description	Genetic	Karmic
Multiple Endocrine Neoplasia	A group of rare diseases in which specific endocrine glands, such as the parathyroid, pancreas, and pituitary glands tend to become overactive, resulting in excessive calcium in the bloodstream (causing kidney stones or kidney damage, fatigue, weakness, muscle or bone pain, constipation, indigestion, and thinning of bones).	yes	Karmic due to conditions in this life
Pendred Syndrome	Accounts for 10% of hereditary deafness. Patients usually also suffer from thyroid goiter.	yes	Karmic to a point
Abnormalities of Sexual Development	Since the pituitary secretes vital gonadotropic hormones that stimulate the testes and ovaries to produce their respective sex hormones, many problems can be traced to pituitary dysfunction. Numerous chromosomal abnormalities may be involved.	yes	yes

Enlightening Voices from the Other Side

Dr. Wren on paying off karma by coming back as a dwarf

Wren just like the bird. And when we are in our spirit body, we can just about fly like the birds. We can think ourselves somewhere and we are there.

I have come this morning to talk about people who are born in a dwarf body. I think that I can speak to that with some authority because I was a dwarf. I am no longer in that body but I did come into this incarnation as a dwarf. I will tell you a little bit about why this was so. In a past incarnation, I was a very normal, good looking man. Actually, I was quite a handsome man and I was extremely vain and very condescending to people. I was born into a very well-to-do family. We enjoyed social prestige in the community. In fact, my family was a very prominent family. My mother and father were very kind and good people to those who were needy, but I was not very kind.

I thought that I was just above everyone because of my nobility. I was English. I was obnoxious. That is the only word that I really can use. I was obnoxious and I had very little to do with people that I felt were beneath me. I was arrogant. The good that I did in that life centered around anything that would bring me some notice of a high degree. It wasn't done for altruistic reasons. I called attention to myself. I really did. But I called attention to myself for the wrong reasons.

When I went back to Spirit after that life, I did eventually do a review of my life. This was a long, long time ago in your earth terms. I eventually got around to doing it. At first I thought I was what you would call on earth "the cat's meow." I thought I was really great, but I had to be brought down many, many, many pegs. When I did the review of my life, I really saw how obnoxious I was. I really had not done a lot of good at all. Then I went through the akashic records and found that in a previous life, going even further back, that I was very egoistical—not as bad as this life I am talking about now. I thought, *I have got to get through this.* So, I planned with the help of guides and teachers and the higher ones to really return in a way that would bring me attention that would be very negative for the most part. I chose to be a dwarf.

I was a very intelligent man and I wanted to do many things, but my size prevented me from doing what I would liked to have done. My soul was very content but my ego wasn't. My personality wanted to achieve something and there were very few opportunities open to me because I was a dwarf. Everywhere I went people would laugh at me. I was the butt of jokes. I attended regular school and I really didn't have many friends. I worked hard in school and because I was bright, the friends that I did have came to me mainly for my help with their studies. And eventually they did become good friends and we have remained friends to this day. They mean a great deal to me.

I was always different. I didn't understand why I had that body. I thought that it had something to do with the endocrine system, something that was malfunctioning. I became a writer because I could send in articles to magazines and they didn't know my physical condition. I made my living that way. It was not terribly lucrative, but I did make my living that way. I published a collection of short stories, but I really didn't amount to a great deal as far as being very successful. My writing was steady. I had great sensitivity as to what people were thinking. I would write about a variety of things. Some were medical problems that I would research and I would contact people by telephone and talk to them, get their feelings, and then submit these articles. So editors of different magazines didn't have a clue that I was not physically a normal person.

Now I did not live to a ripe old age. I was around 41 when I passed to this side. I have to tell you that was long enough for me in that body. I came over here still as a dwarf in the etheric body. I no longer had any physical problems. I did have a heart condition on earth and this is what eventually did me in. And so when I came to this side, I got into a group with other dwarfs and midgets. It was led by a Dr. Vernon, a wonderful, wonderful doctor, who himself had been a midget. He went back to a former life when he was in a normal body. When he came to this side he worked with those of us who were passing over in dwarf or midget bodies. We went through why we were born that way. He explained it was not a fluke. It was something that we had chosen in order to work off karma. And I can certainly tell you that it was a very painful life because we just stood out.

I have noticed on your television that there have been dwarfs working as actors and have made their living this way. I have mixed feelings about that, but it does show people that although our body may be deformed, our minds are active and we are intelligent. And in that respect, it is fine. I don't like it when they poke fun. I really don't. But it does help us to get through whatever it is that we have to experience.

So on this side, with the help of Dr. Vernon and eventually going through the akashic records, I really saw for myself that I had to make changes. I understood then why I chose this body. After I really got through that, I decided I had enough of this body and that I wanted to go back to the life when I was a good looking man, and I wanted to be a very humble and sweet person. After growing as a dwarf, and having the understanding that I could go back to that former life and that I could be a spiritually elevated person, then I worked very, very hard and I have become a doctor. I worked with Dr. Vernon for a long time. Now I have my own group where I work with others, helping newcomers to this side who are either dwarf or midget.

The midgets receive about as much attention as a dwarf, but they are not viewed in quite the same way. A midget is very perfectly proportioned, unlike the dwarf. They are just a small version of a normal person. So while they are viewed as being abnormal, they are not viewed with the disdain that a dwarf is. A dwarf is more repulsive to some people. A midget is just a little person of curiosity. They do get a lot of attention. I would not say it is all positive, but they are here because they did not flaunt themselves to the extent that a dwarf did in a past life. They came back to get attention, yes, for people to know they were not quite like everyone else. But they did not have the degree of vanity that a dwarf usually did. They may have done some negative things, so they come back to get some negative attention.

I do want to tell you a little more about the groups that we have because not all dwarfs were exactly like me in my previous life. Some were just very, very mean. I was obnoxious but I was not a mean, mean person to do ugly things. I just didn't care about people who were needy and I thought I was above them. I did not go out of my way to be mean to them. But some people come back as dwarfs because they were absolutely mean and they drew attention to themselves because they were mean. And now they are drawing attention to themselves as dwarfs because of having been mean. In the previous life, they did unkind things and felt they were great. They had lots of power and then they came back to a life where they didn't have a lot of power. I can assure you a dwarf doesn't have a lot of power. People will make very unkind, derisive comments, giving them a real put-down and it is a put-down! You are small in size and you are literally put down. And many midgets feel they have been put down also, but not to the degree that the dwarf has had to suffer. Midgets are like little dolls.

I am very, very pleased that I had an opportunity to come in so people can really understand that dwarfs and midgets are not freaks, but they are souls that have chosen to come back in a body that is different in order that their soul may progress. They want to pay off the karma—that it is a punishment of their own making. They chose this and they really ought to be commended actually for coming back in that way to work off their karma. It is for their soul's growth that they have chosen. This is true of those who are retarded or have various illnesses. It is a choice. We do suffer. That goes without saying. Many have had to go into sideshows to make a living because nothing else was open to them. ♦

17.

THE KIDNEYS

Function of the Kidneys

The kidneys play a crucial role in the body's circulatory and urinary systems by filtering waste products and toxins from the blood, while returning nutrients to the bloodstream and assisting in controlling blood pressure. In the course of performing these complex and vital tasks, the kidneys are subject to numerous diseases. Diseases of the kidney can affect blood pressure (hypertension) and blood pressure can affect kidney function.

Diseases and Karma Associated with the Kidneys

Some kidney diseases are inherited, such as, solitary kidney, horseshoe kidney (the lower half may fuse instead of separating during the fetal stage of development), anomalies of renal circulation, floating or dropped kidney, polycystic kidneys, Alport's Syndrome (affects men mainly), cystinuria, and renal tubular defects. Anatomical defects of the kidneys are definitely karmic. The same is true of the liver. These are conditions which the soul has chosen in order to get rid of the karma brought into this life. It is not the disease itself that is karmic. The disease or condition provides the tool for a person to work off karma.

Some kidney diseases are the product of karma accumulated in this life time. Worry, anxiety, fear, and criticism produce kidney trouble. A sudden shock and a grief can cause very acute attacks of nephritis, followed in some cases by death. Every mental and emotional reaction to circumstances and conditions should be improved. We cannot worry about every condition. We cannot worry and become emotional over every problem that comes to us. Our mental condition affects the body. The kidneys eliminate the poisons of the body, and when the mind is full of anger and hatred and resentment, we are pouring more poison into our body.

If we created a lot of poison in a past life and never got rid of it, it is back with us to be dealt with. The kidney problems are telling us we have to get to work and get rid of the greed, envy, anger, worries, being overly critical, and all the negatives that are causing the toxic build up. We cannot just carry on as we did in a past life and maintain healthy kidneys. When we have degenerative thoughts, we must turn them into creative energizing and vitalizing thoughts. Now, in all diseases, the mind creates. In order to cure disease, we have to change the thinking.

All kidney problems are considered karmic in nature. Mainly, it is the older person who is affected. This gives a person an opportunity to work off some of his or her negativity in the first part of their life. If changes are made, the individual may not need to develop a kidney problem. The karma will have been satisfied in another way.

Major kidney disorders include hypertension, kidney stones, inflammatory diseases of the nephrons and glomeruli, and the end result of these diseases, if they remain untreated, is kidney failure. Some of the abnormalities that take place in later years are due to how we live our life—our diet and how effectively the toxins are filtered. Not taking good care of the body only compounds the situation. If we are not giving the right kind of nourishment to the kidneys, and we have a karmic problem in the first place, then the kidney trouble will be worse than it would be were it not karmic. When a person is very elderly, the kidneys are one of the organs that will go. Failure that occurs when on the death bed, however, is not karmic, but the body just giving up. When kidneys fail, that is usually a sign of impending death.

Dropsy is associated with kidney failure. It is karmic due mainly to the way the past life was lived, that is, being too materialistic and not giving any thought to spirituality. The fluid does not eliminate properly through the kidneys and the skin. The result is swelling from the excessive accumulation of serous fluid in tissue. In Luke 14:1-6, it is recorded that Jesus healed a man of Dropsy.

Luke 14:1   And it came to pass, as he went into the house of one of the chief Pharisees to eat bread on the sabbath day, that they watched him.

2   And, behold, there was a certain man before him which had the dropsy.

3   And Jesus answering spake unto the lawyers and Pharisees, saying, Is it lawful to heal on the sabbath day?

4   And they held their peace. And he took him, and healed him, and let him go;

5   And answered them, saying, Which of you shall have an ass or an ox fallen into a pit, and will not straightway pull him out on the sabbath day?

6   And they could not answer him again to these things.

Commentary: Jesus was saying to use common sense about what could or could not be done on the Sabbath.

Enlightening Voices from the Other Side

Dr. Kenny:

I have come because I have an interest in different diseases in the body and what they are related to. I am going to talk to you about the kidneys because we know there are various kidney diseases. Some people develop kidney stones or inflammatory diseases. Some kidneys do not function well enough to do their job, so some have to go on a dialysis machine.

First of all, the kidney functions as a purifier. The bodily fluids are taken into this machine called a kidney where the toxins have accumulated and they are excreted as urine. Sometimes the kidneys do not function at all. This can be a karmic condition from a past life, but not always. It can be from mental attitudes, diet and life style during the current life.

If you examine the purpose of the kidneys as a purifier, and if it is karmic, or even if it is not past life karmic, it means that the person has allowed a lot of toxins to build up, symbolic of negativity. When there is a lot of negativity, it means thoughts are not pure, not changed into positive thinking. Then the flow can slow or stop or crystallize into stones which are painful. The pump is simply not functioning properly so that the purifying process can take place. That is when we have to put a person on dialysis. It depends on the toxicity to be dealt with which determines how often the procedure is required.

When they come to this side of life and review their akashic record, then they do see that there are many problems with negativity and being withholding rather than giving to others. Spiritually, the kidneys symbolize generosity. Really, it is a change in attitude that brings about the healing over here. We do not have the problem of having to eliminate over here, so they will realize very quickly that they do not have a medical problem. The etheric body has organs that look like kidneys but they are not functional. Remember, they are just there to provide the pattern for the physical body. ✦

18.

DISEASES OF THE IMMUNE SYSTEM

Function of the Immune System

The immune system is a complex and highly developed system, yet its mission is simple: to seek and kill invaders. If a person is born with a severely defective immune system, death from infection by a virus, bacterium, fungus or parasite will occur. In severe combined immunodeficiency, lack of an enzyme means that toxic waste builds up inside immune system cells, killing them and thus devastating the immune system.

Chart of Diseases of the Immune System

Note: On the following chart are listed diseases which can be inherited, but some are only karmic "to a point." In other words, in keeping with our soul contract, we may have specifically and intentionally chosen a family who could provide the gene to develop a particular "karmic" disease or condition. This is our way of balancing our karma. The predisposition also existed in that family for one of the "karmic to a point" diseases, and we simply picked up that gene as well. Depending on how we live our life prior to the proposed onset of a disorder, we may not develop a "karmic" or a "karmic to a point" disease at all, having already worked off our karma in another way. Or, the disease may be mild and very responsive to treatment.

Disease	Description	Genetic	Karmic
Acquired Immuno-deficiency Syndrome (AIDS)	Human viral disease that ravages the immune system, undermining the body's ability to defend itself from infection and disease. Caused by the human immuno-deficiency virus (HIV) AIDS leaves an infected person vulnerable to opportunistic infections. Can be fatal.	no	yes
Asthma	A chronic inflammatory disorder of the airways characterized by coughing, shortness of breath, and chest tightness. Affects more than 5% of our population, including children.	yes	yes
Ataxia Telangiectasia	First signs usually appear in the second year of life as a lack of balance and slurred speech. It is a progressive, degenerative disease charactrized by cerebellar degeneration, immunodeficiency, radiosensitivity, and a predisposition to cancer.	yes	yes

Disease	Description	Genetic	Karmic
Autoimmune Polyglandular Syndrome	Depression of an endocrine organ as a result of an autoimmune reaction that ultimately results in partial or complete destruction of the gland. Disease affecting one organ is frequently followed by impairment of other glands, resulting in multiple endocrine failure.	yes	yes
Diabetes, type 1	Chronic metabolic disorder that adversely affects the body's ability to manufacture and use insulin, a hormone necessary for the conversion of food into energy. May appear in childhood or adolescence. Affects many organs and body functions, eyes, feet, etc.	yes	yes
DiGeorge Syndrome	A rare congenital disease present at birth, whose symptoms vary greatly between individuals but commonly include a history of recurrent infection, heart defects, and characteristic facial features. The basis for this syndrome is a lack of immune system cells.	yes	yes

Disease	Description	Genetic	Karmic
Immuno-deficiency with Hyper-IgM (HIM)	A rare primary immunodeficiency characterized by the production of normal to increased amounts of IgM antibody of questionable quality and an inability to produce sufficient qualtitites of IgG and IgA. Individuals with HIM are susceptible to recurrent bacterial infections and are at an increased risk of autoimmune disorders and cancer at an early age. Long lasting immunity cannot be maintained without a bone marrow transplant, when a suitable donor is available.	yes	Karmic to a point
Leukemia	A type of cancer in which the blood has too many white blood cells. The white cells produced continually multiply, even though they are not needed, spreading throughout the body and interfering with bodily functions.	yes	To a point in adults - definitely in children
Severe Combined Immunodeficiency	Represents a group of rare, sometimes fatal, congenital disorders characterized by little or no immune response. The defining feature of SCID, commonly known as bubble boy disease, is a defect in the specialized white blood cells that defend us from infection by viruses, bacteria and fungi.	yes	yes

Enlightening Voices from the Other Side

Dr. Adams tells what it is like to suffer from AIDS

I have come today to talk about what it means, what it is like, to suffer from AIDS. I was a gay man and I was rather promiscuous. I did not have a single partner for very long periods of time. When I came down with AIDS it had a devastating effect upon me, absolutely devastating effect, because I knew people all around me were dying. I knew that Liberace, the nightclub entertainer, had died of AIDS, and that Rock Hudson, the movie actor, and many, many others had also. It was terribly frightening.

The drugs at that time were not as effective as what you have now in terms of prolonging life. When my immune system was affected and my body began to waste away, I started getting problems with one thing and then another in the body. There was not much one could do about it.

My family was not aware that I was gay. I lived and worked in another city and they had no idea. They wondered why I wanted to remain a bachelor because I was a nice looking man, in fact, pretty good looking. Women were attracted to me but I was not attracted to them. I really could not tell my family this. I would say to them that I had a number of women friends. And I did. I worked with them on the job.

I was a professional person. As a matter of fact, I was a doctor and I knew that I should not take chances with sex. And for the most part, sex was protected. But then I met a gentleman that I truly fell in love with, and he told me that he was clean, that I was his first partner. And I believed him. He showed no signs of having the disease. This was going to be a life long relationship, but he deceived me. He had had a fling before I met him and he was a carrier.

I did not have a private practice. I worked actually for an HMO. And because I was in that kind of setting, I had many women patients and I worked with women doctors and nurses. We had a lot of fun together. When I really found out that I was HIV positive and that I was developing full blown AIDS, I was asked if I had been careless and contaminated myself in treating a patient. I did not divulge that I had the disease because of my companion. I just let that slide, and people behind my back drew their own conclusions. I was well liked and I know that I was genuinely missed. I really felt a great deal of animosity toward my partner. While he remained loyal to me in seeing that I was taken care of, I did hold it very much against him that I had studied so many years to become a doctor to help people, now I was being taken away. It did not take but several years and I was gone.

I came to this side of life not knowing a thing about it, not even giving much thought to my dying until I saw people on earth dying around me. But then I thought, well I would just be put in a grave and I will lay there and maybe some day will be awakened. It was very different than I expected. People were so very, very kind to me, and so very, very loving. No one seemed to be afraid to touch me or to be around me. They were not afraid they would catch something. I did wake up and I did start to study and to try to raise my consciousness. I reviewed my life. It really wasn't all that bad a life. I wondered why, I asked my guides and teachers why did I have AIDS, why was my life shortened? And so they took me through the akashic records. I was ready for the review because I had really worked on myself. I learned that I had had some sexual problems in a previous life—deviant sexual activities. I was to come to this life to not have an interest in women and to not engage in sex at all.

Over here we learn many things, like why things happen to us, and what we should have done and didn't do. And it is going to be necessary for me to come back and to do this again, perhaps as a gay man again, or in some way to work off my karma. I try to help on this side with men who come over who have had AIDS. I work with a very fine doctor who is very compassionate, and we try to help men see what they have done with their lives. Had they not been promiscuous, which is a problem many had in a previous life, then they would not have suffered. We do not have to have things go wrong with us if we live our live differently. If we live a good life, we don't always have to work out our karma by going through something devastating. And believe me, when you see your body literally wasting away and there is no hope, and there was no hope at the time I came along, it is devastating. Some day they will be able to get a hold on AIDS. Right now, if we could just halt the spread of it. Actually, it would cost so little to stamp it out. If we could give out contraceptives and educate, because it is horrible to bring poor children into this world to suffer. It is unnecessary. I am told that as we elevate as a world, then we will not need to have such devastating things happen to us.

When I had AIDS on earth, it was as bad as having leprosy. People did not want to be around you. They were afraid. Education has helped a great deal. But it was a very bad thing and I have many, many regrets. I really can't do anything about it except to know that I did not infect anyone myself. And for that, I am truly grateful. It was wonderful to come to this side and know that I had a perfect body and that I could start life anew. And so, I leave that with you, and I do wish everyone on earth would be more careful in their sexual relationships.

Comments from the Master Teacher:
Dr. Adams is doing a fine job in helping many who come to this side to gain a new lease on life. You would be amazed at the guilt that many of them bring with them. They were not comfortable being gay, and then to have AIDS as a further stigma, at least in their mind, is very difficult for them. There is a lot of attitudinal healing that goes on. ✦

19.

NUTRITIONAL AND METABOLIC DISEASES

Function of Metabolism

From the National Center for Biotechnology website: "Metabolism is the means by which the body derives energy and synthesizes the other molecules it needs from the fats, carbohydrates and proteins we eat as food, by enzymatic reactions helped by minerals and vitamins. This global statement masks the complicated network of enzyme-catalyzed reactions that occurs in cells." In a chart below, we have listed some of the diseases of metabolism for which inborn errors or inherited traits are due to a mutation in a metabolic enzyme.

Diseases and Karma Associated with Metabolism

Dr. Blake, Spirit teacher, contributed much of the following information. Of the problems associated with metabolism, we will elaborate mainly on **obesity,** which is a known risk factor for chronic diseases, including heart disease, diabetes, high blood pressure, stroke and some forms of cancer. Genetic, environmental, psychological and karmic factors may all play a part in obesity. Controlling weight is a multibillion-dollar business. There is a hormone called *ghrelin* which was discovered in 1999 which is believed to be an appetite stimulant. This discovery has implications leading to treatments for "wasting syndromes" stemming from AIDS, cancer, heart disease, and a variety of other problems. It also may lead to finding a way to inhibit ghrelin's stimulation of appetite in order to treat obesity. When the hormone *leptin* is released into the blood, it signals to the brain that the body has had enough to eat. Most overweight people have high levels of leptin in their bloodstream, indicating that other molecules also affect feelings of satiety and contribute to the regulation of body weight. It goes without saying that with pharmaceutical companies the race is on to find the answers and capture the weight control market.

If individuals have deep longings that have never been fulfilled, or they are upset, or have had traumatic or very negative experiences which have damaged their feelings of self-worth, they may eat to feel better, or to hide behind their bulky bodies. That habit could escalate to binge and gluttony to comfort those unexpressed longings or painful experiences. We become addicted to food. It is clear, however, that losing weight is not just about food.

Obesity is not necessarily a karmic condition. When obesity is a karmic condition, individuals do not have to eat in a gluttonous manner to keep increasing their weight. We can control what we eat. We can exercise. There may always be a problem of being heavy, but one does not have to be a terribly heavy person, getting to the point of being three or four hundred pounds. It means disciplining oneself to work at it. However, some people think if it is karmic, *Oh well, I just have to go through it.* But one does not have to make it worse, causing too much strain on the body, especially the heart.

All of this, of course, is easier said than done. The first step is to honestly face the cause. When and how did it begin? What were the emotions? What is the internal dialogue going on? What self-loathing labels are being used?—*I'm fat and disgusting, I can't lose weight and keep it off because I have tried before, I have no self-control,* etc. What does that thing inside the head say to justify going on binges?

It is so very important to know that we are spirit here and now, and to just know that our appetite and the assimilation of our food is functioning in divine order, if we accept it. A good affirmation to help us achieve some degree of discipline and put it in the hands of a Higher Power is: "Thank you God for perfectly adjusting my weight." Say it with emotion and really believe it.

It is a good practice to say grace, or at least be thankful for the food we eat. Many live to eat rather than eat to live. When we have the thought that we are eating to sustain life in the body and to keep our body functioning properly, then we have a body that the soul can work in. The body is the cathedral of the soul. The soul came to earth to perform whatever it needs to gain perfection, and if the body is not up to par, then the soul cannot accomplish all that it is here to do. It is very difficult for many people to understand that the soul has to use the body to fulfill its contract made prior to incarnation.

In cases where obesity is a karmic condition, we do not have to come into a family that is obese. We can be the only one in the family who is overweight. If it is karmic, we are taking on this metabolic problem in this life in order to overcome the karma we have accumulated in the previous life. We are born with the gene to produce it. Obesity may be karmic for different reasons. It does not necessarily mean that a person has been gluttonous in a past life. It may mean that a person had something that obesity could help them work out. For example, a very beautiful and vain woman in a past life might choose to be obese to overcome her vanity. One could be calling attention to himself/herself to be ridiculed for being so overweight. It is something that a person has to go through to get rid of whatever it was that he/she came with. The difficulty is when we are born, we do not know what we came to do. We know it before we come as it is a part of our preincarnation soul contract, but we do not remember it after we get here.

The spirit teachers say, "If we could just get people to stop and think what they are doing, especially people on a spiritual path, because they can help themselves so much to do the things that they are here to do if they listen to the promptings from their heart seed atom which contains their preincarnation plan. They must be mindful that they are not on earth to want only the finest material things; they are here to do what the soul has to do. Material things are fine and it does not mean that people cannot have them. It simply means to put them in their proper perspective."

Gaucher's Disease is a chronic disorder that affects the spleen, liver, bones, and blood, primarily in the offspring of Eastern European Jewish couples. It is karmic in so far as this race of people is concerned. In other words, in another life those suffering from this disease had a lot of problems with those particular people in a past life. They did not treat them right, so they come back as Eastern European Jews to work out their karma for their mistreatment. How perfectly the scales of divine justice are balanced! And what better way to gain understanding and tolerance than to experience living it yourself.

karmic condition known as **phenylketonuria,** a liver enzyme deficiency, can cause mental retardation if not recognized in time. This may well result from a person abusing his or her body in a former life, probably with alcohol or drugs, and is coming back to have to go through this in order to grow. It is treatable by proper diet and the individual will not need to suffer too much.

Chart of Nutritional and Metabolic Diseases

Note: On the following chart are listed diseases which can be inherited, but some are only karmic "to a point." In other words, in keeping with our soul contract, we may have specifically and intentionally chosen a family who could provide the gene to develop a particular "karmic" disease or condition. This is our way of balancing our karma. The predisposition also existed in that family for one of the "karmic to a point" diseases, and we simply picked up that gene as well. Depending on how we live our life prior to the proposed onset of a disorder, we may not develop a "karmic" or a "karmic to a point" disease at all, having already worked off our karma in another way. Or, the disease may be mild and very responsive to treatment.

NUTRITIONAL-METABOLIC DISEASES

Disease	Description	Genetic	Karmic
Adrenoleuko-dystrophy	Adrenoleukodystrophy (ALD) is a rare, inherited metabolic disorder that afflicted the young boy Lorenzo Odone, whose story is told in the 1993 film "Lorenzo's oil." In this disease, the fatty covering (myelin sheath) on nerve fibers in the brain is lost, and the adrenal gland degenerates, leading to progressive neurological disability and death.	yes	yes
Diabetes, Type 1	Diabetes is a chronic metabolic disorder that adversely affects the body's ability to manufacture and use insulin, a hormone necessary for the conversion of food into energy. The disease greatly increases the risk of blindness, heart disease, kidney failure, neurological disease, and other conditions for the approximately 16 million Americans who are affected by it. Type 1, or juvenile onset diabetes, is the more severe form of the illness.	yes	yes

Disease	Description	Genetic	Karmic
Gaucher Disease	The body is not able to properly produce the enzyme needed to break down a particular kind of fat. It then accumulates, mostly in the liver, spleen, and bone marrow. Can result in pain, fatigue, jaundice, bone damage, anemia, and even death. Common in the descendants of Jewish people from Eastern Europe (Ashkenazi). Other ethnic groups may also be affected.	yes	yes
Glucose Galactose Malabsorption	A rare metabolic disorder in which the enzyme known as galt is missing to convert galactose into glucose. The accumulation of galactose is a poison to the body, and can cause infant death if lactose/galactose is not excluded from diet. Half of the 200 severe GGM cases found worldwide result from familial intermarriage. At least 10% of general population has glucose intolerance in a milder form.	yes	yes
Hereditary Hemochromato-sis or Iron Overload	An inherited disorder that increases the amount of iron that the body absorbs from the gut. Symptoms are caused by this excess iron being deposited in multiple organs of the body. Most common among Caucasians in the U.S.	yes	Karmic to a point

Disease	Description	Genetic	Karmic
Hurler s Syndrome	A series of conditions in which there are enzymatic defects leading to mental and motor retardation and bone changes. Prognosis: death in early teens.	yes	yes
Maple Syrup Urine Disease	The underlying defect disrupts the metabolism of certain amino acids. Because they cannot be fully broken down, they accumulate in the urine, along with their metabolites to give the distinctive smell. Left untreated, there is progressive neurodegeneration leading to death within the first months of life. The Mennonite community of Lancaster County, Pennsylvania is particularly afflicted. In general population, it is a rare disease.	yes	yes
Menkes Syndrome	An inborn error of metabolism that markedly decreases the cells ability to absorb copper. Causes severe cerebral degeneration and arterial changes, resulting in death in infancy. Life expectancy is from three to thirteen years of age.	yes	yes
Niemann-Pick Disease	Cells are defective in releasing cholesterol from lysosomes, leading to excessive build-up of cholesterol inside lysosomes. Can cause death in children.	yes	yes

Disease	Description	Genetic	Karmic
Obesity	Excess of body fat that frequently results in a significant impairment of health.	yes	yes, in some cases
Pancreatic Cancer	The pancreas is responsible for producing the hormone insulin, along with other substances. It also plays a key role in the digestion of protein.	yes	yes
Phenylketonuria	Inherited error of metabolism caused by a deficiency in the enzyme phenylalanine hydroxylase. Loss of this enzyme results in mental retardation, organ damage, unusual posture and can severely compromise pregnancy.	yes	yes
Prader-Willi Syndrome	Uncommon inherited disorder characterized by mental retardation, decreased muscle tone, short stature, emotional lability and an insatiable appetite which can lead to life-threatening obesity.	yes	Karmic to a point
Refsum Disease	Rare disorder of lipid metabolism that may cause degenerative nerve disease, failure of muscle coordination, a progressive vision disorder, and bone and skin changes.	yes	Yes

Disease	Description	Genetic	Karmic
Tangier Disease	A genetic disorder of cholesterol transport, characterized by orange tonsils, very low levels of high density lipoprotein (HDL), "good cholesterol", and an enlarged liver and spleen.	yes	yes
Tay-Sachs Disease	A heritable metabolic disorder commonly associated with Ashkenazi Jews, also French Canadians of Southeastern Quebec, Cajuns of Southwest Louisiana, and other places in world. Varies from infantile and juvenile forms that exhibit paralysis, dementia, blindness and early death to a chronic adult form that exhibits neuron dysfunction and psychosis.	yes	yes
Wilson's Disease	Copper accumulation and toxicity to the liver and brain. Liver disease is the most common symptom in children; neurological disease is most common in young adults.	yes	yes
Zellweger Syndrome	A rare hereditary disorder affecting infants, and usually results in death. Unusual problems in prenatal development, an enlarged liver, high levels of iron and copper in the blood, and vision disturbances are among the major manifestations. Usually results in death.	yes	yes

Enlightening Voices from the Other Side

Dr. Parker on the problems connected with obesity

I am very happy to have this opportunity to come in and to tell you about my work. When I was on earth, I was a pediatrician and I saw a number of obese children. I did, of course, see children for other reasons also. The interesting thing was not all of the parents were obese. Many of the children were obese for karmic reasons, but I had no understanding of that at all. I thought there must be some genes from way back in their family history to produce these children that were really fat. It was sad because they were not always invited to participate in some of the games with other children. They could not run as fast, could not keep up with them. It tended to make the self-conscious child even more withdrawn, or to be one of these "funnies" so that people would laugh and they could get attention that way.

I really did try to help the parents be more watchful of what they fed their child. It was very pronounced when it was only one child in the family who was obese. They wanted to eat more, naturally for some satisfaction. If they were not accepted by the other kids, then they wanted to eat to get that feeling of comfort. And in some cases, parents really had to almost padlock the food supplies. If they were obese for karmic reasons, we were never able to get them to be little "skinny minnys," but we were able to get them to be less overweight. As we were successful in getting the patterns changed in childhood, many of them did maintain a life style that kept them healthy. Some however, as soon as they were out of the nest, gorged themselves with the wrong food and became heavy again.

When I came to this side of life, I became painfully aware of the many problems that stem from obesity. And I have worked actually on both sides of the veil trying to get doctors, nutritionists, dietitians to really help people reverse some of their eating habits. Over here, I work with both children and adult obese individuals. It is a very, very interesting situation.

We have been most interested in what your Dr. Phil has done on TV and the internet. Don't think for a moment that he is not being impressed and guided from this side of life. I am not one of his teachers or doctors, but I am very aware, and do know those who are working with him. He is a very, very fine spokesman. He is tough. He has seen first hand what obesity did in his family. He is very committed and we are extremely pleased with what he is doing. He is right on in trying to get to what happened to trigger seeking food to compensate a hurt, or whatever has happened to the individual. We have to distinguish between those who are born with a propensity to be overweight—it is in their genes—and those whose obesity is triggered by situations in this life. So we have two groups which Dr. Phil is not doing because he is not yet really aware of the role karma plays. But his approach will help both groups equally well. And he is very honest and realistic in telling them they cannot expect to go back to being tiny little things if they are now older. It is just unrealistic. His goal is to get them to be healthy, which is what we want for everyone.

When we deal with obesity from this side of life, we use a similar approach to Dr. Phil with those whose condition was not karmic. We get to the cause. What triggered it? Many obese people, contrary to what they say, are not ready to become slim. They are so attached to that identity for a variety of reasons that they are hiding behind the fat and are not ready to shed it. As you well know, on this side, thoughts are things. We can change our etheric body and go back to any age or any weight that we choose. The etheric body is very malleable. We can mold it as we like. We cannot change the basic shape or change our features, of course, but we can soften our countenance as we grow in the Light. As we elevate ourselves, everything becomes softer and more refined.

We have to work with what is in the heads of those who come to our "obesity clinic," and that is what we call it. Psychologically, many have deep-seated problems. If they are not too deep-seated, they do not need our clinic. They just talk with their guides and teachers about how they can change their bodies and they do it and that is that. Some gradually take off the weight so that their body weight is in sync with their change of identity.

Some of the ones that we work with do not want to be close to people, at least on the surface. They ache inside to be close, but they are afraid of close relationships for various reasons; so they hold people literally at a distance. When you weigh 400 or 500 lbs, and in some cases more, you do literally keep people at a distance. And so we have to work at that and it is not easy. If they have been hurt by a parent or by siblings, friends or teachers on earth, and that individual is in spirit, then we arrange a private counseling session. A lot of forgiveness must take place. If they have been raped, and the rapist is here, then he is asked to come in, if he is willing. You see, the rapist has problems, too. Believe me, we work with sex offenders and they are tough ones also. But we do everything we can to generate an atmosphere of forgiveness, and there are lots of tears shed. We also work in groups. Should they go back to earth for a visit, to a seance, or to a medium who is doing a reading for a relative or friend, they again take on the heavy body temporarily for identification purposes only.

Obesity can stem from a very, very deep hurt. Maybe someone told them they were ugly and they started eating something sweet to compensate for the lack of love. It also, of course, runs in some families who are very poor and survive on too many starchy foods because they cannot afford the balance of protein, and to fill hungry stomachs. Carbohydrates do fill up. It is also ignorance of good nutritional habits. So there are a variety of reasons why they get into this situation. And where there is a karmic condition, then naturally the incarnating soul will go to a family that provides that predisposition.

Now in cases where the guides and teachers tell us that it is strictly a karmic condition to be balanced, we go back, if we are permitted to go back, to a former life and see what they did to bring this about. They may have been very gluttonous in a former life and had to pay the price in the present one. They may have ridiculed someone who was heavy, may have been very beautiful and vain, or they may have been a very mean person. And so they have taken on a heavy body in the current life so they would be guaranteed to receive ridicule or negative attention. That is a great judgment. If they judged others in a former life, they are going to receive that judgment.

Interestingly enough, it is true that even some health professionals working with the obese tend to be repelled by severely obese people. However, the majority are kind and very compassionate counselors doing that work on earth. And I do not mean to imply that many are repulsed or disgusted. But we have, however, observed it over and over again among some workers on earth. It is very difficult to be accepting of someone that you do not think is beautiful. Workers have to learn to look inside and see a beautiful soul, one that has been hurt, and to work from the inside outwardly, while also working on the outside.

Dr. Phil is on the right track. He is liked and he will reach many, many people. This may well be his greatest calling in this earth incarnation.

Now when people get to this side with any problem, no matter what it is, any condition, we initially put all individuals into an intensive care facility where they can rest for awhile to get their bearings, so to speak. Because how many of your churches have really prepared people for an afterlife? They haven't. It comes as a surprise to many. I would say to 95% of them. Even people who think there is an afterlife usually have no conception of what that afterlife is all about. They may think they should stay in the grave when they realize they are dead to the physical world until the Archangel Gabriel blows his horn. Or, they may think they are going to be somewhere in the clouds resting eternally, to be joined by their loved ones some day. And, of course, many others think they will go into absolute nothingness. That is it.

Going back to the obese, we do tell them initially that they are in very safe hands, and that at some point, if they wish to lose weight, that it is very easy to do by just thinking themselves thinner. Now this sounds wonderful on the surface, but it takes a bit of doing for some to want to change their identity or to understand how the law works. So they need a lot of instruction about spiritual laws and how they operate—that thoughts are definitely things. We are pretty basic in giving understanding, whether it is a child or an adult. The children are usually much more receptive initially than the adults because they have had fewer years of reinforcing that obese pattern.

We do have success with those who really want to change. For those who are not ready, we let them know that the door is always open, and when they are ready to come back, we will help them. We even hold what you might call a seminar with a large group of obese spirits who previously turned down our offer of individual help. We give them a little pep talk. If they would like to change, that is fine. If they don't, that is up to them. But we do feel that by changing their weight, they change their image of themselves and are more ready to work on raising their consciousness. A person on earth, or over here, has to want to start thinking well of himself/herself in order to want to make strides spiritually. In working with them, there is a shell we have to crack. It is interesting work.

It is true that self-image does play a very big role in initially getting one on a spiritual path. When individuals think they are not worthy of help to rise to being a spirit of Light, then unworthiness is going to act as a deterrent to making the effort. But we never give up on anyone. We especially don't like to see someone who has been very obese reincarnate without having elevated himself or herself because they have not worked through that. And they frequently simply come back to a family who can provide the chemicals for another obese body and they repeat the pattern over again. This is doubly hard when they again come back to this side.

Now I did tell you that I was a pediatrician. I did go through my akashic records and I learned that in a previous life I had always been interested in helping people as best I could. I was a chef for a French royal family. This was a very long time ago. The French always liked rather fancy foods, and I did try to make things as tasty and wonderful as I could. I used all the ingredients, such as lots of butter and cream, that would put the weight on. I saw how I contributed to making some of the people quite fat and lazy. When I viewed that life, prior to coming back to this one, I thought that one of my goals would be to try to help children, especially, to be healthier and to be able to join in with other children and be accepted. It hurt me to see them left out. That, of course, was not the only reason that I chose to reincarnate. I had other things to work out, but I will not go into those because they do not relate to obesity. So that is my work and I hope that it has given you some idea of what we try to do over here. If you have any questions, please call on me.

Tayde shares how she dealt with her obesity in Spirit

When I was on earth, I literally ate myself to death. If I had not been so fat, I would not have had the problem of cutting off the wind to my chest, so to speak. It is not a healthy situation. You eat the wrong kinds of foods because they are comfort foods and you really do not care. If you live with someone who is also obese, you could care less. There is no incentive to be otherwise. Although it was somewhat karmic, I started getting heavy when I was a young adult and just kept feeding it.

People would look at me and make comments and that did hurt. It hurt a great deal, but it did not hurt enough for me to stop eating the wrong things, or eating less. So when I came to this side and knew that I could be on the road to recovery as far as turning my life around to let my soul express, then I took a look at my bulk and decided I did not need that. And so I have gradually thought myself thinner and thinner and thinner, and from 350 lbs. I am now down to about 140 lbs. I may continue to go down a little more to maybe about 130 to 135 lbs. I did not want to do it all at once, because I don't think I could have coped with such a drastic change. I wanted to do it in stages. Over here, you do not have to diet or take any pills. All I had to do was to think myself thinner. And this way I am comfortable with where I am. I am able to adapt to the change more easily. Being obese is a little different from having a heart condition. With the heart condition, you have to realize you are no longer limited. And that can change when you no longer accept that you are limited and that you do not need medications, etc.

With the weight, it is a little different situation. I believe it is better to do it gradually. One of my guides suggested that I do it that way and I think that was very wise. Because I now look slim and pretty, I naturally am going to act and think better. I am glad I listened to their advice to do it gradually. And so I feel like a new person. I am not the old person, but I needed to change my identity gradually so that I would know that it was me and not someone else in me. And yes I can say that it was a karmic situation that I could have controlled on earth. I had the tendency there and I did not discipline myself to do anything about it.

Dad says I am now beautiful. It is like being a balloon in this etheric body and you just gradually let the air out so that you can change your image. You don't feel the weight over here, but you do feel bulky, and it is nice to have that off and be trim and wear pretty clothes. There is a lady over here who helps me with selecting nice designs. We just think our clothes into existence. The higher we evolve spiritually, the prettier and the finer the materials.

Tayde returned at a later date:

When we come over here, we are so used to eating, and especially somebody like me who really lived to eat, to stuff myself, the starchier the better. When we come to this side, we have the least amount of discipline; so everybody wants some food. And the animals, too, and they give them the essence of food. The essence really means that we can extract an essence from certain foods we crave that tantalize our taste buds. We do have taste buds. And so, we are not actually chomping down on something solid; we are taking in that essence which gives the illusion that we are actually eating. And we get a sensation of fullness, although we don't really have a functioning stomach. It is an illusion. It truly is an illusion. We bring that thought to us so strongly that we can taste it and that satisfies the craving until we become disciplined enough that we no longer need the things of earth to satisfy us.

And the same is true of drugs and alcohol. It gives the desired effect. It is all in the mind because everything over here that we bring from earth is in the head, so to speak. If we think we are sick, if we think we can't do something—all kinds of things—they are all in that subconscious mind, and we really believe things more strongly here. And so, what they do to help us with drugs and alcohol, of course, is to provide the substance from which we can take the essence. Some people go to earth, but it is better to do it here where they can get weaned off.

With food, we are more or less left up to ourselves, but not entirely. In the beginning, they help us, but after awhile, we are more or less on our own. We gradually get weaned away. Some people take a long, long, long time to do it. It didn't take me so very long.

With the animals, the same system is operating. But animals do not go to earth seeking out food like we do. The workers here just gradually decrease the strength of the essence. This is what we who were humans are supposed to do for ourselves in time. That is how it works. Truly, thoughts are things.

We are in a more perfected body here and it is a beautiful body. We have a new life. It does not mean that we have forgotten anyone on earth, it doesn't mean we do not keep up with events and things happening on earth. It does mean we are really in a new world trying to reinvent ourselves. We are reinventing ourselves. We are not the people that we were on earth if we do not want to be. We can go on and evolve to higher planes.

Tayde returned again to add the following:
I did think more about obesity and actually I did go to an obesity clinic, not to get help for myself, but after you had asked for me to give a little more information, I went to an obesity clinic to share with them how I did it. I met with a group of eight "balloons". I know I should not call them that. I told them if you do not like the way you are, you just change it. But change it slowly, if it is too hard to do it all at once. They understand intellectually

that in the Spirit World we can think ourselves thin or any age we like and our etheric body conforms to our thought, but emotionally they are stuck in the condition they were in when they passed over to this side.

I tried to get across to them that if they changed their weight slowly, I really felt they would then be more ready to work on the underlying problem that had caused them to balloon up in the first place. Mine had to do with my lack of self-worth, and while on earth having teamed up with someone who was the same way; so I did not care.

I talked to this group and told them, if you reduce yourself just gradually—in small increments—while you are facing your inner problem, you will find that it will be easier to face that inner problem. As you lose weight you will gain a greater sense of worth, and you will realize that you have some control over the outside. That will help you to look at the problem and know that you have some control over it, too. You don't have to continue the way that you are going. You don't have to carry the memory of being raped, or the memory of somebody telling you that you are no good, that you never do anything right, or that you are ugly, or whatever has caused it. You don't have to carry the weight of that forever. That person, or whatever the circumstance that hurt you, is not more powerful than your own soul. That person, if there was a person, was on a level of consciousness that was very negative, and you do not have to be negative.

And so that is the way I talked to them, because, you see, I am now in a position of having demonstrated that it can be done. They all listened. We all shook hands and I left the group. The group leader thanked me for coming and he felt that I had planted some very important seeds in the minds of those spirits because they have to change their self-image in order for them to want to go on a real spiritual path. They are being held back by clinging to the past. We cannot do that. We have to move on. This is a different day, a different time, and in this moment of now we go forward.

Dr. Glendenning on Starvation

I am what you might call a food specialist. I know that that sounds crazy over here, but I help people to get over some of their feelings about different foods. There are actually people who come over here who feel that if they had eaten certain things, taken certain herbs, or certain vitamin pills they would not have gotten sick and died. I know that sounds crazy but we do have some, and so when the cry goes out to help these people, I answer because some of them are in really bad shape. They are feeling very guilty that they have left loved ones behind when they could have stayed if they had taken better care of themselves. So we have to work with them on the fact that they are now over here. There is nothing they can do about that. We try to convince them that they did not make themselves ill by what they ate, maybe by what they did not eat, and were malnourished. Their problem is very real to them.

I also work with people who were malnourished in some of these third world countries especially, where they simply did not have the food. And we help them to understand that they were in a karmic situation, and they have to change a lot of their thinking of being deprived. It is a horrible life. Many of these people are, like in Africa, or in North Korea where they are starving but are taught to worship their leader. We get those people, and when they come over, let's say from North Korea, they are very, very upset when they look back and they can see how they were used and abused by the system. They are usually young souls who get themselves into the wrong situations when reincarnating. They may come back too soon and without any prior planning.

In Africa where there is so much starvation, they are usually also very young souls, and many are paying off karma. They get themselves caught in situations that they should not be in because they did not plan their lives at all. They wanted to come back and they got into these countries at a particular time when things were really going bad. In India they may have spiritual understanding but there is no real application regarding prosperity. And so we have a lot of people to work with around nutrition, and food and being deprived of something so very, very basic. And it is a horrible thing to go through, to have an empty stomach and parents trying to scratch around and find some nourishment. It is a horrible thing! It truly is because everyone on earth should have adequate basic necessities.

And those who deprive others pay a very dear price when they come over here. I don't work with those. I work with the people who have been deprived. They come very lethargic, having no interest in their surroundings for the most part. Some of them are very happy and grateful to be out of that situation, but many have suffered and they do not know anything else. We have to introduce them to a better life, and explain to them what has happened in the past—that is not the case now. And so it takes a lot of educating these people that come over.

Sometimes I work with groups from one country, and then sometimes with another country. You see the cultural differences. It all boils down to a very basic feeling of hopelessness. It is so pathetic. It is hard for them to accept any responsibility. We have to work on it the best we can, but we try to give them something first to make them very comfortable. We give them lots of the essence of food to let them know that there will never be a shortage for them on this side.

On this side we each find our own little niche and try to do what we can to help others because we are all God's children. No one is better than the next one. Some are simply on a different level of consciousness and we help them to rise.

Comments by the Master Teacher

You heard this morning about people who have been starved. And it is very sad. It is so very, very sad. Some of them do die a very gradual death. And it is pathetic. And especially with the little children, we give them very, very special care over here. They need to be held a great deal; so they go from one arm to another. Spirits take turns holding these children and loving them and giving them a lot of the essence of food. They really have to be dealt with almost like on a physical level. They have to have some form to it.

It cannot be all talk. They have to have nurturing of a little different type than maybe a child who comes over who has been in an accident, or has died from a disease. We can talk to those children, bring them animals to play with. They have more mobility than a little child who has been starved. The latter did not have the energy on earth. The poor mothers are starving themselves. It is pathetic. They require a great deal of attention but they do pull through. They do respond. And when you can see their little faces brighten, it is a wonderful thing. It is a dark little etheric body in a sense, not dark from evil doing, but dark because there is little animation. When we can change that and see them functioning on a higher level it is wonderful. Children are resilient, and we do make headway with them. It is a little sad at first and they do require a great deal of love and attention.

We know that in the coming thousand years of peace we will not see these large pockets of poverty and starvation on earth that we are viewing now. Leaders will become more interested in doing for their people. They, themselves, will become more elevated. And, of course, human rights will improve. This is what we constantly work on, and the day will come. We have had some setbacks, but we will move ahead. There is an immense variety of problems that we have to work on over here. So earth creates conditions by the way they live in ignorance and evil ways. And we try to heal. But more and more healing will take place on earth. You will be amazed at how things will change if you send out love. ◆

20.

EAR. NOSE, AND THROAT

Within the structures of the ear, nose and throat are complex and interrelated mechanisms that allow a person to make sound, hear, maintain balance, smell, breathe, and swallow.

Diseases and Karma Associated with the
Ear, Nose, and Throat

Deafness may result from turning a deaf ear to those in need of help in a past life; so we may return to be literally deaf, or partially deaf in the present life. Deafness may also result from turning away from spiritual instruction in a past incarnation. The soul does work through the eyes and the ears, and the other senses as well, because that is the way the soul functions. Those affected may never have listened to anyone in a past life. They thought their way was the only way and just tuned everyone out. There are cases, of course, where a soul wishes to serve the deaf and their purpose for incarnating is to go through life as a deaf teacher.

Married couples have more deafness than the general population. Where it runs in families there usually have been some members who have been together in a past life and are working out a karmic situation. They are attracted to the family that can produce the necessary conditions. Deafness may also be due to what is going on in this life, such as loud noises in working in a factory, or playing loud music on a boom box, etc.

Tinnitus is an annoying sensation of sound in the ear when there is no sound. It may take the form of ringing, buzzing, whistling, or hissing and may be intermittent or continuous. This tends to run in families. One is attracted to a family that would provide the situations needed to progress, and in order to work out the karma between all of the members. This nerve problem is related to sensitivity of the individual.

Being deaf and mute is generally karmic, but not always. The old and offensive label was deaf and dumb. It did not, of course, mean lacking intelligence, rather incapable of speech. The part of the anatomy affected follows the misuse of the spiritual law involved. As the tongue spiritually symbolizes the key to wisdom's door, an injury or loss of the tongue is a consequence of injuring another through gossip or the betrayal of a sacred trust. However, sometimes these individuals who are deaf and mute come as master teachers, in a sense. Or, perhaps they have done something in the past they want to make up for in this life, and at the same time want to use this incarnation to help others who are going through the same condition. If they simply desire to be of service to a very vulnerable group, then their return has no karmic connection.

In the following *New Testament* scripture, it appears that the recipient of healing by Jesus, a deaf man with speech impediment, was so ordained by his worthiness. In other words, the man was freed from past karmic bonds and could now be healed. As the great Swiss doctor Paracelsus wrote: "The soul's faults of today crystallize into the body's ailments of tomorrow. Spirit is always the builder of the body. The miracles of the Master's healings are only for those who have ears to hear and eyes to see."

Mark 7:31 And again, departing from the coasts of Tyre and Sidon, he came unto the sea of Galilee, through the midst of the coasts of Decapolis.

32 And they bring unto him one that was deaf, and had an impediment in his speech; and they beseech him to put his hand upon him.

33 And he took him aside from the multitude, and put his fingers into his ears, and he spit, and touched his tongue;

34 And looking up to heaven, he sighed, and saith unto him, Ephphatha, that is, Be opened.

35 And straightway his ears were opened, and the string of his tongue was loosed, and he spake plain.

36 And he charged them that they should tell no man: but the more he charged them, so much the more a great deal they published it;

37 And were beyond measure astonished, saying, He hath done all things well: he maketh both the deaf to hear, and the dumb to speak.

This was an interesting technique that Jesus used to perform this healing. First, he led the man away from the crowd and put his fingers into the man's ears, and then with his spit, he touched the man's tongue with the spittle. Looking up to heaven, he said to him, "Be opened." Instantly, the man could hear perfectly and could speak plainly.

Jesus was also successful in healing a mute man as recorded in Matthew 9:32-33:

Matt. 9:32 As they went out, behold, they brought to him a dumb man possessed with a devil.

33 And when the devil was cast out, the dumb spake: and the multitudes marvelled, saying, It was never so seen in Israel.

In those days if a person was what today we would call mentally, emotionally, or physically challenged or disabled, they thought he or she was demon possessed. Any one who had anything out of the ordinary, such as being unable to speak or hear, or was slow, was believed to be demon possessed. The crowd thought Jesus had cast the demon out of this man, but actually, he healed the man of the condition. It could have been due to a karmic debt that the man was born mute. And if so, in this case the man merited being healed so he did not have to live out his entire life in that condition. Marvelous healings can take place if individuals have so lived their life to be able to satisfy a karmic debt before the end of their natural death. The crowds marveled when the man could talk for they had never seen such a healing demonstration.

Chart of Diseases of Ear, Nose, and Throat

Note: On the following chart are listed diseases which can be inherited, but some are only karmic "to a point." In other words, in keeping with our soul contract, we may have specifically and intentionally chosen a family who could provide the gene to develop a particular "karmic" disease or condition. This is our way of balancing our karma. The predisposition also existed in that family for one of the "karmic to a point" diseases, and we simply picked up that gene as well. Depending on how we live our life prior to the proposed onset of a disorder, we may not develop a "karmic" or a "karmic to a point" disease at all, having already worked off our karma in another way. Or, the disease may be mild and very responsive to treatment.

EAR. NOSE, AND THROAT

Disease	Description	Genetic	Karmic
Chronic Sinusitis	This is usually secondary to an anatomical deformity which is either congenital or was produced during the course of multiple attacks of acute sinusitis.	yes	Karmic to a point
Deaf and Mute	Deaf and incapable of speech.	no	yes
Deafness	About 1 in 1000 infants has profound hearing impairment, with half thought to be of genetic origin. If from birth, it is also karmic.	yes	yes, if from birth
Neurofibro-matosis	Rare inherited disorder characterized by the development of benign tumors on both auditory nerves. Also characterized by the development of malignant central nervous system tumors as well.	yes	Karmic to a point
Otosclerosis	An excessive growth in the bones of the middle ear which interferes with the transmission of sound. Onset usually between 15 and 50 years of age.	yes	yes

Disease	Description	Genetic	Karmic
Pendred syndrome	An inherited disorder that accounts for as much as 10% of hereditary deafness. Patients usually also suffer from thyroid goiter.	yes	yes
Sensorineural Deafness	Hearing impairment. Sometimes due to loud noises as working in a factory or boom boxes playing loud music. Can also be a karmic condition.	yes	Sometimes
Tinnitus	Sensation of sound in the ear when there is no sound. May take the form of ringing, buzzing, whistling, or hissing and may be intermittent or continuous.	yes	Karmic to a point

Enlightening Voices from the Other Side

Thomas Edison on hearing loss and recovery

When I came to this side of life, I found that I could hear all kinds of noises, but I also learned that I could communicate without speaking a word. But I did not forget that many people on earth are without hearing, and I have worked over here to try to develop something that would communicate our words without using a physical instrument. I have teamed up with Alexander Graham Bell and other scientists and inventors. Our efforts are not yet ready to unveil. The world is not ready to receive us. And in time people will communicate so easily that instruments will not be necessary.

When I first arrived, my guides and teachers came to me. I knew I had been communicating with some force. I did not know what it was, but I did know that I was receptive to something or somebody in another dimension, a higher dimension, that was helping me with my work.

The interesting thing about being deaf is that you do not require as long a recovery period to know that you are perfectly capable of hearing. In fact, hearing rarely presents a problem. You are receiving impressions even when you may think your hearing has not been restored to the ear. This is because in Spirit we work through thought, mainly. We pick up telepathically what is going on because that is a very natural function of the spirit body. We can communicate without speaking a word regardless of which language is spoken. The thoughts come just as plainly as if they were something one was hearing. In other words, thought is so strong on the spirit side of life, one hears it as a voice.

Psychologically a deaf person gets to the point, if he or she does not have a hearing aid, to kind of tune out everything anyway. I was able to develop some kind of amplification but it still was not too satisfactory.

My life has been very rich and I still work mainly on helping to improve and to bring new things to the world. I was happy that I had a few years on earth when I heard well, so that I would know what I was missing when my hearing was so badly damaged. When I was a boy I sold newspapers on the train. I also did some of my experiments on the train. And one day one of my experiments blew up. The conductor not only threw me off and my equipment, but he cuffed my ears so severely that I lost much of my hearing. That was a karmic thing that I had to go through and do my work with a handicap. I think that this happened in order that I could rise above that handicap and invent things that had to do with communication. Probably in a past life, somewhere back there, I caused a situation where someone became deaf; so I had to pay the price. But let the people know that deafness does not continue on this side. We have perfect hearing and we have a perfect way of communicating regardless of what language a person speaks. And so I leave that with you.

Helen Keller on overcoming enormous handicaps

I was born in Alabama on June 27, 1880. I was a very normal, happy baby. Everything was just fine until I was 19 months old, when I contracted a very severe illness and became blind, deaf, and mute. Now you call the disease meningitis. Of course, back at that time there was really nothing they could do. So I was a 19 month old baby who had been able to see, had been able to hear, was starting to talk, and then all of a sudden it was all gone. But I did carry with me the memory that I had been able to see, hear, and speak.

I became very, very, well I guess you would call it mean—oh yes, as a baby, as a child. Growing up I knew full well that I was totally different than everybody else. Can you just imagine a small child at 19 months that could not see, hear, or talk? I felt very helpless. My parents would put me in a chair and there I would sit all day. I would throw things. I would break things. Oh, I was terrible. I was very frustrated. I was very unhappy. My life was a constant pool of darkness. It is hard for anybody who can see, hear, and talk to even begin to believe what that is like for a person who was normal, and then to get that way. It was a total pool of darkness. It is very hard for me to even think about it now, it was so terrible.

So then my parents hired Anne Sullivan who was partially blind. She could see some things. She empathized with me. She was wonderful. It was part of our preincarnation plan to be together and for her to help me. But at first, when she started working with me, I was very bitter. She tried working with me with signs, to get me to know things by signs. All right, to do a sign with a person who can't see, hear or talk, she would have to take my hand and make a sign with her hand, and she would take my hands and put them up to the sign so I would know what that was. Let's say she was trying to teach me to say "I." She would make the sign, hold my hands to it, and then she would point to me to show me that I was I. Sometimes it would take a day or two just for one sign, because I had to feel it. Then she tried to get me to say, "I want a drink of milk." She would have to show me what drink was. She would have to get a glass and put it to my mouth to tell me what a drink was. It was terribly difficult to get the concept. We worked on signs. She had a terrible time getting me to know what milk was. Oh my, we would end up spilling all down the front of me because she would get the milk, put it to my mouth so that I would know this was milk. And we would do that maybe for two days before I would get that. Then we would go back to the whole thing, "I want a drink of milk." Then I would have to work on that. It was terrible. I would end up being so frustrated that I would throw things. I would hit her, but I was a child. It was very frustrating, but she stayed with me throughout my life. I could never, ever have done the things that I did without her.

So, I worked with the hand signals for several years. But when I was 8 years old, we had what we called a well house outside of our home. The well house was where the water was. We went to the well house. I wasn't very happy because I wasn't really interested in where I went or what I did. But I did go out to the well house and I felt something very cool flowing over my hands. And all of a sudden, right at that point, the mystery of language just came to me. It awakened me. And I knew the word. The way it came to me was w-a-t-e-r. I got it in my head with this cool stuff running over my hand. And I knew that was water. I knew that there was something, a much higher power working in me. That actually awakened me. I had worked for years trying to learn these signs. All I needed was this water running over my hands. It was so cool and it was so refreshing. All of a sudden, I felt the letters and I knew that was water. You could never imagine how awakened I felt. I felt such a feeling of joy, and such a feeling of hope that simply encompassed me. I knew there was something working within me, there was some kind of higher force. Remember, I was only 8 years old at that time. I was still a child, but at that moment I felt that I was set free. I no longer felt that terrible darkness.

Anne and I left the well house. And as we returned to the house, I would reach down and pick up a rock or anything that I felt. And it felt that it was alive. It was so wonderful. Everything that I touched made me feel so alive. I had not felt alive in my whole life since I was 19 months old. I got inside the house and I remember a doll that I had broken up, so I went over and picked up the pieces. Oh, I had broken that doll into many pieces. I sat there and tried to put them together, but of course, I couldn't because I couldn't see. I couldn't put them together so I began to cry. Then I became very sorry for all the things that I had done, and I realized that I had a very bad attitude and I felt repentant. I was very sorry for all that I had put my poor parents through, because it was terrible raising a child like that. From that day on, I really started to progress.

I started working with hand signals. Then I started to work with Braille. I started to learn to read and write Braille. After Braille, I began to try to communicate with the people who could see and hear. And you know, I was the very first blind, deaf, and mute person to effectively communicate with people who could see and talk. When I could learn to read and write Braille, my speech came back and I was able to speak. It was when I progressed that my speech returned, but my hearing never did, nor my eyes. I needed help to learn to pronounce things. I had to start putting words with the signs. Then it was important that I knew the signs. That must have taken me 4 to 5 years. It was very rewarding. Much of the karma was my parents', and it was very hard for them to watch me going through all of this, learning the hand signs and learning Braille, going to school the way I was. It was very, very difficult for them.

I went to Radcliffe College and graduated in 1904. Everything was put into Braille for me to study, and Anne Sullivan was right there with me. At graduation, I announced to everybody that I dedicated my life to the amelioration of blindness. And I did. I dedicated my life totally to helping educate the blind. But if it had not been for Anne, I could never have become the international celebrity that I was. She was just wonderful. She helped me all the way. We went on numerous tours. They were all on behalf of education for the deaf. I visited 35 countries on 5 continents. I did all that between the years 1939 and 1957. I really became a powerful symbol of triumphant over adversity.

I started getting a pretty bad ego because I knew I truly was doing some pretty wonderful things. My ego began to get pretty bad. And actually, I can say that I did become a little egotistical. But I did work for what I did. I truly did work, and I truly did try to help the entire world. Winston Churchill called me "the greatest woman of our age." It was quite an honor. I met every President of the United States from Calvin Coolidge on down to John F. Kennedy. At that point, I had my speech. I also had my speech when I went to all those various countries. I was able to get across my education for the blind to all of them, to show what they could accomplish. That was my purpose.

Then I wrote 14 books that were published. There were two that I liked the best, *The Story of My Life,* published in 1902; and the second was, *Teacher Anne Sullivan Macy,* published in 1955. Those were my two favorites out of the 14 books that I did write. Then I died in 1968.

I achieved a great many accomplishments and I know they were made with Spirit's help. I could never have done all that I did without the spirit guides and teachers that I had, but I wasn't always aware of them. Many blind people do become clairvoyant, and I know that I was clairvoyant, but I didn't know from whom I was getting it. I could see a shadow and I would know what the shadow was. But I think I was seeing it with my eyes, but it really wasn't my eyes. I was seeing with my spiritual sight, but they would come more like shadows than a person. I wasn't too aware that I was receiving from Spirit, and yet I knew I was getting some kind of help. Do you understand?

When I came over here and went through the Akashic records, I learned I had come to do exactly what I ended up doing. And I had to become blind, deaf and mute in order to fulfill what my soul wanted. I came to be a teacher. It wasn't so much to work off karma as it was to come and give. My soul decided that I was going to come back to be a very definite example of how people could get through all the tragedies of their life. This was not what I would call karmic except for the period between 19 months and 8 years. It was at age 8 when my karma was completed that I had the awakening experience at the well house, and my life from that point turned completely around. I did try to do my service well and feel I was rewarded by having my speech return. If it had been karmic, I would have been born with this and I was not.

I did not really know what the afterlife would be like, but I had absolutely no fear. I had no problem seeing once I got to this side. Everything was lifted. It was so wonderful. When I passed, for three days I was down around earth and I could not see or hear. But as I was met by spirit, and I was taken over, immediately it was all gone. It doesn't always happen that way with many, but I had lived my life exactly the way I was supposed to and that made a big difference. I have worked over here with those who had been blind and deaf, and very strongly with those who could not speak at the end.

I have worked with Alzheimer's quite a bit because they are in very bad shape when they come over here. I try to go in, first of all, to see if what they have is karmic. And then I try to let them know what they have done in past lives that brought this about. I get permission to go through their akashic record, and as I see what they have done—you see, they become more aware on this side than they ever could have on earth. I try talking to them about a past life and to realize why they had to go through the misery and the tragedy that they did. Yes, I take them back to the past life, but I still want them to be aware of what they went through so they would never have to repeat it. And why they went through it. That is the big thing. Most of the time they can recall the onset and very early stages, and then it just gets to a point where they don't remember anything. Some don't get to that point because their karma is finished. Their attitude also plays a part, and the attitude of the care givers and the people around them. We have to work with the whole picture to get them to understand.

Many were very intelligent and productive people. I work with them, showing them what they accomplished on earth, and usually they have accomplished a great deal in their earlier life. And then I go to how they misused themselves, or caused something like that. I go through that and they understand. It is not too difficult to get people to understand if you describe it very simply, and it may take a long time to get them there. If I can't do it my way, I turn them over to a psychiatrist.

I am hoping so much that I have taught and have gotten through to people that no matter what happens to you, you can work through it. You can get past it. I have worked so hard for the education of the blind and the deaf. I went to many schools and taught and gave lectures, and tried to help those who were very poor and could not advance themselves in education. You do not have too many places that really teach the blind or the deaf, not specific places. Your computers are wonderful now for the blind and the deaf. There are special computers and are set up with Braille. They are very, very expensive but they are available. Sometimes by going through a school, they will provide one. It is a totally different type of computer from the normal one.

The point must be gotten across: No matter what the tragedy—I am not just talking about blindness or deafness or being mute—you can get the ability to work it off. Just because something is terribly wrong, you can cope with it. Maybe you can't get over it, but you can cope with it. Like with me, no, I never got my sight back. I never got my hearing back. I did get my speech, thank goodness. I could talk to the people. I could give them the information. I could help them in every way. A lot of the credit I received truly should have gone to Anne Sullivan Macy also, because she was right there for me, every step of the way. She married late in life and her husband was very helpful to me also. She went to Spirit before me, but by that time I was so well known, if I had to go on a tour or something like that, I could get somebody in high places to go with me for security. I will leave now and I am so happy that you wanted me to come through.

Ludwig von Beethoven on how he kept composing music despite a total loss of hearing.
I didn't have an easy life. I was 18 years old when my mother died, so I took care of my younger brothers practically all of my life. My father was an alcoholic. So it was not an easy life. But, you know, I had some of the best teachers that you could ever have. So I did have a lot of training.

I was musical from a very young age. In the 1780's I was studying the music of the German composer Johann Bach, so that was my cornerstone of instruction. I had this buried inside of myself, so even after I became deaf, I still had a remembrance here. I met Mozart but I really didn't get a chance to study with him while he was on earth.

When I went deaf, that was the most terrible thing that I could ever have gone through. I was in despair for quite a long time because I knew that was going to be the end of my performing career, and I had just emerged on that. I wrote to my brothers and I told them just how much in despair I was. For two or three years I was terribly despondent, then all of a sudden, I decided this is not the way to go. And so I started putting faith in God and putting faith in myself. This wasn't the end of my life. So I went back to Vienna and stayed there the rest of my life and worked with Joseph Haydn.

No one will ever know what I went through when I was in the depths of despair. It was terrible because I thought I was done, finished. See, I wasn't thinking from a spiritual level. I was thinking from a materialistic level at that time. It was very frightening to feel that all you had done and could do was taken from you. I was in a very, very despondent state. I was doing a great deal of concerts. Then I honestly decided, *hey, I'm not going to quit*. I did have very generous patrons who helped me after I was deaf.

I decided I had to do something, and I started reading some spiritual books and decided that life was not just making money. It was doing something good, so I began to tune in. I gained an awareness of how I could be contacted by Spirit. I did a great deal of meditating, a great deal of tuning in, because I knew that was the only way. I knew I was too young to give up. The very first time that I saw a note, oh, I was just shocked. Where is this coming from? I thought it was from my higher self. But then the more I worked with it and the stronger and stronger and stronger my clairaudience became, I realized it was coming from Spirit. And it was wonderful. It was right there reborn. So I had no problem with hearing when I came over to this side of life. Those who are deaf on earth have no problem hearing when they go to Spirit.

I started doing compositions and I could hear them clairaudiently, not in my physical ears, but in my spiritual ears. I could hear and receive from the spirit realms. I think I did very well because I did do several masterpieces. Some of my most beautiful work was done then, but actually it was a different style of work. I called it the heroic style. It was a more forceful and stronger kind of message that I was putting forth in my music. I was doing whatever it was that I was told clairaudiently or whatever I saw clairvoyantly. A lot of times I would see clairvoyantly the music and I would take it from there. I was being helped by many, many on this side of life. Johann Bach was a great teacher. He helped me from Spirit. My style was different from his, but, you see, when he would give me whatever it was, then I would see the notes. And then I would take it from there and I would change it to my style. I worked with many who were wonderful, wonderful teachers, including Mozart.

All of these things that I had done before I became deaf were still a part of my memory. So I could use some of that along with what I was receiving. I just incorporated it. I was very happy that I was able to do the things that I did. I was happy that I got out of my depression because that was terrible. I was like a different person completely.

In going back to the akashic records, I learned that I had abused my musical talent in a past life. That is why I had to go through deafness in this life. So it was taken from me, at least what I thought was taken from me, until I realized that, *hey, this is caused by something I did.* But the despair was terrible because I wanted a concert career. I wanted a lot of money. I wanted a lot of fame. My soul decided that was not what I needed. That was a very hard lesson. But I did make a lot of money even after my hearing was lost. People appreciated me. We had patrons in my day. I was very happy that I learned that I could still go on. Because when this happened, it wasn't too bad at first, but finally I was totally deaf, so I had to depend on Spirit. I thought I was depending on my higher self, but I was actually depending on Spirit. I really feel that I worked out my karma.

I had completed quite a few of my compositions before I went deaf. My Ninth Symphony was the most famous of all classical music and it is still in existence. In the last movement, I put to music the poem Ode to Joy written by a German poet named Schiller. My symphony depicts the struggle with adversary and then it concludes with the uplifting version of freedom and social harmony. That is so important today. In your world, if more people would send out their thoughts and prayers and really work for freedom for all mankind everywhere, and harmony throughout the world, things would change. That is what I am working on Good music is harmony and that is healing.

Many of us came to earth around the same period. This was by prior planning so that we would be here together. We were together in past lives also. Our music was actually developed in past lives. I would say in three or four past lives that we had. Generally, that degree of development does come from having worked at a talent in past lives. I'm not talking about a normal person, I'm talking about someone who has made a big contribution to music. We had the talent and just refined it each time.

It will probably take 50 of your earth years before the music on earth really changes. What you have now all sounds alike and you can't understand the words when they sing. It's terrible. We try to do something from Spirit to make these young people think differently. There is no real good music unless you go back to the past. The young people today are not even aware of the great composers of the past. They are not taught. There is so much information they could get. You have the internet which is just wonderful. But if they could just get back and see what we have done and see what can be done. The music in my time was very spiritual, very uplifting. When you raise your consciousness, you don't want the type of music you hear today. You can take a plant and you can play this stuff today and you see it not thriving as well. And then you play more spiritual stuff and you will see that plant revive. It does not have to be classical, but something that will raise your vibrations. Some of this modern stuff takes your vibration right down. It is in keeping with the low morals of today. We are trying to raise the vibrations. When you raise your consciousness you want things that are more refined. Even the churches are not doing a good job.

I do a lot of work over here. We are trying very hard to change the vibrations of your earth. We have to have people on earth to work with us in order to do that. It is very, very difficult. I am very happy that I was asked to come. It is very nice to be able to come in and talk just like you are on earth. •

21.

THE EYES

The eye is often compared to an extraordinarily sensitive camera. Spiritually, the eye represents the soul faculties of awareness and perception, and the sense function of deception.

Diseases and Karma Associated with the Eyes

When a person is born blind, or if blindness occurs in early childhood, it is a karmic condition. It can be the result of a neglected effort in the past life to think clearly. A warped and twisted mental viewpoint will eventually produce a similar condition in physical sight. This is true because the eyes are the windows of the soul. If we are not trying to progress ourselves spiritually and we do not use our soul powers, then we are going to lose the functioning of the corresponding physical organs—the organs that the soul is functioning through. In the case of the eyes, closing ourselves off from spiritual truth during one or more incarnations tends toward physical blindness in some future incarnation, or vision which is blurred or very imperfect.

Paracelsus, the 15th Century Swiss physician, was particularly interested in blindness. In his practice he differentiated between becoming blind with age and being born blind. He pointed out in our trance contacts with him, "that in a past life a person may have inflicted cruelty on another individual in the area of the eyes, like poking the eyes or putting hot coals on them. Blindness in a new incarnation becomes the karmic price for inflicting such torture. Another cause of blindness in one eye in later life is due to using the eye to hypnotically suggest other people to one's way of thinking and to do one's will. Some people will stare at us trying to make us do what they want. They are using the eyes to control. They probably did this in many lives until they reached the point where they were blind in at least one eye in later life. Selfishness and not sharing or caring can also cause blindness—turning a blind eye, then in the next life being blind. That is a condition that cannot be corrected for the karma must be balanced out."

A dishonest and suspicious person will exhibit shifty eyes. Schizophrenics will frequently not even look at another person because they cannot emotionally involve themselves. When eyes have no luster, it shows a person who is feeling hopeless, very desolate, and very fearful because he/she is not using the sanction of the soul. A person may reincarnate because there is something they choose to go through and their eyes or ears will be affected. Sometimes it is actually a physical imperfection in the organ. We cannot attribute everything on karma.

Nearsightness runs in families. Usually what we inherit, we inherit for a reason. We come back for the situation. We have chosen a particular family because maybe in a past life we were not on any kind of spiritual pathway. We may have been very materialistic or very hateful. Members of our family were the same way. Like attracts like and forms the law of attachment. That is where karma comes in. We come back to that family and that inherited gene is there; so we are going to have to work it all out. Glaucoma is also inherited and falls into the same category as nearsightness. Remember, the eyes are the windows of the soul.

As we know, the etheric body is perfect. However, upon arriving in the Spirit World, it is more difficult for the blind person to accept the restoration of sight than for an amputee to accept the wholeness of his/her body. The spirit doctors or guides encourage them to open their eyes and to tell what they see. At first, they will say that it is all black. They see nothing because it is in their head that they cannot see. The doctors persist, telling them no, that is only because they think it is black. Thoughts are things. This is especially observable in the Spirit World. Again, they are patiently told to open their eyes again and they will see there is light. And so, that is how they are worked with. They do not need glasses there, although many times spirits will continue to wear glasses with no magnification strictly for identification. That is their choice.

Chart of Conditions of the Eye

Note: In the chart below are listed diseases which can be inherited, but some are only karmic "to a point." In other words, in keeping with our soul contract, we may have specifically and intentionally chosen a family who could provide the gene to develop a particular "karmic" disease or condition as our way of balancing our karma, but the predisposition also existed in that family for one of the "karmic to a point" diseases, and we simply picked up that gene as well. Depending on how we live our life prior to the proposed onset of a disorder, we may not develop a "karmic" or a "karmic to a point" disease at all, having already worked off our karma in another way. Or, the case may be mild and we are very responsive to treatment.

Disease	Description	Genetic	Karmic
Best Disease	Also known as Vitelliform Macular Dystrophy Type 2. Heritable disorder occurring primarily in European Caucasians. Gradual loss of visual acuity starting in teenage years. Severity of symptoms is highly variable.	yes	yes
Blindness	From birth is not genetic.	no	yes
Cataracts	Can cause blindness if not removed.	no	no
Color blindness	Affects 10 times more men than women. Picked up with the family with which they come back to work out karma.	yes	Karmic to a point

244

Disease	Description	Genetic	Karmic
Diabetes	Retinal damage due to Diabetes.	yes	yes
Glaucoma	A term used for a group of diseases that can lead to damage to the eye's optic nerve and result in blindness. Can occur in infants. Affects 1 out of 25 Americans.	yes	Karmic to a point
Graves' Disease	Overactive thyroid. Eyes may bulge and take on a staring appearance, goiter may develop.	yes	yes
Gyrate Atrophy of the Choroid and Retina	(Choroid is the thin coating of the eye). Progressive loss of vision, with total blindness, usually between ages of 40 and 60.	yes	Karmic to a point
Hyperopia Farsightedness	Eye is too short so that rays of light cannot intersect on the retina.	yes	yes
Macular Degeneration	The macula is the part of the retina with the sharpest sight. If the surface of the macula degenerates this can cause legal blindness. Usually due to poor blood flow to the retina, but can be inherited.	yes, in a few cases	Karmic from conditions in this life

Disease	Description	Genetic	Karmic
Myopia	Nearsightedness often begins in early school grades. The growing eye becomes too long, so that rays of light from distant objects focus before the retina.	yes	Karmic to a point
Presbyopia	Affects most people in their 50s and 60s. As the lens accumulates more fibers, it becomes less able to accommodate to near vision.	no	no
Retinoblastoma	Occurs in early childhood. The tumor develops from the immature retina the part of the eye responsible for detecting light and color. In the hereditary form, multiple tumors are found in both eyes, while in non-hereditary form only one eye is affected and by only one tumor. Highly treatable, but if untreated, it is almost uniformly fatal. Second most common childhood cancer most often found in children under 4.	yes/no	yes
Waardenburg Syndrome	Main characteristics include a wide bridge of the nose, pigmentary disturbances such as two different colored eyes, white forelock and eyelashes and premature graying of the hair, and some degree of cochlear deafness.	yes	Karmic to a point

Enlightening Voices from the Other Side

Dr. D. Cowan on working with those blind from birth

I am very interested in your book. I think it is really novel. I certainly hope that because it is, that it will sell. I know that your primary interest is in helping people and not money to be made from it. The important thing is to help people understand that life does not end with physical death. It goes on and it goes on very painfully for some people who have lived a pretty miserable life on earth. But we on this side try hard to radiate our love to all who come, not judging what they have done or have not done on earth. We try to evaluate what we can do for them here. And we are successful sometimes, and sometimes we are not, in our efforts to get them to consider a review of their life and to go on to grow, and to become a better and happier person.

The work that I have taken on is to work with those who were blind on earth. Those who were born blind were blind because of karma that they had accumulated for various reasons. I will not enumerate them because I understand that you have been given a number of possible reasons why this can happen. So suffice it to say, if born blind, it is because of karmic bonds that need to be loosened. If the blindness occurs later in life, then there is that possibility again that it was karmic, but it does not necessarily need to happen. It all depends—and we wish we could get this across—on how a person is living his or her life on earth.

To lose one's sight is especially a very, very difficult thing for those who have had their sight because they do miss it, and feel a sense of helplessness until they can adjust. Those born blind are actually able to make a better adjustment than those who become blind later in life. We know that blindness is terrible and obviously that is why some of the punishments meted out centuries ago, or maybe not that long actually, were to take someone's sight away. What worse thing could they do?

When they come to this side, if they have not elevated themselves, or have not developed clairvoyance, then it is difficult for them to accept that they can now see. It isn't a matter of just saying, *open your eyes and look*, because the thought of blindness is so firmly embedded in their mind, especially those who were blind at birth. They cannot believe they have a perfect body with perfect sight. They may open their eyes and truly not see anything but darkness in the beginning. We do work with them over, and over, and over. It depends on how rigid they are in their thinking. Those who have clairvoyance were able to see because they did not need the physical eyes for their spiritual sight. They are much easier to convince. They, of course, are few in number at this point. There will be more with clairvoyant vision as the New Age progresses.

Coming over here and not understanding why this happened to them is the thing we really have to work on most. We get them to open their eyes eventually and see, but then we have to deal with the underlying cause of their blindness on earth. When we are given permission to go back into the akashic records and take a look, then we can share that with them. They are not ready to go through the akashic records themselves; so it is necessary for a spirit teacher who is evolved to do this with permission. We never violate anyone's privacy without their permission. Sometimes it is very hard for them to accept the cause that they did anything cruel to the eyes of another person, or that they turned away from conditions that they could have helped with, and so forth. They turned a blind eye to helping when they could have helped. Many of them will stay in our groups for awhile, but when it comes time to facing their part, they may bolt out of the door. Others are grateful to have an understanding and we work with them to strengthen them and to guide them to do a review of this life just passed on earth. They are relieved to know when karma has been satisfied. And many of them become our wonderful helpers to help others in the group, or to even follow up with those who have left the group and to encourage them to return.

I got into this work because I had a blind sister when on earth, and I felt like she was missing so much. I felt almost guilty when I could see beautiful scenes, and I tried to describe them to her as best I could. But how do you describe to a blind person beautiful colors, beautiful workmanship, beautiful nature scenes and things. She was always a pleasant and productive person. She worked as a counsellor to the blind and was very good at helping blind people go out and live productive lives.

I came to this side of life before she did, and I took care of her first dog, Rex. We waited for her to come over. I wanted to be the one to help her open her eyes and see. And so I was given that privilege to work with her, and because she trusted me, it happened pretty quickly. I would tell her to open her eyes. She would say she did not see anything, that it was just nothing. I would keep working with her. I would take her to a beautiful scene over here and I would describe it to her and encourage her to open her eyes. That is how we did it. And this is how I do it with others. I decided that I would help others. My sister assists me sometimes, but she has gone on to do other work.

When I am permitted to do so, I take others who think they are still blind out to beautiful places. We work looking at Mother Nature first, because we have many beautiful scenes here. Then we also work in groups. Sometimes I have even taken a small group of three or four. Others help me, of course. We don't do it by ourselves. We have a little contest to find out who can see first. And it helps them. We use a little bit of the old ego to compete. Now, we don't like that ego to take over too strongly on this side of life. We want the soul to guide and so we don't encourage the ego to rise except in very special situations. But it is very interesting work. My people do not stay with me too long because I get them to see, and then we counsel them as to why the blindness occurred. Once they get through that, then they can go through the rest of life, reflecting upon what happened. Their guides and teachers help them with their further progression. Mine is pretty much strictly related to the blindness aspect of attitudinal healing.

And so I thought perhaps you might be interested in knowing that. I do sincerely hope this book will go far and wide, and anyone who has a blind person in their family who has passed over will know that they are sighted now, and that a blind person still on earth can look forward to having perfect sight over here. It is all 20-20 vision over here. No one needs to wear glasses, although they sometimes do for identification, and that is the only reason— no magnification whatsoever. I thank you for the opportunity of coming through and sharing this with you today. •

22.

FALSE GROWTHS

False growths such as tumors, cancer, gall stones and the like indicate obviously that something is growing inside of us. How does a tumor or cancer start? Cell division gets out of control. It becomes a growth and we are feeding that growth by every destructive emotion or thought. So, in time a few cells separate themselves and then they begin to grow in a destructive manner.

We must realize that our thoughts are things. What we are thinking is bringing about the things that are affecting our health. Destructive emotions, destructive ideas, and destructive desires all produce disease. Behind every disease is thought. If you have a lot of hate, that is definitely a destructive emotion. How many people will say, *Oh, I hate them. I can't stand them*? That is a destructive emotion, or, by being so jealous or envious of others. People whose ideas are very destructive to other people, or to themselves, produce disease within themselves. Behind all disease is thought, including ungoverned sexual desires.

Let us say, we find that we have a tumor, or have gall stones, or cancer, then we should erase the negative thoughts about the condition. We do not want to be constantly thinking about it. We have to dissolve the idea of false growth because there is nothing in our body that can grow unless we feed it. It cannot grow unless we feed it. We can continue to feed it by continuing the thought that caused it in the first place. We can also feed it by thinking constantly that we have the growth itself. We have got to remove from our mind any thoughts that are not good. There has to be a positive outlook with faith. That can produce perfection in the body. So whether it is cancer or fibroid tumor or cysts or gall stones, those growths are neither person, place or thing. They have no life to sustain them unless we give it to them.

Cancer is karmic in the sense that we have chosen the particular family that we came into because of some situations that had to be worked out from a past life, and that family would help us to work it out by providing the predisposition for cancer. In that sense, it is karmic, but it is not karmic to the point that we have to develop cancer. Let's say we are born into a family where cancer is a predisposition, and we are aware of that. What is the first thing we should do? Clean up our thoughts, not dwell on negativity. And people will dwell on the negative. They will say, *My mother had cancer, my dad had cancer, I know I am going to have cancer.* What are they doing? They are feeding it. Many with family histories of cancer, and other diseases which have inherited components, are getting genetic tests which can predict their risk of getting the disease. They have to realize if their soul contract is to pay off their karmic debt, then they have consciously chosen, prior to incarnation, to come to parents who will pass on the necessary gene.

When a person has cancer and is cured, it frequently returns in a different place or in the same place. Even if a person does have cancer and it has gone from one place to another, then to another, they can still stop feeding it. The growth is not going to enlarge. When a person has cancer, it might be to help or strengthen somebody else in that family, but more often it is to pay for something done in their own past life, or something done in this life. It is for the individual's soul growth.

If there is anything that comes about that you do not think is right, the best thing to do is go to a physician. By all means, seek medical help. Physicians are here to help with their knowledge and understanding. Get it checked out. Get help with it and change your thoughts. Think of all the people that say, *Oh, everything is all wrong in our world today. There is a lot of sickness and there is a lot of unhappiness and everything is wrong, and why did God let this happen to me?* That kind of thinking produces false growth. Your inner emotions can create outer conditions.

How many religions teach that we are feeding things by the way we think? We have to understand that as we sow, so shall we reap. We are going to pay for our karma, but most are thinking more of karma from their past lives than the karma they are creating right now. And that karma is going to go with us at our transition if we do not get it taken care of. It is a vicious cycle, if we do not stop it. People hate to think that they are causing their own disease because, by doing so, it means having to accept personal responsibility.

Thoughts are things. The spirit doctors tell us that seventy percent of all diseases are the result of suppressed emotions. It can be any suppressed desires. Suppressed emotions and suppressed desires can very definitely cause disease. This does not just apply to sex, but desires for a beautiful home or something material that is way beyond what we can provide for now. It could be an unrealistic ambition to attain to something for which we are not qualified. Talk to yourself and use reason. We can desire to have something, but when we are constantly thinking about it and it is bothering us, then it becomes a problem. St. Paul said: *I have learned, in whatsoever state I am, therewith to be content.* (Phil. 4:11) It does not mean to give up a desire, but to put it in proper perspective. Be content with where we are right now while reaching for something better. If only we could be content with whatever comes, we would find a greater inner peace.

There are all kinds of false growths. Some of them can be benign and some can be very serious, like cancer. Are the thoughts different? It could be negative thoughts about anything, but when it is as serious as cancer, the negative thoughts are more concentrated, or the emotions more suppressed. Many tumors can be removed successfully. The least successful at the time of this writing is with tumors of the brain, although advances are being made. From a karmic standpoint, it indicates that something went on in a past life that did not get solved and it just grew and grew and grew and the propensity was there for it to materialize in this life. Any problem with the brain has to do with abuse—letting thoughts and desires overpower us. So we come back into this life and we could have a tumor on the brain or some other condition that would prevent us from thinking properly.

There are more than a hundred different types of cancer, all characterized by the uncontrolled growth and spread of abnormal cells. The survival rate continues to increase. Although cancer is a tool by which karma from a past life can be erased, treatment is now more effective.

Enlightening Voices from the Other Side

Dr. W. Scott added the following about cancer in adults

I am a doctor on this side of life. I was a doctor of oncology when I was on earth. I had many patients, running the gamut from children to adults. I know that you have already had someone come and talk to you about children with cancer. (*See Chapter 26 on Special Treatment of Children, Dr. Bacon, page 277*) I am going to concentrate more on the adult. Children are so much more open than adults. When adults have had cancer and died from it and come to this side, they are in very, very bad shape before they leave earth. They are frequently emaciated, depending where it really hits. They can be in very, very bad shape and in a great deal of pain. The kidneys have shut down, and this organ and that organ is affected. It is kind of a domino effect. It goes through the body and I guess I am concentrating on those mainly with cancer in the main body, not in the limbs. With the limbs, we usually are able to control the spread to some degree.

When they come over, having reached the stage of being so, so sick, and the body is so racked with cancer, they need a lot of rest. And this we give them. We come periodically and talk to them. We tell them that they are in a different body. DO NOT IDENTIFY WITH THAT OLD BODY ANY LONGER! Forget about it. It was either burned up or put in the grave. Whatever happened to it, let it be. Don't even think about it. This is a new life, a new body, a new way of looking at things.

Acceptance of the etheric body depends on how far they have evolved. If they are spiritually evolved to a point, it is not going to bother them. If a person is not on a spiritual pathway at all, then they have a hard time with it. They cannot accept that it is a totally new body.

And so we work, and we work and we work. The mind does not want to give up this stuff. And until we get them ready to go through the akashic records, and no longer have that subconscious mind, we have to work hard. We really have to be persistent, if they will let us be. We can't force them. Some of them do not want to do anything, absolutely do not want to do anything. This simply holds them back. And so we can only do so much. You can lead the horse to water but you can't make him drink. But we are willing to help. We are there to help.

I think with people who have cancer, it is a very, very frightening disease because it has long been associated with death. And if it is to go to that point, then all the medical profession can do is retard it in one place and it is going to affect another part of the body, or they will not be receptive to the treatment. So they come with a pretty heavy kind of burden. If they have licked it while on earth and they come over for a different reason, then that is a totally different kettle of fish because they are feeling rather confident, and they can look back and review the akashic records and they can see why they had it. They usually are much more accepting than those who have died from it. Those who have died from it, even with some understanding of afterlife, are much more difficult to work with. But eventually, it all gets cleaned up. We do not do chemo or radiation, or any of that stuff. All we need to do is change the attitudes of mind. I think that is about all I can say except that the caregivers, where there is a long term illness, are usually involved karmically. I really believe this is true of all long, terminal illnesses. ◆

23.

LEPROSY

Leprosy or Hansen's Disease is an insidious, chronic infectious disease, which, if left untreated, can result in severe disfigurement, especially of the feet, hands, and face. Although it is a contagious disease, it is not as easily transmitted as once feared. It may have originated in India and spread throughout the world by various travelers. Today the disease is found primarily in tropical areas.

Leprosy is an ancient disease. Cases were recorded in the *Old Testament* and in documents found in India dating back to 600 B.C. Worldwide, leprosy has been one of the most feared diseases. An enormous stigma has been attached to it, causing those afflicted to be shunned by family, friends, and society. At one time, probably around the Middle Ages, individuals with leprosy were declared dead. A symbolic funeral and burial was held, after which the infected persons were banished. They either begged on the street or went to leper colonies established to isolate and care for them.

In view of the fear surrounding the disease, and the ostracism of lepers, it is understandable they would feel enormous rejection. It is to pay off karma that one develops the disease. Leprosy and cancer are on the same level. Cancer takes the heavy toll in modern life that leprosy did in the past, and for similar reasons. Both are "fire diseases," which some say are the consequence of an ungoverned desire nature in either present or past incarnations. According to the *Old Testament*, one reason for leprosy was the result of slander. Others say the karmic cause of leprosy is due to the unbridled misuse of the creative life forces during incarnations in ancient Lemuria and Atlantis. It is certainly a disease symbolizing spiritual uncleanliness in a previous life.

It is recorded in the *New Testament* that Jesus healed the lepers that approached him, as in the following passage from the Gospel of Luke.

Luke 17:11   And it came to pass, as he went to Jerusalem, that he passed through the midst of Samaria and Galilee.

12   And as he entered into a certain village, there met him ten men that were lepers, which stood afar off:

13   And they lifted up their voices, and said, Jesus, Master, have mercy on us.

14   And when he saw them, he said unto them, Go show yourselves unto the priests. And it came to pass, that, as they went, they were cleansed.

15   And one of them, when he saw that he was healed, turned back, and with a loud voice glorified God,

16   And fell down on his face at his feet, giving him thanks: and he was a Samaritan.

17   And Jesus answering said, Were there not ten cleansed? but where are the nine?

18   There are not found that returned to give glory to God, save this stranger.

19   And he said unto him, Arise, go thy way: thy faith hath made thee whole.

According to Mosaic law, lepers were required to keep their distance from other persons and cry "unclean" to warn anyone who approached them. When Jesus entered the village, they cried to him to have mercy on them. He looked at the ten lepers and said, "Go to the priests and show them that you are healed." Only a priest could determine whether a person was afflicted with Leprosy or had a minor skin disease, so before rejoining the community the priest had to give them a clean bill of health.

Only one, a Samaritan whom the Jews despised, returned to Jesus to show his gratitude. "Does only this foreigner return to give glory to God?" Jesus blessed him and told him his faith had made him well. His healing was no doubt permanent because he recognized the source of his healing. When we have sufficient faith, healing can take place immediately. If we do not make changes spiritually after a healing, the condition can return. Not all lepers were cured. Some were not ready to break their bonds.

Leprosy has proven difficult to eliminate for several reasons. Scientists do not yet understand how the bacterium is transmitted from person to person. Many exposed to an infected person do not get it. In other words, many exposed do not need to get it to erase karma.

Doctors have not yet learned how to identify people who are infected but have not yet developed the disease. Also, efforts to eliminate leprosy are hampered by the stigma still attached to the disease. Many do not seek treatment for fear of being abandoned by family and ostracized by society. Despite the seeming obstacles to eratication, great strides are being made in effective multi-drug therapy and the prevalency has been reduced. What is not understood by the scientific community is that this disease is being superseded by cancer as the tool by which karma can be erased. ✦

24.

THE SKIN

The skin is the sensitive outward cloak of the body. Because the skin is the buffer zone for both internal and external environments, it is affected by inner thoughts and internal activity, as well as, external conditions such as chemicals, injuries and over-exposure to the sun. Its clarity and color will indicate much about our physical and emotional states.

Diseases and Karma associated with the skin

In his concern about what we are doing to ourselves here and now, Dr. Blake, spirit doctor, has given us his insights.

When the skin is in near perfect condition, this indicates there is a deep calmness inside that person. The calmer we are, the more attractive and clearer our skin will be. Outwardly, we may some-how express differently, but inwardly we feel a calmness based on self-confidence, a knowing that what we are doing is what we are supposed to be doing and that we are doing it right. We may get out of patience with others at times, but on the inside we are say-ing, *I know I can do the things that I have to do. I know that I am doing this right.* That is the inner calmness that produces beautiful skin. On the other hand, if we are a nervous wreck all the time and we are worried about this and worried about that, then there will be some breakout in the skin. Prolonged unrelieved stress will pro-duce adverse affects.

Most detrimental, of course, is condemnation of others, jeal-ousy, greed, hatred and the like continued over a long time for it does affect the condition of the skin. We probably have all ob-served people who are constantly jealous, or who really hate some-one to the point where they cannot say anything good about them— really and truly hate them. Take a look at such people and you will find a lot wrong with their skin. Or, observe the skin of some married couples whose long standing relationship has been an unhappy one. In time the skin may erupt with pimples or there will be some disfiguration. One stress related condition is rosacea in which the skin becomes red and thickens in affected areas of the face. Blotches or pigmentation changes can occur.

Many teenagers suffer from acne. Frequently, it is related to oily skin or from the outside environment, and in time clears up and leaves no lasting imperfections. However, in very serious cases of acne where it just seems like it is never going away, that usually stems from something within the family and it leaves scars. Is it a family that is always condemning someone else, or always condemning them? When these teenagers are told over and over they did not do this right or did not do that right, they can be scarred emotionally and, in turn, their skin will be scarred to reflect their inner feelings.

As indicated above, many skin diseases and blood disorders can be traced to a lack of harmony in the life. If you are a person who is never harmonious, is always griping about somebody or something, always finding fault with somebody, you very definitely can have a skin disease or a blood disorder. Although the blood is a spiritual flow, it can become contaminated by constant negative expressions.

Boils and eczema and other skin irritations can be helped if we realize that our blood is pure, and that blood can change every day. Eczema or dermatitis may have many causes, among which are allergic and toxic reactions, irritations, infections, and genetic predisposition, all of which are treatable. You could even get rid of psoriasis which is believed not to be curable. However, it may return if there is no permanent attitudinal change. We do not need to accept hives or shingles. We have to recognize that the blood is really pure, and that we are the ones that contaminate it. No one else does it to us.

Some people have very rough skin. They look as though they are heavy drinkers and yet they may not touch a drop. That is caused by the way they live, either exposure to the elements, toxic chemicals and irritants, or inner turmoil. People who can get themselves calmed down and just take things in their stride will have more perfect skin.

Disease	Description	Genetic	Karmic
Atopic Dermatitis	Red Blistering rash, or thickening and discoloration of the skin.	yes	Karmic to a point
Birth Marks		no	yes
Cutaneous Porphyria	Enzyme deficiency causing manifestations on the skin.	yes	Not necessarily
Diastrophic Dysplasic	A rare growth disorder in which patients are usually short, have club feet, and malformed hands and joints. Particularly prevalent in Finland.	yes	yes
Disfigurations		no	yes
Ellis-van Creveld Syndrome	A rare genetic disorder characterized by short-limb dwarfism, polydactyly (additional fingers or toes), malformation of the bones of the wrist, dystrophy of the fingernails, partial hare-lip, cardiac malformation, and often prenatal eruption of the teeth. Often seen among the Old Order Amish community in Lancaster County, Pennsylvania.	yes	yes

Disease	Description	Genetic	Karmic
Male Pattern Baldness	Disturbances in 5-alpha reductase activity in skin cells might contribute to male pattern baldness, acne, or hirsutism.	yes	Karmic to a point
Marfan Syndrome	Inherited connective tissue disorder affecting many structures, including the skeleton, lungs, eyes, heart and blood vessels. Characterized by unusually long limbs, and is believed to have affected Abraham Lincoln.	yes	Karmic to a point
Malignant Melanoma	The most aggressive kind of skin cancer. More common in people with lightly pigmented skin. High risk of developing new melanomas.	yes	Karmic to a point
Menkes Syndrome	An inborn error of metabolism that markedly decreases the cells ability to absorb copper. Diagnosed by looking at victim s hair. Death in infancy.	yes	yes
Psoriasis	Instead of taking the usual 26 to 28 days to form the epidermis, the process is speeded up to take on 3 to 4 days. This causes an abnormal outer layer of skin which we see as round or oval red patches of skin covered with silvery scales.	yes	Karmic to a point

Disease	Description	Genetic	Karmic
Vitiligo	A skin condition resulting from loss of pigment which produces white patches. Any part of the body may be affected. Melanin, the pigment that determines color of skin, hair, and eyes, is produced in cells called melanocytes. If these cells die or cannot form melanin, the skin becomes lighter or completely white. Affects to some extent 1 or 2 of every 100 people.	yes	Karmic to a point

Enlightening Voices from the Other Side

Dr. A. G. had this to say about skin problems

I was a doctor in the tropics, but I also worked a great deal in the U.S. And I saw a lot of skin diseases. Many people come to this side of life who have had a problem with psoriasis, hives, shingles, acne, impetigo, cellulitis, skin rashes, scarring, bad burns and disfigurations. Disfigurations frequently are of a karmic nature—something that they have carried over from a past life that they have had to face, like birth marks that they bring with them. When people are born with birthmarks, it is because they needed to call attention to themselves. Birthmarks are karmic. They were either very arrogant or judgmental of others, and so forth, and now they have a mark on them which they cannot erase. When they come to this side, there is no mark on the etheric body. They have no disfigurations. The etheric body is perfect.

Now, when people have these problems, or have disfigurations or horrible blotches, etc. that occur to their skin, they come to this side and they see part of their body and see that it is perfect and is rather translucent. They then want a mirror. They want to see what their face looks like. And when they no longer see the disfiguration, or whatever it happens to be, they are very, very joyous. And we explain to them that they have worked off that karma, if it is karmic, and that they now have a very perfect body and they have nice skin. The skin is naturally going to vary somewhat from person to person. I don't want to give you the impression that when someone arrives on this side of life that their skin suddenly looks like that of a baby, because that is not the case.

It is true that the etheric body looks like the physical body did on earth, with the same features, but it does not have the grossness that may have occurred in the life on earth. If their skin is kind of porous or coarse, it is not going to be like baby skin if they are an adult, but there will be a definite refinement over the earth complexion as the person progresses. Even though they may have wrinkles, there is a definite refinement in the skin. And they do not have to have the blotches and disfiguration. If that is a karmic thing, that certainly is erased. You have seen people on earth whose faces are twisted from strokes and that is no longer a problem here. Of course, that condition goes deeper than the skin.

In truth, you do not have actual skin over here. This is just the etheric body; so it is not skin as you know it. It is like skin but it is not actually skin. The etheric body is a solid form composed of ethers. And as they elevate themselves, that so-called skin becomes more refined and more full of light and more beautiful.

I also would like to mention that I believe, seeing from this side of life that even though someone has a predisposition toward developing any kind of skin problem, if they have elevated themselves before the onset is to take place, in accordance with their soul contract, then it does not necessarily occur. We do not always have to pay the karma that we have brought over with us from a past life through the act or condition that was preplanned, because it can be worked off through good deeds prior to the proposed onset.

Dr. Pisak on plastic surgery

I practiced cosmetic and plastic surgery. I worked with some very well-to-do ladies and gentlemen who were extremely vain and I played right into their vanity. I would perform cosmetic surgery on their faces and necks, and when they would come back for a follow-up visit, I would say, *Well, next time we could work a little bit more on this place or that place.* And when they healed, many of them would come back for more surgery. It really wasn't necessary. It wasn't necessary at all. They looked good after the first operation. Then maybe I would suggest a tummy tuck, or maybe this or that or the other. I got the ladies, especially, into doing so much and never being satisfied so that I would be able to make lots of money.

There have always been people who are vain and wealthy and who what to stay young forever. I don't believe a little bit of cosmetic help is wrong. It is when so very much is done over and over and over. A surgeon should call a halt to it and counsel a person not to continue this. It is not in their best interest to be so vain. My goodness, when I finished with someone they didn't even look like their former selves. So plastic surgery, if it is done for purely cosmetic effects on an otherwise healthy but aging face, should not distort one's appearance. It should make a person look younger, but not like a different person.

I gloried in all the money I made, and I really thought nothing of it until I got to Spirit and saw what I had done. I not only was greedy, I took advantage of rather neurotic people. I could have helped them had I had a different attitude. A fellow plastic surgeon once said to me, "Are you still working on Mrs. So and So?" And I said, "yes I am." He just shook his head. I was not considered too ethical among the plastic surgeons of my acquaintance.

Plastic surgery first came about, as its main purpose, to help those who were disfigured from birth or from accidents by reconstructing their features to a point where people would not be repulsed by their appearance, and more importantly, they would feel physically and emotionally better about themselves. In the case of a baby born with a cleft palate, this condition really needs to be taken care of because it can interfere with food intake and digestion, and it is a rather unsightly condition when it is severe.

I did very, very little charitable work. I wanted to be paid. Could I take all that money with me when I came to this side? No, not even a copper penny. And did I merit a beautiful home? No, it is okay because I did help some people who really needed it, if they could pay something. I put my heart and soul into my work if they could pay.

Well, I found out that we have to pay for everything we receive. There are no freebies. We even pay for the air we breathe by making our lungs pump. And so you pay ahead of time before you get into the next realm or plane over here. I am working on it now. I have elevated myself and I am talking to people. Some are my former patients. I help them see that all that surgery had nothing to do with their souls, and I really ask their forgiveness for encouraging that more and more work to be done on them. My motive was not pure by any means.

Now I work with those who became disfigured on earth who still think they are disfigured over here. And even though we show them a mirror so they can see their reflections and tell them their etheric body is perfect, they do not see themselves as perfect. Can you believe that? They do not see themselves as perfect. They look at themselves and in their minds they still see the disfigurement because it bothered them so much. And so it is a matter of changing their attitude, and when they change their attitude, they accept that they are good looking, just as they were before an accident disfigured them.

I am working hard to elevate myself and to really help those truly in need. So I want to mention this. There are two categories that we work on. One group includes those who were born normal and maybe wanted a little change to look younger or fix a minor problems. Included in the same group are those who were normal but through accidents or cancer or something else were disfigured. We can take them to a mirror, and in time, because they had a normal face, help them to see that they are perfectly normal. Their etheric body was not damaged.

In the second group are those who were born with deformities and severe birthmarks. Those are the ones who require different treatment. We explain to them that their earthly appearance was karmic and that occurred because of something from a past life. Perhaps in a past life they had big egos and flaunted their egos by saying, *look at me, how great I am*. And people did look at them. Then they came back with a disfigurement and people would look at them, and the expression on someone else's face was painful. With birthmarks, we have great success. With the severely disfigured, it is much more difficult. In time, with counseling, many elect to go back to a former life and use that etheric body which is free of disfigurement. They are then capable of using their bodies correctly without all the bloated egos.

While on earth some of them found jobs in side shows of a circus billed as freaks. Many of them earned a living that way. And in some parts of the world still do. When they come here to this side of life, we have to counsel, sometimes for a long time to mix with others. When they were making their living being billed as a freak, there usually were other so-called freaks with them. They had their own little colony and were accepted in a circus. They were just accepted. So they tell us they just want to be with their own people over here. We have to really work at it sometimes to get them to see that they can change their appearance if they are willing to understand why they look the way they do. Then we can go back to a former life, go into the akashic records, and determine the "why". That is how we really bring about the change in attitude. Having learned to bow their egos, they may then elect to go back to a former life when they were in a perfectly normal body. They will use that body with a new attitude.

I got into the work of being a plastic surgeon because in a former life I was around people who were disfigured—a whole family had the cleft palate. I thought that God had done them a terrible injustice. They were poor and I saw the problems they had with eating and digesting their food. So I thought I could come back and be helpful to people who were disfigured, but I learned to help myself. Yes, I was good at my craft, but I was better at making money. And I charged plenty. I would increase my fees regularly for those who could afford them.

I hope people will think twice about plastic surgery because you have earned the appearance you got, and that is the way it is. ◆

24.

SEXUALLY TRANSMITTED DISEASES
AND DEVIANT BEHAVIOR

Venereal diseases are not karmic in the sense that a person has a genetic predisposition for gonorrhea, syphilis, genital herpes, vaginitis or chlamydia infections. The karma is that they have not learned how to control sex. So they go from one situation into another situation. It is the situations that are karmic. They may have been a prostitute in a past life, or were a pedophile who gets his kicks from little boys and young females, or engaged in promiscuous sexual behavior. They will come back and be tempted to do the same type things they did in a past life in order to have the opportunity to be strong enough to refrain. Some are obviously unable to discipline themselves not to engage in sexually deviant behavior or activities.

Acquired immunodeficiency syndrome (AIDS) is a human viral disease that ravages the immune system, undermining the body's ability to defend itself from infection and disease. It is caused by the human immunodeficiency virus (HIV). AIDS leaves an infected person vulnerable to opportunistic infections. It can prove fatal. Although exposed, it will *only* affect those who are working out a karmic debt for past life sexual problem behavior.

Enlightening Voices from the Other Side

Dr. Monroe on working with pedophiles and rapists
I work on this side of life with people who engaged in sexual deviation, pornography and various things like that—the pedophiles and rapists. They all stem from a different basis, so we usually try to keep them separated when we work in groups. Those who are into pornography sometimes will get involved in pedophilia and so forth. Rapists really have a problem with anger and violence, of wanting to inflict harm on the opposite sex. And while it does not necessarily have any connection with their mothers in this life, it does go back to a past life in which they were abused

by their mothers or other significant women and they have carried it over, not to consciously hurt their present mother, but to hurt women who represent the mother or women who abused them from the previous life. And it is very deep seated. They do not hurt their wives usually, sometimes yes, but not usually. They can have a very "normal" family life. Being a rapist is an extra-curricular activity, so to speak. They can love their wife very deeply and divorce her completely from women in general that they want to hurt. It is just that great need for revenge. They do not know the women. They just pick easy targets.

When they come over here, the treatment consists of taking them back to a past life and working through that, and if the mother from the past life is here, then we try to bring her into the treatment. So that is what we do. We certainly would not want this kind of person to reincarnate before working this out. They come back to earth, really not to rape someone, but to develop a healthy relationship with their mother or with women, and they are unable to do it, but that is on a subconscious level. Consciously, they usually have an acceptable relationship with their mother in this life.

With the pedophile, they do have problems in having a normal relationship with an adult woman. And so they seek their pleasure with a vulnerable little soul. And it is really very hard because, in a sense, they are a rapist to a child. But the dynamics are different. Usually, they have done this in a previous life and have come to try to establish a normal relationship with an adult woman and are not successful, so they revert to what they were comfortable with previously. It is a very traumatic thing for a child to experience, and it is a dear karmic debt for the pedophile. Again, it is deep seated and it is difficult to cure. Perhaps some day, when therapists realize it goes back to a former life, they can successfully regress their patient, and then they might be able to bring this out and be helpful. Or, if they are mediumistic and can get help from the guides and teachers, they can work it out that way. But there is a missing link in the treatment that is done today. And that missing link, of course, is tapping into the akashic records of a previous life in which this was also a problem.

Some people are just sexual deviates on a consenting basis. They do not see the beauty of the sexual act, and try to enhance it with all sorts of ways and so forth.

I got into the work frankly because I was all mixed up when I was on earth. And when I found out why I was, and I got through that—it took a long time—then I felt I was qualified to try to help other people in the same position. The one thing we want to keep them from doing is to go back to earth and try to impress someone to perform certain acts that will give them some satisfaction vicariously because it is still in their heads. So we want to change what is in that head so that they don't continue to desire the gratification that comes from the deviation. And they won't have the desire if they permit us to really work with them. Certainly enough of that goes on in your earth plane without having those from this side go back down and tear people apart.

Comments by the Master Teacher:

These problems are really very difficult and they are on a very, very low vibration. And yes, they do need people here to help them. And we commend anyone who is willing to dedicate his or her service to bringing them up.

B. Vargas on molesting a boy when he was a priest

I was asked to come to you today to talk about the kind of work that I am doing over here and what led up to it. I was a Catholic priest. I left the church because I had molested a little boy of about 8 or 9 years of age. He had Asthma and a heart condition. He was a frail child. The molestation occurred only once and when he complained that I was hurting him, I immediately stopped. It was very shortly thereafter that I resigned the priesthood. I felt I was not worthy to be a priest. Every day after that occurrence I prayed to God for forgiveness.

I moved to another state and went on to marry and have two children of my own. We regularly attended the Catholic Church, but I made certain my children were never alone with a priest. I worked with children and with youth groups but had no inclination to hurt them. I guess I was not a true pedophile, but I was aware that it was not uncommon among the priests.

The young boy lived to be about 20 years old. I went to Spirit many years later, and after I had gained some knowledge about spirit life, which was a great surprise to me, I looked him up. I wanted very much to seek his forgiveness. He told me that he had long ago forgiven me. He was aware that I included him in my daily prayers. Also, knowing I was working with children, he wanted to make certain I was treating them appropriately. He was satisfied that my conduct was proper. I had made a mistake which caused him great trauma but he was too afraid to confide in anyone.

I did review my previous life and learned that I had been involved in some deviant sexual behavior which I had to atone for. I chose the priesthood, not to find a safe haven as some priests have for their deviate sexual activities, but to truly serve God. I did fail to live up to my soul contract while in the priesthood, but did try to make up for it on the outside.

I have followed some of the new reports exposing priests and am glad a cleansing is taking place. More careful screening must be done of those who apply to attend seminary. Pedophiles can cause a child to have great emotional trauma in their young lives. Pedophiles incur heavy karma.

Alex describes his involvement with child pornography

I was involved in child pornography when I was on earth. I was not a pedophile. I did this strictly for money. Well, I may have gotten my kicks by doing this, but I never actually physically injured or molested a child. I did psychologically scar some children who were my subjects. I did some adult pornography, but was only interested from the standpoint of observing and making money by selling my pictures.

I was caught. I was prosecuted. I served a prison term. I was not particularly liked by some of my fellow prisoners, but when they understood that I did it for money and did not molest a child physically, it helped protect me a little bit. There is a code in prison that you do not hurt children. I served my sentence fully, because when I came before the parole board, apparently I did not convince them that I would not do this again. There was one member of the board who was violently against pornography and was determined that I was to fully serve my term. I did this, and knowing what I know now, I am very glad that I did serve it because I worked off my karma for doing the pornography while still on earth.

I was a middle aged man when I was freed from prison and I had a rough time getting a job. So I moved to another state. And because I was physically fit, I got a job working in a warehouse where they did not check my past. And I lived my life as best I could. I did meet several men on the job who were not well educated but who were very good people. They would invite me to their homes but I never discussed my past with them. They were good churchgoing people and got me interested. So when I came to this side of life, I was more open to something on a religious level.

I did question some of the teachings I had been given on earth because they just did not seem to be right. I received a great deal of help from my guides and teachers when I got over here, and I elevated myself. And I have really asked for forgiveness for what I had done because pornography is abnormal. It is not the kind of thing that is uplifting. It creates a lot of fantasies and it leads to inappropriate acts and behavior.

When I learned more about sex on this side—we don't have sex here—and how it affects people on earth, I realized the magnitude of the low vibrations that I had created and propagated, promulgated, then I felt that what I had done was truly wrong.

In a former life I had engaged in some aberrant sexual activities. And actually I came back into this last life on earth to clean up my act, so to speak. I cleaned it up in the sense that I did not physically engage in a lot of things I had done before, but I did not improve my situation with my photography. I could have been a fine photographer to have brought in beauty, to have captured much, much beauty. However, I used my talent as a photographer in the wrong way. And I do want to come back to earth and get it all straight this time. So I am struggling with that. I know that no matter what we have done, God forgives us. And those who are here to help us do not judge us, but we must learn to forgive ourselves or we cannot grow. We will be stuck. We will be stymied. We cannot progress unless we forgive ourselves and move on to something better.

Comments by the Master Teacher:

You can see the variety of activities and situations that people get themselves into. Alex was quite right. God does forgive and we must forgive ourselves. We can ask the forgiveness of others that we have hurt, and we can ask God to forgive us, but we must forgive ourselves. That is so very, very hard for so many people to do. They cannot be free to move on until they forgive themselves. ◆

26.

SPECIAL TREATMENT OF CHILDREN

Enlightening Voices from the Other Side

Martin on the care given to babies and young children

If the children are very, very young, they are taken to nurseries where men and women care for them. The caregivers are very good about bringing them back to earth to visit their biological parents, even when there is an abortion. They are brought back so that connection remains. They do grow in Spirit. We grow as far as we want to grow, depending on the work that we want to do.

One adoptive mother loved her daughter a great deal, but did not really like children in general. When she came over here at sixty plus years, she chose to take care of babies in order to work it out. She has done that for all these years and is still doing it. She did not like the children's antics and their fighting and so forth. She raised her daughter more as an adult than a child. She knew this had to be corrected, so she took on the little ones as her service over here.

Children grow just like they would grow on earth in the sense they have to learn to communicate with words. If you had a newborn baby that went over, that baby would probably carry over a lot of memories from the previous incarnation, a previous time in Spirit actually. Those who take care of babies would teach them how to communicate, just like you on earth teach a young one how to talk. As the little soul progresses then we can teach it to talk. They will grow in size. The etheric body grows. It will not stay a baby in the etheric body the rest of its life. They do not have to become an adult if they choose not to, but most do. Some choose to go back to a child size and work as a joy guide to someone.

For example, if a stillborn baby came back four years later to communicate with its mother, it would come as a four year old to be identified. They would come back at the age they normally would be had they lived. They are fed the essence of food and milk. In time they no longer want it. Sometimes people on earth are asked by their joy guides to put out ice cream so they can take the essence from it.

Children are raised by a group of spirits, not just one caregiver for that would be too much of an attachment to one spirit. We still want them to be attracted to their earth parents. If there is a relative in Spirit who wants to take care of the baby, then that is a different story because that baby would then bond with the grandparents, etc. If not a relative, they would not have a total bonding, because we would want them to still bond with the biological parents. We keep bringing them back to get used to the parents who had them. Many people do not believe the child lives on. In those cases, the poor child cannot bond with them.

With an abortion where there is a rejection, usually they will bond with the Spirit who is taking care of them because the parents have rejected them in the first place. There are reasons for that, too, very good reasons. The mother could not raise that child. It could be karmic. Even if aborted, the etheric body is already perfectly formed. Passing from earth state to Spirit is really a birth in which the etheric body becomes perfectly formed although the physical body may have been deformed.

Sometimes even the aborted child will be taken back to play with other children in the family. They will be taught how to play with the little children. You hear so much about a child talking to somebody and the grown-ups do not know who it is, that is usually a stillborn or child who died when very, very young or a child who was aborted. They are brought where they know the child will be played with and talked to and helped.

The children have their schools over here. They start out very young receiving some spiritual insights. They are not taken to churches, just helped with spiritual growth. They get pure spiritual teachings. They are not corrupted by the intellects of earth.

Trained workers are required and this training is given to anyone interested in working with babies or young children. There are no unwanted children in the Spirit World. They grow, are educated and trained for service to which they are drawn and best fitted for. The child grows, is taken to the parents for visits and forms a bond, and when those parents go over, they may be helpful to the parents in their first stages of their new life.

Dr. Bacon talks about children with cancer

I have been invited to come and talk to you about children with cancer. Until a few years ago, this condition was usually fatal. We are now making some progress with reversing the symptoms. First, let us talk about the fact that cancer is a karmic condition. When it affects a child, it is primarily for that child to work off karma. Many of them are very old souls that only need a small dose of something, that is, only need a comparatively few years of suffering. At the same time, this is a condition which affects the karmic needs of the parents. It is to help them to work off their debts as well.

Usually, in the case of the parents, they have not been good parents in a past life, allowing their children to suffer unnecessarily in some way. It did not bother them during that incarnation, but now that they have a child that they really wanted to bring into the world who might not be with them very long, they are suffering intensely. So it is a matter of both parents and children trying to balance their karma. Or, on the positive side, it could be that the parents themselves were the recipients of poor parenting, neglectful parenting, and so they wanted to come back and be good parents and give their child the great care a cancer patient, or very ill child would require.

There are various forms of cancer as you know. It depends really on what part of the body or organ is affected. The particular form puts a different aspect into the mix, so to speak. You can better understand the underlying problem of the child's past when you are familiar with the symbolic representation of the various parts of the body. It could be that the child had a lot of emotional problems, grew up not being able to work them out, and so came back with cancer this time, perhaps in the stomach area.

With some children, it may be leukemia, cancer of the lymph nodes, or of the bones. These little children suffer a great deal, but they do not have as many years of suffering as they would possibly have, had they chosen a different form of illness to work off their karmic debt.

Many children have not been on earth long enough to totally forget life in the Spirit World, and so their connection is much closer than it would be in the case of an adult. The exception might be with the terminally ill adult in the very last stages when the veil between the two worlds becomes very thin. For the young child, that veil is still rather thin. Sometimes they talk about their little spirit playmates whom they see so clearly. Their souls are aware that it is a land that they will be returning to, and it is a beautiful land. Their soul just knows this, even though they may not be consciously aware. And that soul knowing gives them a certain sense of comfort. They do not usually face death with the fear that the adults have because of their recent residency in the Spirit World. However, they are often faced with the sadness and the tears of their parents and loved ones.

Hopefully, the time will come when there will be greater understanding of why these things take place. People will know that God's divine justice is perfectly balanced as we move along on the continuum of life. Those scales finally reach a point of perfect balance. And if those on earth truly understood this, parents would realize they are the instruments to help a child work out karma, while at the same time, working out some of their own. There should be no guilt on their part, simply understanding. I do not mean to bring this into a focus which is devoid of warm feelings. It is not a cold kind of situation to face by any means. But with the knowledge that the little ones come to this side (Spirit World) to be well cared for, and that they can visit their parents on earth, should be of great comfort to their loved ones. The day will come, not right away, of course, but will come when those on earth will be more elevated and will be able to see spirit more clearly. In fact, the time is coming when those on earth who are sufficiently elevated spiritually will be able to see spirits with their physical sight.

The children come to this side and it does not take them very long to really understand that they no longer have to suffer. It is a matter of attitudinal change. They are very open and receptive to attitudinal healing. They are in a nice little etheric body which looks like the physical body they left behind, only this one is perfect. It is pathetic to watch them try so hard to come back to their parents to let them know they are okay and to comfort them. So often the parents are not open to communication. Rather, they blame God for taking away their precious child. It is very sad, but we can only explain to the children and they catch on in a hurry.

I have worked on this side for a long time with children who come over. I was a pediatrician on earth. I watched children, and it literally broke my heart to see them suffer, especially with cancer. In my time we really had nothing that we could do, except try to make them more comfortable with medication. Now there is hope for many. And if it is meant to be that they are to work off this karma in early life and to go on to live a normal life, of course, that will take place. But again, it is related entirely to the amount of karma involved and how soon it can be balanced out. With all karmic conditions, although they may not be cured, help should be given to alleviate as much pain as possible.

We bring animals to the children, or we take them down to the animal realm and let them play with the animals. This helps them so much. And, of course, the animals love the attention. I know that in your hospitals on earth, you have stuffed animals, but we have the real thing over here. And when children on earth are taken from dysfunctional homes to be placed in foster homes, stuffed animals are important to give them a sense of security. Something alive that they can cuddle is so very important. Live puppies are especially comforting. On this side, the puppies frequently stay with the children and they both grow up together. It is a beautiful thing to watch.

We have a lot of music, art and some spiritual studies to progress their souls. If they are in their last incarnation, they chose, if they like, to go back to a former incarnation when maybe they were a teacher, or whatever they did at that time. Taking on that etheric body, they can function to their fullest potential. That is entirely up to them. Usually, when they decide to go back to a former incarnation, they were not too close to the family that they went to as a child. I am saying that when they go back to earth to suffer cancer or another serious disease, they do not always go to a family that they have incarnated with previously. So the ties are not that strong. They may remain a child for awhile to help the family, but then they will go on. They might even wait until that family comes over, and then they will go back to a former life. It is contingent upon the elevation of the soul and the karmic links with the parents, because you do not always go back to the family that you may have had problems with. Many times people go to families simply because they can provide the conditions and experiences needed by the soul to progress.

If they are old enough, usually by age 12, they can go through the akashic records, and we are there to help explain things to them. Very young children do not always understand when they are reviewing the akashic records. So we find it helpful to let them be here longer and then go back over it when they are a little more mature so they can understand fully. Many of these children truly are old souls in the sense of spiritual elevation, and they just needed this particular earth experience. It may well be the last incarnation required to erase all karma—the last incarnation they wish it to be. They may not chose to return to earth. We are not always dealing with just young souls beginning their soul evolvement because many may be very elevated children.

Interestingly enough, I had a very lucrative practice on earth, but I did develop a heart condition in late life. And I suppose that it was to finish up my problems with love. I gave a great deal of love to my patients, but apparently, from reviewing the akashic records, I had been a pretty loveless person in the past life, and I needed to finish it off. So I developed a heart condition, which is certainly symbolic of not giving enough love, and finished off the last of the love karma before coming to this side.

I was really intrigued when Dr. Cranston talked to me about your project. I think this book will be wonderful in answering many questions. It is the first time I have been asked to talk about this from both sides of the veil.

Dr. Perkins speaking on deformity in children
I was so pleased, intrigued to know that somebody cares enough about what we are doing on this side to help their loved ones. Yes, I was delighted to accept an invitation to come and tell you about my work.

I deal with children who were born deformed. And I am talking about badly deformed children who did not live long on earth because of the severities of having things like a brain born on the outside, or being so badly crippled that there little knees were actually pushing into their organs, being born with a heart on the outside. I don't want to go into more description of these conditions because they are not pretty. When these things happen, the infant does not live more than a few hours, or a few weeks at the most, or gives up life and is stillborn. I do not want to make it such a gruesome sight that it is difficult for the reader. Suffice it to say, there are some terrible, terrible, terrible infant bodies. These are primarily to help the parents with their karma. Because this little soul has such a short life, if at all on earth, it really has no memory of the earth experience and can come back to this side of life without really having lost the memory of the Spirit World. When they come back to this side, they do have a perfect etheric body.

And because they came as a baby, they can come back to this side as a baby, or they can elect to be an adult or an older child, if they choose. If they were an adult and came just to have that birth experience to help the parents work off karma, they really can come back over here and take on their previous etheric body. I help them to make this decision. We go through a little review of what they looked like at birth, which sometimes is a shock to them. So they need a little help, but then we explain that this was a decision that they had made to help these particular parents. It is a karmic thing.

The soul of the parents felt they did not merit having a perfect child because they had not treated a perfect child very well in a past life. And so, in some cases, a child who is imperfect comes to really shake them up. Karma is not for the purpose of punishment, and I don't mean to give that impression. It is for enlightenment. It is to help them. It really does shake them up and they do ask, "Why did God send me this child." Well, God didn't send it. Through the karma incurred by the treatment of a child in a past life, this is all they could receive—a child taken away from them. Of course, it is a child many of them would not have wanted, had the child lived. But it does give them much pause for thought when this happens. I think that is about all I can say about this.

Sometimes there is a little guilt on the part of the returning infant, and we dissuade them quickly, assuring them that was the way it was to be done. Because when they view that body, it is pretty awful, but they come over here with a perfect body again.

Comments by the Master Teacher

I do want to say something here. I don't want you to be confused about an infant who comes with great deformity. That soul does take on a different etheric body in order to produce the physical deformity. If it is stillborn or dies immediately, it goes back to Spirit in a perfect etheric body and can immediately revert to the original etheric body, the etheric body of the previous life. It has no earth experience so the etheric body that was used to produce the physical body is simply discarded, and the soul takes on the body of the previous life. There are many interesting twists to things over here.

Roy Carr describes techniques used in working with children

I have just come in here at the request of my doctor, Dr. Monroe, who just spoke to you about heart conditions. He was very helpful when I was on earth and I outlived him. When I came to this side, I looked him up and he did help me greatly to get through my thinking.

I am now working with children who have come over with congenital heart defects. We do interesting little things with them in trying to help them to understand what happened and why they had just a short life. Part of it was to help their parents. It is a little difficult sometimes at first to explain to children that we have many lives, not just one. And so we do little books and we write little stories about the different lives. The teachers are very, very helpful. Some of these children are really too small to understand the akashic records so that is put off for awhile. Usually they do not go through that until they are around twelve years of your earth time. In the meantime, the teachers know who they were for the last couple of incarnations. So they will suggest to me to tell the child, let's imagine that you were Jack and you were a carpenter. And so we draw things about carpentry. And we may regress them a little bit without their being too consciously aware. These have to be very short sessions. We will say to them, what do you think that Jack was thinking about? What was he doing? Where did he live? And what kind of family did he have? And so I help them with their art and the teachers are there to help with the regression. Then we move on to the next life when they were named Eric, and we go through the same thing. And then we get to the last life.

And so this helps to prime the pump, so the speak, so that when they are ready to view the akashic records, it makes a lot more sense to them. They have kind of a foundation and it is not all so very new. They go to spiritual awareness classes and they learn many things. So this is part of the programming. I am very happy that I am able to do this because children are wonderful to work with. It is so much easier to express love to them than it is to some jaded old soul that comes over with bitterness. But I will eventually work with those types. I hope this has given you a fresh little idea of what we do.

Dr. Laverty on emotionally disturbed children
I understand that you have had a number of others come and each has talked about his or her particular interest. We have so many problems to deal with on this side. You would just be amazed at how specialized our efforts become because of so many problems. There are so many helpers here to help elevate the consciousness of people.

I was a psychiatrist when I was on earth, and I know that you have had Dr. Clayton come in and talk to you about several illnesses. And he is a wonderful, wonderful doctor. My particular specialty was working with children who were, I would say children who were emotionally neglected because their parents were unable to really give them the kind of nurturing they needed. These were families that were socially upper class, monied people who were too busy with their social activities and taking their trips, and so forth. The father may have had a good position and was very busy at his work. You would be surprised how many children are neglected because of this situation. They have baby sitters or nannies to take care of them.

It is not until the child exhibits some very bizarre behavior, very exaggerated behavior, that the parents seem to notice at all, and then they want to shunt them off to a psychiatrist and ask us to do all the cleanup work and straighten out their children. And they do not want to be too involved in the treatment program, only minimally. This was not my only work, because I did work with other children who came because of other circumstances. This was what I became known for, however, and I kind of specialized in. I tried so hard to work with the children, but without real parental support and involvement, it was very difficult to make great strides. Some of these children I saw for periods of years, and I perhaps was most helpful to them when they reached their teens. That is a rebellious time against authority. I did help them more at that time than I was able to when they were younger because I could talk to them differently and help them to see and to accept where they were and how they could get out of it. Some of them carried scars for the rest of their lives. There were a few suicides which was very, very sad. And the parents felt that I had not been helpful enough. That was socially disgraceful to them.

Sometimes I wondered why I was in the profession, but then I would have somebody come along showing improvement. That would make it all worthwhile. I did the best I could knowing what I did. Had I known the dynamics of the karma that was being worked out, I probably would have used a very different approach.

I think the reason I wanted to come to talk to you today is to help any psychiatrist, social worker or psychologist working with children to try to understand what the underlying problems might be, and to try to sort these out a little differently. We work on this side more openly when they come over still hurting. In the case of the parents, when they are ready to evolve, this information is given to them; so we work with everything being open and laid out. This is how it has all come about, and if they want to grow, this is what we must do. We must go through it. We must hash it all out and then we can move on with forgiveness.

It is going to take a real education on earth about reincarnation and karma. And your churches are very definitely going to have to make some changes in what they teach people. The first step, of course, is to teach them there is an afterlife. There is continuous life. We simply shed our physical body, but we take our personality and our mind and our soul with us to continue in life. We have got to get that across. And then they have got to teach about reincarnation and karma so that counselors on any level can broach the subject with them and try to figure it all out. The time will come when you will have more mediums who are working in these counseling or psychiatric settings. And they may be able to obtain enough information to really help their patients move ahead. It is going to take time, but the more information that we can get out, the better. And we are trying all the time to share more of the techniques that we use over here with those on earth. Some of these are being picked up very clearly and are being put into practice. They need the understanding in order to add another dimension to their treatment.

As I mentioned earlier, I was not always successful. I did the best I could. I was very frustrated frequently. I did not have the understanding about guides and teachers. I really was not tuned in enough to receive impressions clearly, so I have continued this work on this side because I wanted to give enough of myself that I could really help people. So this is what I am doing over here. I do work individually and in groups, and when the parents are available and willing to come, I bring them into the group setting so that they can see what they did, how the patient reacted, why the patient had to go through it, and so forth. There has to be that kind of open dialogue. We don't always get through the resentment immediately, by any means. We keep hammering it out, and eventually there is a real clearing of the air. There is forgiveness, and frequently a true friendship forms between parent and child.

Many are not children when they come over here. I work with those that have had that kind of background. And I am a very determined person to make sure that we help as much as we can in every situation where those involved are ready for the help. We can't beat our heads against a brick wall if they are not ready. We have to wait for them to be ready, but we still try informally. We talk to them. Guides and teachers work very closely with me and we all use the same approach of trying to get them to want to rise, to elevate themselves. And we will take them to higher realms, planes and let them see the beauty, and we hold that out as the carrot. They, too, can be living on those planes, but it does mean they really have to cleanse themselves of the garbage so they can move ahead. So that is the carrot we use by taking them to see the beauty of a higher plane.

I hope that I have helped you to understand better what we do with the emotionally disturbed child. I should not leave you with the idea that these children in every case deserve the neglect. They are not all paying karma, because some of these parents have truly created a situation that the child did not merit. So it is not karmic in all situations, but it creates an enormous amount of karma for the parents when they do this to the child.

Dr. Pendergast on treatment of cripples

I was invited to talk to you about working with children or with adults who were cripples in childhood, some crippled from birth, some with cerebral palsy that eventually crippled them, spina bifida, or other disorders. When a child is confined to a wheelchair, it is usually a karmic condition. But it does not remove from the child their frustration, their envy, their jealousy when they see other children who are free and able to move around and do the things that they would like to be able to do. They do question, *why me?* And some of them are able to work through this, and they in their own way become as productive as they possibly can. They can develop to be cheerful individuals, but it really depends upon the degree of spirituality they have when they incarnate.

When they come over to this side, that is when I work with them. And some of them are very bitter and feel that they had a rotten life. *Why did God do this to me?* attitude. So we first have to convince them that they no longer are in that physical body; they don't need it. I have actually been around some who panicked when they didn't see their wheelchair beside them. We told them they no longer needed it. But there are some cases where they are so deeply, deeply convinced that they are helpless that we have had to put them in a wheelchair temporarily. We will not allow them to keep that wheelchair for any length of time. We will take them, if they get too resistant to our treatment, and give them water therapy. Their first reaction is to think they are going to drown and they start instinctively to move their arms and legs, and they find that they have mobility. Thoughts become so ingrained in a person's head. They are extremely difficult to dislodge. Even when they can look at their bodies, even when they can stretch out their arms and legs, some of them still think they are crippled. We have to do a lot of convincing, an awful lot of convincing that they are just fine.

If they are old enough to really understand, we try to explain to them that they went through an earth experience to work off some karma for bad things they had done in a previous life, but that is all past. Their slate is perfectly clean. They have a new life. They have a new body to move around in which is perfect. Now, what they need to work on is perfecting some of the thoughts in their head. When we can make a break through, it gives us such a sigh of relief that they finally accept, *Hey, I am a complete person.*

We find, interestingly enough, many of these individuals want to become involved in some form of athletics over here. We have different games. We don't play games here to win for the ego sake of winning. We play just to enjoy playing and to win because we have done our best. It is not to say, *I deserve a trophy for what I have done.* It is none of that. Many of them do want to be involved in something very athletic to really prove that they are real perfect beings. You would be amazed how they get out there. When some of your well known athletes do come over, they usually are very happy to work with these children or adults and help them. They like nice fresh recruits, and they have done some wonderful work. Lou Gehrig has been wonderful in helping. He was paralyzed. He knew what it was like to be a great athletic, and then to be crippled. And so he has helped us immensely, and so have many of the other athletes. They have been absolutely wonderful. We are so glad to pass our individuals on. That is something that I am involved in doing.

I was a Catholic priest for awhile in my life. I did not stay with it. After a few years, I felt I could be more helpful by being out of the priesthood than I could in it, so that is what I chose to do.

Dr. R. Gaynor on caring for child murder victims

I want to tell you a little bit about the work that I am doing with murder victims, especially children who come to this side— those who have been sexually assaulted and brutally murdered. You have had some cases that have received a great deal of public attention. I want to talk a little bit about why these things happen. They are not always karmic. The perpetrator of the crime has usually been a bad seed in a previous life and has come back hopefully to be strong enough to make up for what he (and usually it is a he) has done. They come back to do good deeds for children, but instead, because they had not managed to have normal and good relationships with adult women to satisfy their sexual desires, they become pedophiles who carry it too far. Many times they would not murder if they were not afraid of being caught, and of course, by murdering they guarantee being caught. Or, at least guarantee there will be a massive search to find them and bring them to justice.

It is so sad because the children are so terrified by what has happened to them. They come over here and if there are no close relatives, especially grandparents that they may have known, it is sad. If there are close relatives, then they immediately take them into their arms and give them the comfort, the love, and the security that these little ones need.

There are occasions where this has been a karmic thing. The child has brought over things from a past life, and they wanted to work it out by being attacked and murdered so that they could affect some changes in the law. They chose this, and it is also a karmic thing for the parents to work through. So it usually affects the entire family if it is karmic in nature. As I said previously, it is not always karmic. It is just a horrible thing that has been done to a perfectly innocent child. And it certainly adds to the karma of the perpetrator.

The treatment over here would be the same in caring for the children in making them feel secure, loved and wanted regardless of whether or not it is karmic in nature. Eventually, they are old enough to understand what they did, what happened to them and why it happened to them. In the case of a child who is at least twelve, we are able to take them through the akashic records shortly after they arrive here so they can understand what happened. In some cases, the parents remain very active in helping other children who have been kidnapped, or start foundations whose purpose is to help in some way. The TV show, *America's Most Wanted,* has helped another father whose son was kidnapped and murdered. Some of these actions that the parents have taken were planned before incarnating; however, it does not lessen a parent's feelings toward someone who has murdered his son or daughter and who has no remorse. These perpetrators will go to a very dark realm and will suffer terribly. We are hoping that all parents will forgive them before they leave the earth plane for their own soul's sake. It is not to make a murderer feel better and to lessen his guilt, but it is primarily for the growth of one's own soul that we encourage this. We want the parents to find peace and freedom.

I got into this work because when I was on earth I almost caused the death of someone. I was in a blind rage over something that had happened and got into a physical fight and almost caused the death of that person. I did a lot of damage, and I believe it was only through the prayers of everyone that this man pulled through. It definitely must not have been his time to go. I had so much remorse. I did go to him immediately when he was in the hospital, and I did pray for him, and I did tell him how very sorry I was.

And because God had let him live, when I came to this side, I wanted to work with those who did not make it. I had carried much, much guilt although this man did finally forgive me. He said, "I was as much to blame as you." I figured I was one of the lucky ones.

And so I hope this has given you a little insight into what we go through, and how we try to make amends. But we have to be sorry for what we do in order to grow. We have to have remorse, but we cannot allow that remorse to go on and on and on. Guilt is the cancer of the soul. It affects the whole person. We cannot dwell on it continually. We have to have the remorse, we have to ask God for forgiveness, ask the person we hurt to forgive us, and then we have got to forgive ourselves. We must forgive ourselves. We must put the whole thing in proper perspective to know what happened at that time to trigger whatever it is that we did, and we have to move on. And if we can do it while still on earth, that is wonderful. But that is the purpose of reviewing our life through the akashic records because it gives it to us straight. There is no way that we can change it, color it, modify it. It is the absolute truth that we face. And when we can face truth and accept personal responsibility, then we can grow, but not before. I think I have talked enough but I am so grateful to be able to share this and to know that it is going to be published and to reach other people and to help them to stop and think. •

27.

MULTIPLE BIRTHS, MISCARRIAGES
AND ABORTIONS

Enlightening Voices from the Other Side

Dr. P. Henney talks about multiple births

I have come this morning because I was one of triplets. I was on your earth many, many, many years, way, way back, several hundred years ago, as a matter of fact. I will tell you a little bit about my life. Growing up as a triplet, and it was a little unusual in that day to be something more than a twin, if there were multiple births. This was because if there were more than two, usually one would be too small to survive. It would be very unusual to make it. You have had seven who are thriving, and quintuplets, the Dione quints were very famous. They did survive and that really was very unusual because we did not have the medical knowledge or care at that time.

Being one of three boys, it was very interesting because we were very different in some ways. We wanted to do different things when we grew up. My parents encouraged that. They did not understand why we weren't more alike, although we were identical. We were all from the same egg. It split three ways and we looked alike. We used to fool our teachers and do all kinds of tricks on people. We loved doing that.

We did take up different vocations. I became a medical doctor. One of my brothers was a very good chemist, and the other became a lawyer. We respected each other's differences. We were normal boys. We fought and at times were jealous of each other, if one was able to do something better than the others. But as we grew older, we truly respected each other. I think that our parents helped us a great deal. They did not understand that it was a karmic thing for us to come back to be so close to each other, but they were spiritual—they weren't just religious, they were spiritual— and they taught us to have respect for each other. This was great. I think in some respects in adult life I was closer to my brother who was a chemist because I would ask him things that would help me with my profession. But then when my lawyer brother would have a case and if it had anything to do with chemistry or medicine, he would call on us for our expertise.

We stayed close to each other. We lived in the same town and we did much visiting back and forth so that we were very close knit. In that respect, we did what we were supposed to have done. That was to respect and love each other. Now, in a previous life that I viewed going through the akashic records, I saw that we had truly been enemies. We had hated each other. Two of us were brothers and the third was a cousin. We were jealous and we were just at each other's throats all the time. My cousin lived with us off and on because his mother became an invalid. Our parents were very healthy and they took this boy into our home. We really resented his coming and having to share anything with him, and he resented being there. We were very mean to each other. We really were. When we were grown, we went our separate ways.

After going to Spirit and reflecting on our life together, we decided that we really should come back and be forced to be together again, but to do it in a different way. We kind of started our lives as triplets being a little nasty to each other and maybe jealous, but our parents did intervene. They really did bring out the best in us in many ways. I don't say that we were perfect by any means, absolutely not, but we did grow up to love each other and to respect each other and that continued. We were great friends. We truly were great friends. When others in the world seem to be against us at times, the three of us stood together. There were times when we were criticized for our work. My brother lost some of his cases and he was branded as not being a good lawyer, but he did his best. And we stood by him. It was hard for him to even make a living at one point, and we stood by him. We knew he was a good person and sincere and competent. He was able to pull through that. It was partly karmic. He pulled through that and was able to be very helpful and successful in later life.

I lost a few patients on the operating table. I lost a few babies. They were meant to go, but I had no understanding of that, and I felt terrible, terrible! My brothers consoled me, but to this day I have pain because I brought anguish to families. I did my best and I am still struggling to get over that. I am grateful to have an opportunity to come through and tell how much it hurts. I want people to understand that we can't always save someone. I want people on earth to know this. We can't save them when it is their time to go. We try our very best but it is not always meant to be that way. It isn't. And now, I feel better if this is going into a book to tell people it is not always meant to be. You have better methods now and sometimes people are saved when it is really their time to go. You have prolonged life when you should let them go. Eventually, there will be more knowledge. There will be better understanding in the future.

So on this side I work very hard with people who come over as part of a multiple birth to help them to understand why they chose that life. Some of them just hated each other. They never got over what they had done in a previous life. They came back and did the same thing all over again. They may not have been twins or triplets in a past life, but they did have some strong connection. Frequently, they were members of the same family who came back to be close to each other and to work things out. So often they did not do it.

I have also worked with conjoined twins. That is very rare. It goes without saying that they had a pretty difficult life in one of their previous lives and did not want to work it out. Usually, what happens is that in one of their former lives, they did not get along at all, not at all. And they came back to work it out. They may have been twins or just part of a family and they still did not work it out. So then they chose to come back as conjoined twins where they would absolutely be joined together and to have to have that experience. They called them Siamese twins at one time. They had to get along. They forced themselves to get along because they wanted to grow spiritually. In some situations, medical science has been able to successfully separate them. Even when they are separated there is some physical reminder that they have been closely joined. They have that reminder to help them to form a good relationship and love their sibling.

When they get to this side, we do help them to review their life and see what the problem was, and why they chose to work off their karma being conjoined, or part of a multiple birth. It is very interesting to listen to them in a group setting—the things that they did to each other. It's most helpful when both twins or triplets or whatever are here so they can all be in a group together to face it. But if one is still on earth, we still work with them individually or in a group, so that when their siblings come over, they can be more advanced and more helpful.

I hope that I have helped you with this. It has certainly been helpful to me to come and talk about this and to really try to get people to understand that there is a reason, a karmic reason, for being part of a multiple birth. And that they need special help from parents, teachers and counselors to really live the kind of life they chose in their soul contract. They are to live in peace and love with each other and to get through the past negative relationship.

Not all twins are identical. Some are from a different egg entirely and will look different and may be of different sex. In those cases, the karmic bond is not as binding. They just need to be close. Or perhaps they just want to do some work together in this life. It could be for very good reasons, having nothing whatsoever to do with karma. Or, it could be karmic and yet they do not need to be identical to work out their differences. We will all try to help you find a publisher because this truly should go out to the world.

Dr. Hunsinger helps women who have aborted or miscarried their fetuses

There are so many, many conditions that people come over with. I am sure you recognize that no matter how well put together they are, there is always something that someone can help them with in making the adjustment to this side of life. We give the most attention, of course, to those who are badly in need. The ones who come over who don't have too big a problem usually can be helped by their guides and teachers. And they stay with them. Sometimes, the guides and teachers will stay as long as ten or fifteen of your earth years, simply because they are growing together. They are learning together. They become very good friends. The guides are not ready to go on to guiding someone else because they want to evolve higher, especially, if they are new guides and teachers. They have studied here but they have not had someone to guide previously. This is their first experience. They realize they could have been more helpful while the person was on earth. Of course, this does not happen all the time because frequently, the guides and teachers have been with a person for multiple life times.

If a person is particularly needy, the guides and teachers stay with them to be helpful. If they cannot be as helpful as someone trained to work on particular problems, then they will bow out and let someone else take over who is more specialized in helping with the residue of some diseases and other problems. We have all kinds of counselors over here. There is no end to them.

I was actually a tailor on earth. Over here, I was so interested in how things work and how people are helped, that I talked to many about their reactions to the Spirit World.

I decided to help women who had miscarried their fetuses and came to this side with a great deal of guilt. They thought they had done something to cause the miscarriages. And so my job was to help them become reunited with the souls that had not developed, who actually had decided that the situation was not correct or appropriate. The soul comes into the aura of the mother and observes whether the mother is truly the right one to come to. The soul considers how the parents interact and if it is the right environment for that soul. Can the family provide the right opportunities for that soul to grow?

In working with these particular ladies, I will describe one in particular. She was not a bad person by any means. In fact, she was perhaps too nice a person to have given this particular soul the opportunities that this soul needed to overcome certain stressful experiences related to its past life. Assessing the situation, the soul backed out. In this particular case, I had to explain to this lady that she could not have provided what was needed and that that soul had gone on to someone else, and actually, that soul was now in a physical body on earth. When she understood this, it alleviated her guilt. She had suffered a great deal feeling that she was not qualified, that God did not want her to have this child and took it away. Understanding brought her so much relief.

I also work with some women who have aborted. If the abortion takes place early in the pregnancy before the soul enters into the fetus, then that soul has the choice to decide whether it wants to stayed tied to that mother, or if it wants to go to another potential parent. If the soul elects to be a part of the situation, then it usually is for karmic reasons. It will stay related to the mother and grow up in the Spirit World.

If the fetus is about three months old and the soul has entered, and an abortion takes place then, it is definitely a karmic thing. The soul will grow up as a baby over here, if they choose, or go back to a former life. Usually, when that happens, that is, the fetus is aborted after three months, that soul knows that this is going to happen before entering and only wants a short experience, or, is providing an experience for the parents. When women come over, they are frequently very surprised to find their babies have grown up in the Spirit World. ♦

28.
ALCOHOL AND DRUG ADDICTION

Alcoholism, Drugs and Attracting Wrong Influences
The spirit teachers have explained that using a ouije board and the wrong methods of communication, black magic, etc. attract spirits who have not progressed. It is not the fault of the spirit guides. It is a matter of the person being so easily influenced and wide open. The guides can only do so much. That is something that people do not understand. They think the guides can do everything. No, they cannot. If people attract something to them, the spirit guides will try to get them out. They will try to help them in every way they can, but we still have freewill. The guides would talk to these undeveloped spirits and try to convince them not to bother the people on earth, but they do not always pay attention. It is a game.

An alcoholic may be in control of drinking, only to test himself by going to a tavern to see how strong he is. There are spirits who frequent the tavern because they want the essence of the liquor. The person will attract them and they may well give into temptation. It should not be. Any one with a vice should not be around those types of people because they are going to attract the same type of temptation that they went through before. Don't tempt temptation.

Enlightening Voices from the Other Side

Paracelsus, the Swiss physician
Let's say, you have an alcoholic who really drinks and drinks and drinks and drinks. That person has attracted an entity who did the same thing on earth. The entity is there impressing them to drink, and they simply think they are the entity. They cannot distinguish between their thought and the thought of the entity. The entity is making them worse all the time. The entity is getting the essence of the alcohol. The individual has to stop going into places where those entities would be and throw this one out by quitting the drinking. It is difficult to get them to quit drinking.

especially difficult with alcohol and drugs. It is very hard to get them to realize that this has to stop because they are possessed, but they don't even know they are sometimes. And that leads to doing things to get money to buy the alcohol and drugs, and the entity is encouraging them. That is a difficult situation. But it is not really karmic, it is simply they have gotten themselves in a bad situation. A lot can happen, and the alcoholic is really going to have to end it himself or herself. They can get help. They can go to a withdrawl center. And if they are willing to help themselves, then the entity is going to leave because they are not getting what they want. I had cases where I knew there was possession. I would get a person to a hospital where they would dry out and the entity would leave before the alcoholic entered the door in some cases.

Dr. Allstair describes his work with drunk drivers

I am here today to tell you about the group for which I am a facilitator. I see myself more in the role of a facilitator. I work with drunk drivers who have come to this side, and every one of them has either caused an accident to hurt someone or to kill someone.

Usually when they first come over, if they have done something really serious, have been in jail or prison, and they have served some time on earth, and if they have served enough time, they have worked off their karma. They still carry the enormous guilt over what they have done. And so this is what we are working with. When they first come over, they are in the same category as 95% of the other people, being confused and not knowing what spirit life is all about. And we do try very hard to catch everybody in the beginning and offer them classes and personal, individual help to get them over what they experienced on earth. Some of them are very eager and want to begin very shortly after they arrive. Others are just not ready to face themselves, and we cannot force it. And so they just sort of rest and do absolutely nothing. They will visit friends, play card games, or something to amuse themselves. It is a perpetual vacation for some of these people. Eventually, if they want to rise and get tired of all that, they will ask their guides and teachers or someone to help them.

Some of the drunk drivers that I get are very eager from the early stages of arrival to work on their enormous guilt. Some have been here a long time and they have allowed that guilt to really eat away at them. Some of them, and you won't believe this, are not too worried about it at all. They say, "the kid shouldn't have been running in front of my car. The parents should have been holding on. Or, some old fool shouldn't have been out in the middle of the street." They have not accepted their responsibility and there is nothing that we can do for them until they want to change. We can try, and there are many workers on this side who do try to reach them.

I have a group that is seriously interested in progression because they are there on their own freewill. We have not lassoed them and dragged them in. They are there because they want to grow. They want to ask for forgiveness from those they have hurt or sent to this side. And so we help them to really work through this. Frequently, we go with them to the person that they have injured or killed when they are ready to ask for forgiveness. Our presence gives them a little support. Where there is true forgiveness, we might even ask that person to come to the group and to talk about this, and to give courage to others in the group so that they, in turn, go and ask for forgiveness of those whom they have hurt. Forgiveness is so healing and essential for progress.

It is a very supportive kind of approach. It does not mean that we tell them that what they have done is okay. Far from it. We insist that they own up. They have got to admit that they were very, very, very wrong, that they did not exercise any discipline in drinking or being under the influence. So many people on earth are obese, and I know it is a billion dollar business. I am aware of Dr. Phil on your television who is trying so hard to help people to reduce and be healthier. But just think, if all of those obese people were drinking to excess instead of eating to excess, what a horrible situation you would have. So, we are thankful the alcoholics are much fewer in number as compared to the foodaholics.

If they are truly remorseful, that is the first step. We can work with them. And then the next step is for them to ask for forgiveness from God, from the person they have injured, and definitely to ask for forgiveness for the level of consciousness that brought about this tragic situation. Carrying guilt is truly like a cancer on the soul. We have to forgive ourselves, no matter how horrible a thing we have done. We must have the remorse, but we also must have the forgiveness so that we can move on. And the determination that we are going to take charge of that weakness. Many have vowed that they will come back and be workers to help those who are weak.

My group that I am currently working with are working on getting through this life. They are not yet ready to go through the akashic records to look at any of their previous lives to determine if a previous life influenced their alcoholic addiction. I do not work with drug addicts because it is a little different. The dynamics are very similar but a little different. So I stay with the alcoholics.

I got into this kind of work because my father was an alcoholic, and growing up in that kind of environment with its lack of stability, a mother having to go out and do housework in order to keep food on the table because my father lost his job frequently. I know what it is like from that side. Fortunately, he did not kill anybody or have any accidents, and I am very grateful for that.

In my previous life, I had been an alcoholic. I did not properly care for my family. I came back to be in an alcoholic family so that I would know and understand what it is like to be in a family where I was a helpless, vulnerable child at the mercy of someone who should be taking care of me and was totally derelict in assuming the duties and responsibilities of parenthood. So I got paid back. And that is what it is all about. I do want to help others, and I will come back again, I am sure, to work more in this area, or in some area of helping people. I am grateful I had the opportunity to come and talk about this. It is a very, very serious problem and it definitely is one that I am delighted that Alcoholics Anonymous and Alanon are helping with.

Dr. Wilson describes how he treats medical dependency

I was a pharmacist when I was on earth. I had a drugstore in a small town and I got to know a lot of people. I helped them a great deal. I was very aware that people could get hooked on certain drugs. And when the doctors would prescribe certain things over and over I got very concerned. And on occasion would even call the doctor and try to diplomatically tell him these things were addicting. I wondered if he even realized how addicting they were because doctors do not have a great deal of pharmaceutical knowledge. Some of the doctors took it very positively and appreciated my help and would ask what I would suggest, and some told me they knew exactly what they were doing to keep their patients quiet, or something of that sort.

I never believed in really drugging people. It is interesting that when the person comes over here and they have had so many medications all their lives, they want their pills. It becomes such a habit. They are so dependent upon them. We have to explain to them that they do not need pills here. We do not need pills over here because the etheric body is absolutely perfect. But if they are so insistent and we see that it could possibly be part of the treatment process of weaning, like by being weaned from food by giving the essence, then we will give them placebos—perfectly harmless little pills. If they say they do not look like the ones they have been taking, then we ask them to describe the ones they had been taking and we duplicate them in size and color and it makes them very happy. But we work very, very hard to get them off as quickly as possible so they can grow. We do not want them tied to the earth. We want them to be able to get strong enough so they can go through the akashic records, they can review their life and move on. This does not mean that we discourage them from reaching back to their loved ones on earth. I do not mean that. But they have to sever their emotional dependence on earthly things in order that they might grow.

So this is what I do. I tell them I worked as a pharmacist on earth for many, many, many years and I know exactly what they need. After they have been on some of these pills for awhile, we start cutting down on the number and we work that way. When they finally accept that they do not need them, we cut them out completely. I thought you might be interested in knowing that we do have to work at dependency on medication. And with people who are so dependent, they usually have other problems that caused their death, so those have to be worked on, too, but I am not involved specifically with those. Sometimes, yes, it all depends. We try to get their guides and teachers to work with them, and we have our experts also.

Dr. A. on the treatment of drug addicts
I am here this morning at the invitation of Dr. Cranston and I

was very much intrigued by what you are trying to do. We have very few opportunities to speak to anyone on earth. We try to impress them, but we do not get through most of the time. And even when those of us have had an opportunity to get through, our guidance is not always followed. And so our work can be very frustrating if we lose sight for whom we are truly working. We are working for the Light, and we try to shine our light and hope that we get some reflection from those that we are trying to help.

Well, when I was on earth, many, many, many years ago, I was Chinese in that incarnation. I smoked opium. We had opium dens and it really did weird things to our minds. It was not, it goes without saying, the right thing to do. You don't get your highs that way. The American Indians have their own methods of getting high to feel closer to Spirit. No drug is necessary to get a spiritual high. I won't go much into that life because it was a dark life. When I got to this side after that life, it took me a very, very, very long time to get out of that fuzzy, lethargic state and to really want to turn my life around. Frankly, in terms of your earth time, it took centuries to progress.

I came back to a family in which there was some drug abuse going on. This was quite some time ago. Drugs have been around a very long time. I came back to a family where my father was a heroin addict. We were from a wealthy family. There was much money in the family so that my father could afford his drug habit, and of course, it certainly was not as expensive as drugs are today on your earth. At that time, heroin was not the drug of the so-called affluent, but my father got involved with some low-life people. And once hooked, he did not have the strength to give it up. My father had buddies who were into it also, and some of them could not afford their habit, so he would buy drugs for them.

Our physical needs were taken care of because of family money, but I really had only a part-time father. I saw what this could do to a family. My mother stayed with my father. She loved him, and I think he loved us, but he loved his heroin more. I got to see what it was like. That is the environment in which I grew up. I had no desire to take any kind of drug myself. I was very much turned against it all.

I became a successful business person. I had the money to initially back my business. My father was generous. I never knew any physical deprivation while on earth. I was not a religious man but I did try to be ethical and I was fair with my employees. I would say I was an average decent person.

When I got over here and really got my feet on the ground, because it was a shock to know there was an afterlife, I learned I had to go through a reflective period and get on a spiritual path. I chose as my work over here to help drug addicts who came over because I did have resentment toward my father and I wanted to get through it by gaining a greater tolerance and understanding of the problems of drug addiction.

Drugs can get an absolute death-hold on a person. You have treatment programs on your earth now which help people, and I am very happy that you do. But many get to this side never having gone through treatment, or may be back on them again. Many of them overdosed and found themselves here. With drug addiction especially, it can cause the door to open wide to very undeveloped spirits to walk in and possess them and get the person into a pack of trouble, to say the least. Many crimes have been committed under the influence, or when possessed and not in control of themselves enough to know what they were doing. Many crimes have been committed to get the money for drugs.

In the group I work with, there are usually some pretty tough addicted people. The craving is there, and we have to go through withdrawal on this side for many of them. It is a very intensive, very intensive kind of work because it is so hard for them to quit cold turkey. Actually, we help them by giving them something over here that is an equivalent to what is done on earth. In fact, it was through our intervention that we got through to some doctors on earth to give their patients methadone. It helps them to get through the severe withdrawal symptoms associated with heroin detox. Of course, they eventually have to get off that.

On this side, we give them something which does help, and they gradually withdraw from the craving. It is kind of like the essence of methadone to get them weaned off. Believe me, it is harder on this side than on earth. We are successful with that phase of it to a large extent because they are really hurting. They do not always want to go the next step to get into group therapy and we cannot force it, but we do try very hard. We know if they relapse, then they are going to go back to earth and encourage someone there to stay on the habit and do things they should not do. They will get the essence of the drug through the addict on earth.

The treatment that you are using on earth really started over here. It is our techniques that we, not me personally—I am only following what many fine spirit doctors figured out long ago— were able to impress those on earth to try. There is a success rate up to a certain point, and we are hoping that it will get better and better all the time.

We personally would like to see drugs legalized. It would cut down on the enormous profits that the drug dealers are making. It would put many of them out of business. You could get people into rehab. I do not believe that it would increase the usage of drugs at all. I really do not believe that. I think that you would have much better control because you would be able to stop the drug trafficking. The drugs would be sold legally. The cost would be less than they are now, therefore, people would prefer to buy them at a lesser price than to go to a drug dealer where they would pay enormous sums. So the control I think would be here, and I do not feel that it would be widespread. I think there would be greater monitoring, and there would not be the pushing and trying to get people hooked. There could be greater intervention. In order to buy these drugs, you would have to go to classes to really understand what they do to the body. No one wants to get hooked on anything. This is a big problem. Even prescription drugs can be addictive. We are trying to impress doctors to be more aware of this. It is a huge problem, but it is not being addressed by your leaders as it should be.

It is really sad when we work with people over here and they look back at their life on earth. They do have to review every single day of it and really look and feel what they went through. And what a waste of precious time on earth to have done this to their body, mind and soul. They have to face it, and some are not able to do it. They just go so far and are not strong enough to face it, so they take a rest. We have many, many, many helpers to support anyone who is ready for help. There is enormous remorse with the drug addicts of how they did steal in order to support their habit, and the things they did to their families. The anguish they caused their parents, their siblings and their friends, and how much they regret and wish they could undo and to have set a better example. Some of them were in the performing arts—musicians and acting, etc. where they just didn't need to get a high.

Comments by the Master Teacher:

You can certainly see the ramifications of alcoholism and drug addiction. It affects not only the person, but all of those around them. It is not a very pretty sight for us to view. We are not always able to intervene when undeveloped spirits come in and temporarily possess someone on earth. They want to perpetuate their habit and they do not listen to our pleas, but the day will come when this has to stop so that the earth will become more elevated. And you will have your thousand years of peace. We are very grateful on this side of life that we have such wonderful workers who are truly dedicated to help these individuals turn their lives around, if not on earth, then over here. We are always given another chance. That door to reformation never closes on either side of the veil and that is so important for people to realize, but they should not wait until they come over here because it is much more difficult to progress. You do not have the buffer you have on earth. You are with like-minded people and it is more difficult. ✦

29.

CHIROPRACTIC CARE

Enlightening Voices from the Other Side

Dr. Reed on breaking the pattern of needing Chiropractic help in Spirit

I was a chiropractor when I was on earth. I did not get into the Atlas Orthogonal method that you are receiving though I have been able to observe that it is a very fine technique, a really advanced technique. I worked very hard as a chiropractor and I believe that I helped many, many people. I did not believe in being too invasive in my technique. I preferred the more gentle kind of ways. I worked in the South on both black and white races, and I do believe I saved people a great deal of money from getting surgical procedures. I was honest and I did give of myself to the best of my ability. I highly recommend chiropractic help for many, many situations. I got into the work because in a former life I had some problems with my back and my limbs that I believe would have benefitted from chiropractic adjustments. I decided when I made my soul contract to return to earth that I would help people in a way that was not as invasive as surgery, so I followed my contract and did exactly that.

Now it is interesting that when I came to this side of life, there were people who had practically survived, they felt, by regularly seeing their chiropractor. It was so ingrained in their head that they would have a certain ache or pain, that when they came over, they carried that mental cycle with them and could not believe that they had a perfect body that did not need adjustment. I had to learn that the physiology and the musculosketetal make up of the etheric body was totally and completely different from the physical body. I had to learn this. And so then I had to work with people over here to convince them what their body was really like, and to get it out of their head. It is all "head work" over here. It is attitudinal healing, the very thing that your book will address.

You would be surprised at how big a part the mind plays in keeping a person attached to the physical ailments of the earth body. And the same is true of somebody who wanted physiotherapy. So I work with those as well to convince them that it is not needed over here. You can do whatever you want with your etheric body. Someone crippled could go out and play tennis immediately upon arrival, if they would get the crippled consciousness, or any kind of pain consciousness, out of their mind, and substitute a healthy consciousness.

I wanted to share with you that no matter what bothers a person, we can work it out, physically, no problem at all. Mentally, people carry guilt and all sorts of feelings that do sometimes require very long periods before they can truly be healed. •

PART THREE

HEALING MENTAL, EMOTIONAL, AND SOCIAL PROBLEMS

This is Dr. Clayton. I have been invited to say a few introductory words about this section. I feel qualified because I was a psychiatrist on earth and I am doing psychiatric work on this side of the veil. I am not going to comment individually on each of the mental, emotional and social disorders that are included here. I simply want to emphasize that many of these disorders have been brought about by negative karma.

We, over here, are deeply grateful that this book doesn't just give a description of the various disorders or problems, but includes many stories or case histories which show how an unresolved problem from a past life greets you in the current life. In other words, mental illnesses and some emotional disturbances are carry-overs from past incarnations. The soul has chosen to work them out in this manner. You may think of mental illnesses and emotional problems as related only to earth life. But believe it or not, these are all conditions or problems which, if not successfully worked out on earth, are brought over to this side for us to finish the job, so to speak. In Spirit, there are expert therapists waiting to enable you to heal your earthly scars. Varying techniques are used to try to reach each and every one who is ready to progress.

It is certainly wise to correct whatever errors you are making now so that you don't carry them on to the next life. The wise will learn to raise their consciousness and be very aware of what they are thinking and doing at all times. We would like to see the day when we didn't have so many suffering from painful and very disturbing conditions. But until the consciousness is raised, that is how it will be.

The last two chapters of this section deal with things like taming the ego, feeling guilty, having regret, holding grudges, handling the bully, and so forth. These can certainly cause a lot of damage to the soul, so the reader should pay special attention to these two chapters and not get caught in doing things that could easily be avoided. Put the brakes on now.

This material is invaluable. You are receiving information that we have tried for so very long to get through to those of you on earth. If those who are in a helping position will only study what is presented here, and have the courage to talk about past lives, they will come up with the answers to many present disturbances.

It has been my pleasure to contribute to this section. ♦

30.

ALZHEIMER'S DISEASE

Enlightening Voices from the Other Side:

Dr. Clayton, a former earth psychiatrist explains the techniques used in the Spirit World to reach a person coming over with Alzheimer's Disease.

(Note: Although Alzheimer's is a disease of the brain, the ramifications of this disease include mental, emotional, intellectual, and social problems., therefore, it is given a place in this section.)

Alzheimer's is definitely a karmic condition which some people have chosen as a way to work off their karma from past lives. They make a plan prior to coming back to earth which includes attraction to parents who have the ability to produce the genes necessary for them to develop Alzheimer's. In other words, not all individuals have the potential to develop the illness, only those who have made a preincarnation plan will do so.

People on earth are trying hard to figure out what causes this condition, what kind of chemical reaction takes place in the brain to bring it about, and so forth. They may detect that certain genes are involved, but what they must understand is that it is karmic. And when it all gets figured out, then some other condition will need to replace it to give individuals a method to work out their karma. We will just be moving from one method to another. That does not mean research should not continue in the field. It should, but there always has to be some way of balancing one's karma. As the New Age progresses, and especially during the eventual coming Thousand Years of Peace, there will be less need for *traumatic* kinds of things to happen to more spiritually elevated people. Nevertheless, as long as we come back to earth, there has to be something because we are not perfect and we will always be doing things that are not perfect to some degree.

You will notice with people who have Alzheimer's that the condition usually occurs in their advanced years. It does not usually happen when they are young. This is because during that person's incarnation, they wanted to accomplish dual goals. To reach their first goal, they functioned very well. They may be very bright, mentally strong and active individuals for the greater part of their lives. Take for example, President Reagan, who aspired to a high position and was successful in achieving it before the onset of Alzheimer's. We can take other examples, such as, Charlton Heston, who is well recognized as a fine actor. He was very actively serving as president of the National Rifle Association until he was diagnosed with Alzheimer's. What I am trying to say is that people with Alzheimer's have made a plan prior to incarnating which would allow them to make some contribution, in addition to working off *major* karma. Major is the key word here. Hence, the first part of their life was to try to realize soul growth by contributing something worthwhile, and/or by resolving *minor* conflicts carried over from a past lifetime.

To fulfill their second goal, the last part of their life would be spent vegetating mentally to work out karma resulting from something of major significance, or an accumulation of a number of wrong actions. There is very definitely a karmic tie, not only with the caregiver, but with the family or someone close to the family. This gives the caregiver an opportunity also to work out his or her karma by taking care of someone who requires a great deal of looking after. Given time, the law of cause and effect never fails to be fulfilled.

The Alzheimer's patient has chosen to live on earth without the benefit of being consciously aware of his or her environment during the period of this condition. The soul has tucked away the memory of why this has come about; hence it is the function of the subconscious to cause the soul to review what happened in past lives. It is not the personality or conscious mind that is reviewing; it is the soul. The conscious mind is not aware of what the subconscious is bringing through to the soul. When the conscious mind is functioning on such a very, very limited basis, if at all, as in very advanced stages, it indicates the subconscious mind is in total control. The subconscious is actually acting out the things which are relative to what has gone on in a past life. If individuals misused their intellect then, the subconscious is not allowing them to express it consciously now. However, this ability may vary depending upon the stage of the illness. In the early period, some days may be better than others, and some tasks more easily performed than others. Mild disorientation and memory lapses may give way to frustration, agitation, and confusion as they realize they are losing their ability to be in control of their life. Initially the body remains vigorous, while the mind slowly and inexorably wastes away in advanced stages. Eventually, helplessness obliterates the personality. Benefit from medication may offer limited help, ever in keeping with the circumstances and extent of the karmic debt.

It is important to understand the role that the subconscious mind plays with all people. When we make our transition to Spirit, the subconscious mind is a part of our spirit body only until we review the akashic records. It is no longer needed after that reflection. We then draw from the superconscious or soul memory while in Spirit. At the time of transition from the earth plane, all that was stored in the subconscious during the earth experience is transferred to the akashic records or Book of Life in the Spirit World. When we reincarnate, we are again given a subconscious mind, into which is stored all of our past incarnations, as well as the plans we wish to accomplish on our earthly sojourn. The heart seed atom is another storage unit, located in the etheric body, which also contains the memory of all our incarnations. The heart seed atom works in conjunction with the subconscious so that at the predestined time, the onset of Alzheimer's is set into motion. The appropriate chakra or spiritual center also plays a part in carrying out the plan of incarnation.

At some point in our eternal life the garbage in the subconscious has to be emptied. With the average person who has done something seriously wrong, the subconscious would either bring up that garbage during life on earth, or it would be dealt with in the next dimension. In the case of individuals with Alzheimer's, however, they have badly abused their consciousness and did not wipe out their karma while on earth and were unable to resolve it in Spirit. Therefore, they chose to reincarnate and to suffer from Alzheimer's so their soul could progress. For these particular individuals, it is immensely more difficult for them to work it all out in Spirit. In fact, they probably would just freak out having to face their past.

Actually, coming back and developing Alzheimer's is a kinder way for them, in a sense, to resolve the abuses of their past. That way they would erase karma from about four or five incarnations during one lifetime—a huge accomplishment!

In an advanced stage when they are no longer able to communicate verbally, this indicates the conscious mind is no longer functioning. The memory bank of the subconscious has been locked away from conscious retrieval. The conscious mind does not store information, so when it cannot contact or draw from the subconscious, it is unable to function. The conscious mind has no way to work after it reaches such a point.

The progression and degree of disability a person goes through is directly related to the extent of his or her transgressions that must be forgiven. The more advanced the condition, the greater the amount of karma that is erased. So in very progressed cases, most, if not all of it, is finished when they cross over. Some people never reach the very advanced stage because they are called home due to problems of a medical nature. They may have a heart condition, liver or kidney problems, or any one of a number of diseases to bring about physical death.

It is understandable that when individuals make their transition, their memory of those years when the Alzheimer's was so advanced is a blank. In such cases, the karma is erased so there does not have to be a record. Nothing was recorded in the heart seed atom or soul memory to be transferred to the akashic records. Therefore, when we work with them on this side, we are working with souls whose soul memory is blank for that period of time. And it takes many evolved spirits to help them.

The person who goes over has no idea why he or she went through this ordeal because there is no real record of what was going on in this life in the last phases of Alzheimer's. When they come over here, they are very, very confused because they are still living in the immediate past. It is not the immediate past that we are dealing with to help them. In order for them to progress, they have to understand why it happened in the first place. This may go back to many lifetimes ago. Spirits whom they knew at that time would be brought in to help them make some connections. In the course of treatment, they have to relive what occurred in the past life to find the reason for their condition. By having spirits they knew in particular incarnations come and speak to their soul and share experiences they had together, it jogs the reason for what occurred. Treatment also includes eventually reviewing the akashic records with their trusted teacher.

With most of these conditions that involve mental dysfunction, very evolved spirit helpers work with the spirit's conscience. When the conscience is triggered, remorse and understanding surface. We try to get across to them that they have paid the price for their transgressions. We want them to be remorseful, but do not want them to feel they will have to go through all of this again. They now have been purified.

If the Alzheimer's patient lives a very long life, it usually indicates it is becoming more a karmic thing for the caregiver. Sometimes the caregiver, who may be a spouse or close relative is unwilling or unable to take care of the patient, in which case the karma of the caregiver does not get worked out. If a person is put in an institution and the loved ones continue to visit and to show interest, then that is a different situation. But to abandon the patient, the karma waits for another lifetime to be balanced out. It is frequently very difficult for the caregivers to reconcile themselves to their part in this relationship. When they come over, we have to work with them also to give them the understanding of what went wrong. Many times they have done a wonderful, wonderful job with the patient and they have freed themselves from the karmic tie with the patient.

It takes a great deal of patience and loving understanding to work with these people when they come over. Their willingness to progress is the determining factor of how long it takes in terms of earth time to recover. The whole thing is very similar to a bear who goes into hibernation. They are functioning at a very low level, a bare existence when they make their transition. When they come out of their hibernation and go back to where they were functioning before going into the "den," the den symbolically being the period of suffering from Alzheimer's, they can pick up their life on this side. Then they can go about very, very nicely, having worked off a great deal of karma.

If they have medical problems which take them before Alzheimer's has progressed too far, spirit guides will help them to come back rather quickly and try to communicate with their loved ones on earth. For example, a man might come back to see his wife and knowing her love was there it would help him to go on to progression in Spirit. He may not be able to actually communicate with her but the guides would bring him to visit her and take him back again. In more advanced stages, this is not possible, for they need extensive help from many spirit helpers to overcome the condition.

The important thing for people to understand is that their loved ones, in time, will be perfect and whole again. As humanity becomes more accepting of the afterlife and the fact that they must accept personal responsibility for their thoughts and actions, then this understanding will be well received.

A. M., Recovering Alzheimer's Patient

I am here to talk as a recovering Alzheimer's patient. I was an artist and an entrepreneur when I was on earth. I was a very active, energetic, creative person until I was in my late 50's, close to 60 when I realized that I could not remember things as well as I did previously. I had a very good memory, very retentive memory up until that time. And I started forgetting things and getting confused. My art work was showing the results of that. It was very frustrating, very, very frustrating. And people would come to me and say, "Oh, you know, I was downtown the other day and I ran into so and so, and they asked about you." Well, I couldn't remember that person. I could not place that person. I started failing for very recent things. And it got so, as time went on, that I wasn't really able to drive. I could not remember the route that I was to take.

Fortunately, I had a sister who helped me a great deal because my husband was still working. He would help, of course, at night and weekends. They were getting worried that I might forget something and go out and get lost, or that I might turn the stove on or something. It did get to the point where I really needed supervision. I resented this, that I could not do for myself because I had been so self-sufficient. Well, it reached a point as the condition progressed that I had no recognition of my family and they had to feed me and so forth. They told me about this when I recovered on the other side. It just reached to the point where there was nothing recorded in my soul memory because I was so out of it.

And when I got to this side of life, I still was very much out of it. There was just the tiniest, tiniest bit or recognition that there were people around me, very, very tiny. Some patients who come over here whose condition had not progressed as far as mine have a better time of it and have more awareness. I lived about 12 years on earth with Alzheimer's, and it was a great drain and strain on my sister and my husband who had retired during that time. I know they took good care of me. I know they did because they were both very loving people.

Well, over here, they regressed me to an earlier incarnation when I had really done some pretty awful things. They were pretty awful. I had a position of authority and I really took advantage of people. I overworked them, I underpaid them. I made life absolutely miserable for them. I was, in fact, a man then, and these were serfs who were working on my estate. They were almost like indentured slaves in a sense. And I really mistreated them. So when I came back into this life I decided I wanted to be productive, and yet I wanted to work off karma. I was productive until the onset of Alzheimer's and then I became totally dependent on my caregivers. In a sense it paralleled my earlier life when the serfs were dependent on me. But I had worked hard enough in my earlier years in the current life, and I supposed somewhere else in another incarnation, to have merited good caregivers. But they were also working out karma that they had with me. And so, it got rid of a lot of karma for the three of us, which was what was intended to be.

In the treatment process, those who were to help me, had gotten permission from higher authority to go into my akashic records and find out where the bulk of my trouble had occurred. So they regressed me to that lifetime and they brought in people that I had known during that particular life. And through that process of recognizing those that I had known before, and understanding what was going on, I was able to then come back into the present life and go to an earlier age when I was functioning well. I needed to be regressed to that earlier life in order to reawaken the soul and my mind because you do take your subconscious mind over with you until you work things out. So it was a reawakening by going back to a previous life and then transferring that, in a sense, to the current life.

I am living and working over here as an artist because I really did like to do a kind of flamboyant type painting—splash a lot of color. It is kind of a cross between modern art and realism, somewhere in between. It might be considered vague realism coming through, but sort of veiled. I try to put a story in each of my paintings, and I try very much to help others who have come over who don't seem to be opening up, but yet kind of wishing they had been an artist. We help them to express themselves on our type of canvas. It is not quite like yours. We have to express ourselves more with our thoughts. On earth you are working with thoughts, of course, but a lot with your hands. Over here, thoughts really are things. It helps them to open up when they can express in this manner.

I hope that I have helped you. I wished that all of my family who are still on earth would realize how well I am. It is so difficult for people to know that we function beautifully over here. This is the real world. I am so very, very pleased that you asked for some one to come and tell about their recovery.

Comments by the Master Teacher
There are a few details about the treatment of Alzheimer's which are very important for everyone to understand. There is no record in soul memory of the period when the disease was so progressed that the person had no conscious awareness. Their conscious mind had reached a point where it was no longer functioning and so nothing was really being recorded or stored in the subconscious mind. Even the treatment can be a little confusing to an Alzheimer's patient because we do regress them. That is true. And we have them functioning for awhile in the etheric body of that previous life. Then we have to enable them to make the transition to this incarnation when they had Alzheimer's and they are made aware of what really went on during this life and why it took place. They are able to review their life on earth and then go through the akashic records. They are regressed to an earlier age prior to the onset of Alzheimer's; so they appear younger and fully functioning. It is a very difficult and delicate kind of treatment that requires skill and dedication on the part of the doctors and workers on this side. •

Chapter 31.

PARANOIA AND SCHIZOPHRENIA

Enlightening Voices from the Other Side

Dr. Clayton on Schizophrenia

I did work in a mental hospital with those who were Schizophrenic and I can tell you a little bit about that. When they are on earth, they have recollections of a previous life, and these come and go. Unlike Alzheimer's Disease, Schizophrenia can affect young people. Sometimes they do respond to medication and treatment but that depends on how much karma has to be satisfied.

In very severe cases, the families are simply unable to care for them during periods of great delusional distress. They are put in institutions which is sad because they observe others similar to themselves which makes them wonder if they are that crazy. And they do use the term "crazy."

There is a chemical imbalance and malfunction of the chakras, the sixth and seventh especially. Sometimes they will reach a period where they have worked off the karma and live a pretty normal life for many years, or for the rest of their life.

When they come to this side, we have to regress them to that life that they were tapping into while on earth. We then help them to understand what went wrong so they can face it and put it to rest. It is painful for them to relive it, but we are very patient and supportive. We assure them that they have worked out their karma. It is important that they accept this and there is no further need to be tormented by being split, so to speak.

There is no reason for anyone in the Spirit World to have any kind of mental or physical handicap or illness, if they will permit helpers to work with them. If they refuse, then naturally they remain in a lower realm of consciousness. Most individuals opt for help.

The mind is delicate. Frequently, Schizophrenics are born into families that tend to be withholding of feelings at times. There can be a mixed message that is sent out by the parents. People tend to shun them because they are uncomfortable around them. In some families they are considered possessed by evil spirits. It has been the cause of breakups in family, parents accusing each other of having bad genes. Unfortunately, they do not have the understanding that it takes parents with certain genes to provide the type body necessary to develop Schizophrenia. In fact, the parents are actually helping to work out God's plan to free individuals from their wrongdoing. Instead, there is much guilt and rejection thrown about, or perhaps overprotection stemming from guilt. The thing to get across to your readers is that we work diligently to help any spirit with a psychotic background to become free individuals again, and to get out of their self-made prison or torture chamber.

Going back to Schizophrenia, that is like double personality. Are they exhibiting the personality from a past life? Yes, they are. Does it frightened them that they are doing this? Are they so split they are not aware? They are not really aware of it. Sometimes they do become aware of it, yes. You have heard people say, well, they are two different people. Then they are aware.

A Schizophrenic can be a pretty decent person, and then all of a sudden, they will do something that is terribly wrong, like stealing, or even commit murder. But that is another person. Something evil has taken over them for a period of time. It is the evil that they have done in the past. It is not a spirit possession.

When we think of them as being delusional, it is because they are living a part of that past life. They respond to medication in keeping with the extent of the karma.

Comments on Paranoia by the Master Teacher

Paranoia stems from things going on in the current lifetime, although it is related to something brought over from another life. Maybe in a past life a person had a very difficult life—many things that happened in that incarnation which were not good, not necessarily that they did, but things that they had to go through in that life. Perhaps someone did something to them that was not quite fair, so they brought that back to earth with them. So they become paranoid over every little thing that goes on to hurt them. They are thinking this is going to happen because of that, or that is going to happen because of this. In other words, whatever it is, it is going to happen again.

Do they necessarily connect that with the people they feel mistreated them? Oh yes, that part is karmic. This is also connected to the heart chakra because there is no love there. Also, the throat chakra because the throat chakra is what is used to create things. Instead of being positive, it is a negative influence. And they seem to draw more and more negative influences to them because like attracts like.

If the spirit guides and teachers cannot get through to them while they are still on the earth plane, they have to work very diligently on this side to get them to understand and eliminate all negativity. Many of them will bother people who are still on earth. The paranoid individual and some schizophrenics will come back and try to influence with their negativity.

A paranoid individual who goes to Spirit is always looking for the negative. We break through that by showing them the love and the affection and the beauty and all of the good in the Spirit World. Some religions teach hell fire and damnation which is totally wrong. It does not exist, however, they are convinced that hell fire and damnation does exist and they will come looking for it. And they don't find it; so we have to convince them that does not happen. Then they think we are hiding it and not showing it to them and they refuse to accept otherwise. The hell fire is within oneself. If a person honestly believes that it is what he or she deserves, they are going to feel it on this side, as well as on earth.

We have to get them over resentment because usually paranoid people are very resentful. Their whole life, as far as they are concerned, has been terrible. It is pretty miserable to always be looking over your shoulder for fear someone or something is going to do you wrong. They are always expecting the worst. That is one of the reasons why people have panic or anxiety attacks. They think things are bad and going to get worse. They can be pretty miserable, but they can do a lot in their life on earth to change their thoughts. Unlike Alzheimer's Disease which cannot be changed, paranoia and anxiety attacks can be overcome. It is not totally karmic. You may be around those with whom you have karmic ties, but you have to learn to get over them. It is not nearly as serious as Alzheimer's and schizophrenia.

Dr. Maddox on Paranoia

I know that you have had others give you some information on paranoia, but I would like to add a word or two. Paranoia is fear based, and it is fear of a type that is very difficult to dispel. We can tell someone who thinks that someone is doing something evil to them that it is not so, but that falls on deaf ears because the intensity of the fear and the distrust is of such magnitude that it truly falls on deaf ears. They cannot be convinced easily at all.

While paranoia may lessen to some degree by change in environment, when they come to this side, it is difficult to treat because they get the idea that thoughts are things, which is true. But then they take that to reinforce their earthly ideas of people doing them harm because they know that if someone on the spirit side thinks evil of them, that is a more powerful direction of energy toward them, which is also true—the thoughts that spirit may be thinking are so strong. They are actually stronger than when they are on earth.

I hope I have made that clear that by their own demonstration, those who are paranoid have sent out thoughts which have returned to them as a thing. They can think something, such as thinking they are somewhere and they are there. Or, they can think of something they want to eat, and the essence is there. Therefore, with that kind of knowledge, it strengthens the paranoid tendencies because they feel people can do them harm by their ability to send thoughts which would become things literally hurled at them.

Now I want to comment a bit on how we try to break through that. We have to help them through an avenue of love. Because of their fear, they feel that people hate them or do evil things to them. The opposite of hate is love, so we try to convince that they are much loved. And we try to get them into work which will help them to help others, to give love. We work better in groups, but we also work individually. In groups, sometimes they will come out with pretty wildly exaggerated tales of persecutory thoughts directed toward them. Usually someone in the group challenges their statement. It is the peers who are the most helpful. We simply act as facilitators, keeping the group moving. But the real help comes not from us as group leaders as it does from their own peers who recognize the lunacy of some of their delusional ideas. We emphasize that we want to help them rid their thoughts of someone or something doing them in. We want them to be happy, and when they feel happy, they are at peace. For when they are at peace, they no longer will have these delusions.

Some of them are very difficult to help, especially, when it is combined with schizophrenia. We try to get them to the point where they can view the akashic records. In viewing a past life it is a very touchy thing. We have to get them to really trust us, to have an enormous amount of trust in us, their doctor or someone who has chosen to work with them. If we do not reach that point of great trust and we talk about these records that are hidden away, so to speak, it could make them extremely paranoid about the "secrets that people have gathered on them." So it takes time to explain how the seed atoms within gather this information in every one and that it is very, very private information. That it is only known to God, to them, and a few trusted souls who want to help them to understand and find peace. They are tough customers, believe me. But the effort that we make it well worth it. Our goal in Spirit is for everybody to find peace and be closer to God.

When relatives and friends come over to this side, and the paranoid individual accuses them of things, we try to involve the relatives in helping that person to see things differently. By the time we get to the akashic records, we are in pretty good shape because they can see the beginning of their problem. Some have gotten that far only to say, "I think you just made it up." It is tough but we keep at it.

I have worked with these people in Spirit for some 50 of your earth years. I was a psychiatrist and I continued to work on this side because I wondered why I had not made a better break through while on earth. It was over here that I realized that it was, in some cases, a karmic thing, a carry over from a past life of some situations they had to work out in this life, and also where it could have developed while in the immediate past life on earth. It has been a privilege to come and talk to you in this way.

Dr. Clayton on Paranoid Schizophrenia

When Paranoia and Schizophrenia are combined, you have a Paranoid Schizophrenic. In other words, someone who was paranoid in a past life and who comes back in another incarnation as a schizophrenic not only goes back to that past life but brings all of the garbage connected with that event to the present life. If they were paranoid and actually killed someone in a past life because they were paranoid, they did it because they thought somebody was really after them. It was not in self-defense, it was a delusional thing. Then, if they incarnate as a schizophrenic, they bring that paranoia with them. So it is a combined thing and when you have that combination, it is much more difficult to treat those people than just being schizy. The more paranoid they are, the more paranoid they become. They really are dangerous at times when they go into these psychotic episodes.

It is a matter of having a basic psychoses to which is added the paranoia which becomes worse. Treating their chemical imbalance helps schizophrenics in many cases, but does not help much with those who are paranoid because that takes therapy and helping a person feel a sense of security. When they are so suspicious, they believe that God is helping others but has turned against them. They are really tough ones to deal with when they get to this side. We have a compound mental illness to help them sort through.

Why do they choose to come back as a schizophrenic? It is, of course, to work off karma. And in that preincarnation plan, they feel that they will be strong enough to deal with the situation while on earth and they can work out their karma on earth. That is why they choose that method. You are never without choice, no matter what dimension you are in.

I sometimes personally think some people returning to earth are ill-advised, but that is their right. I think some of them are not strong enough when they are permitted to go back. We try to make the plan of incarnation include all of the opportunities favorable for soul growth, but that soul has to be strong enough to go through those things in a positive way, not just add more karma. I am not a negative person, but I am a realist. I do question at times that their choice has taken precedence over sound judgment. Everyone needs an opportunity to go back to earth if he or she wishes, but they should be discouraged from going back before they are ready. It will be a requirement, condition, or criteria during the coming "thousand years of peace" not to allow a spirit to reincarnate who is not "ready" to do so. There will have to be some preparation and plan. At present, many spirits do jump right back into a physical body and that is not the fault of spirit teachers, that is the insistence of the person.

Many young souls will come for the experience. Parents may not want a child, only want sex and pregnancy occurs. That will attract young souls who will get all kinds of experiences in this life. The soul may choose the wrong parents. A young soul is not experienced and they come just to be coming to the earth—any port in the storm. A more elevated soul will be choosey. They make their plan, but many souls have no plan. Their only plan is to get on earth. They may be born at the wrong time to take advantage of the unseen influences of the universe. All the factors that would be favorable to someone who planned might be negative for those who do not plan. As the New Age comes in stronger and stronger, there will be more and more old souls and fewer young souls. The gates will not be open. The old souls know what they want, the young souls do not.

Esther Houser on attitudinal healing through art.

I was an artist when on earth. I taught art and was more a teacher than a practicing artist, because I was interested in helping people to express themselves through art. I worked primarily in a mental hospital. In an institutional setting, you are somewhat limited in what you can do. But we worked with Schizophrenics and people who were very paranoid to get them to express their feelings. And then I would take their drawings or paintings and would sit down with their psychiatrist, and we would analyze as much as possible where they were in consciousness.

I was not aware that I was receiving so much spiritual help in doing this, but I did receive very strong impressions. I just did not realize these impressions were coming from Spirit. The art work of these patients would frequently open up some avenues that the psychiatrist could pursue. And so it was very nice work, and very rewarding. There were times when it was sad because you could see the darkness that was within. There were never enough psychiatric hours to give these people the intense work they needed. But I think that the expression through art was a helpful release.

When I got to this side of life, I wanted to continue that work to see what results we would have over here. In working with paranoid people, especially, it is very difficult because you can be accused of doing all kinds of things. And it is hard to break through that. We have to work at it and use different techniques on different people. We need to reassure them of our continued interest in them. Our love for them is what motivates us to want to help them. And when they draw for us over here is not very different initially than what they were doing on earth. They have to learn to use different materials, of course. Their thinking comes through more strongly than on earth, and we can tell more easily whether they are growing or not by the light of their body. Is that light shining forth more strongly?

We do work hard to get them to change their attitude, and it takes a lot of doing. It is hard for them. I think it is more difficult actually for someone who is paranoid to go through a review or reflection of their earth life because they want to project the blame for everything outside of themselves. Most people do that until they are elevated. That goes without saying. But it is a very exaggerated example of projecting outside. We do eventually, if they are willing, and they must be willing, we do break through. And the ones who do become beautiful, beautiful souls. And frequently they become helpers to help others who are mentally disturbed.

That is what I do. I think I got into being an art teacher because in my previous life I had artistic ability, but I really had no one to encourage me. I was a very shy, withdrawn child. I would draw and adults would make fun of what I drew because it wasn't perfect. I felt very rejected. And so when I came back in this last life, I wanted to help bring out the feelings of those who were in a vulnerable state, who needed some support and encouragement. So that is how I worked that out for myself. Of course, I had many other things to work out, too. Don't think that is the only thing by any means, but I wanted to do some service and it did help me a great deal to be free of any wrongdoing from the past. When I got over here, I did work on myself a great deal, and eventually was able to go through the akashic records.

I have been privileged to get to Master Joseph's school on occasion and I have met your husband. He is a wonderful, wonderful, wonderful man, a beautiful man. And it was he who thought it would be interesting for me to come and talk to you. And so, Dr. Cranston came to me and asked if I would like to participate in this little project. I understand that the project is growing and growing and growing steadily, but I am glad I was invited to come. I understand there are many, many more who are lined up to come in and speak to you and tell you about their work. I am glad I had this opportunity. And it was really fun to be able to come and talk through someone because this was my first experience. And actually, it is very easy.

Comments by the Master Teacher
Art does provide a wonderful avenue and opening to express the soul. And using different colors, of course, brings about a healing vibration, and when there is support for their efforts, naturally they are going to work harder to do more drawings and paintings and then they will put themselves more into what they do. •

32.

THE MENTALLY CHALLENGED

Enlightening Voices from the Other Side

Charles Bostwick on working with Down's Syndrome patients

It is important to understand that those who are mentally challenged or retarded have *chosen* this condition prior to incarnation for the sole purpose of working off karma. As part of that prior plan, they chose parents who could actually provide the type of physical body needed. Taking on this condition provides a way to balance one's debts more quickly. In fact, one could possibly work off more karma as mentally challenged person than one could in two or three "average" lifetimes.

When the mentally challenged make their transition to the Spirit World they need a great deal of help. Not all accept that help initially, but eventually they will come forth and want to progress. Many blame their parents for the way they are. It is very sensitive work to help them realize what actually did go wrong. We all have done things that we should not have done. We all have things we could have done and did not do.

Parents who bring children into the world who are less than perfect are simply the vehicles by which those souls are able to come to earth to work out their karma. They should have absolutely no guilt about this. If they understood better that they were the vehicles, they would embrace these little ones and give them every opportunity and all the love and needed protection that is required to help them to live a healthy life while satisfying their karmic debt. Sometimes there are parents who simply are not able to cope and send their mentally challenged children off to institutions. There are extenuating circumstances and, again, they should not suffer guilt for what they must do.

This group of people frequently do not have a long life because it is a very difficult life for many of them. Then, too, they only need to stay on earth long enough to make restitution for past errors. When they make their transition to the Spirit World, helpers there try techniques to get them to utilize more of their "brain power," which has, in a sense, been shut off, to a certain extent, for they are very child-like and their reasoning ability is limited. They have been living in a cocoon, so to speak, and now that they are on the other side, they can come out like a butterfly, fluttering their wings and using their real potential.

"Brain power" is used very loosely here because when we cross over after awhile we no longer have a conscious or subconscious mind. The spirit workers, therefore, are drawing on the soul memory (superconscious mind or soul) to go back to an earlier lifetime when they were functioning very well. When they review a prior incarnation in which they have done some pretty awful things, then the spirit teachers or helpers must move them to the realization that they have paid their dues, so to speak—they have worked off whatever was not good by living a mentally challenged existence. They are now free to embark on a fuller and richer life. The Spirit workers have to go step by step by step in getting them to do this. These Spirit workers can be anyone sincerely interested in rendering this kind of service.

Those of us who work with the mentally challenged do so under the supervision of highly advanced Spirits. With this work it is indeed rewarding to know that you can actually be an instrument to help someone. We are only instruments. We are not the ones that effect the change—it is the inspiration that flows through us to trigger the right response. Part of my enjoyment in the work is because I am able to look beyond the exterior into beautiful souls. What I really see is a soul who has chosen a difficult life in order for that soul to grow. When you think of it that way, you are very cognizant, very aware, of how much that soul, that spirit, has been willing to go through in order to progress. They are deserving of every ounce of effort and help that we can give them. We really keep that in mind. We do not focus on the exterior. We focus on the interior.

I have been working with a young man who made his transition when he was about thirty-two years of age. Spirit has given me permission to tell that this man was a brilliant scientist in one of his past lives. He was a scientist working on some chemical reactions in the cells of the body. He was responsible for doing some things that were very harmful to others. In fact, his experiments caused a great deal of torture to animals and to some humans, as well. He was far more anxious to see that his ideas had merit than he was in what harm his efforts would bring to others. And so he racked up a very high karmic debt. He chose to work it off by coming back mentally challenged, an advanced moron. When we have shown him what he did, he had enormous remorse. And it has been through his remorse—his conscience, which is part of one's soul, that he has had an awakening to his intellectual abilities. This is a very, very traumatic thing for a person to face when they have done something of such large measure which has hurt others. Now sometimes a person will have an accumulation of different things from several incarnations and they will elect to return as mentally challenged to work them all off at one time instead of doing it piecemeal in a number of incarnations.

In the beginning, we are not told what a spirit's karma is based upon. The higher teachers want us to work for awhile before they tell us that because they do not want us to be prejudiced in any way. They want us to know that this is just a little soul who is eager to be made whole again. In time we will know, and the spirit will know about the past.

In working with them, it is interesting to see how the light dawns bit by bit by bit. Before we actually tell them what the akashic records reveal, we will use the approach of something like the following: *What do you think about people who do things to hurt others?* And we start with the simplest of examples and we work up to the awful things. For instance, by gently treating them almost as we would a child, in a sense, we start with little examples like pulling the wing off a bug, etc. As we work toward the really dreadful or most damaging thing they have done, we keep telling them that not everyone understands that a particular thing is not right to do; nevertheless, God does forgive those who do hurtful things. This wonderful Father who exists inside them, and in everyone else, forgives them and loves them and gives them another chance to do what is right. And if *they* have done something wrong, they will be forgiven also. We try to explain to them that people go from one life to another and that they look different in each life, and they act differently in each life. We give them a great deal of loving support through each of these steps. And then it finally dawns on them to ask, *Did I do anything that I should not have done in a past life?* At that point we then can share with them what they did, and we share this in bits so that the impact will not be too traumatic. It is going to be to a certain extent regardless, but we buffer the impact as much possible. These are beautiful souls we are trying to reach.

It might be necessary to go back a number of incarnations, and it is a very delicate thing. They are working with guides who are helping the individual go to the akashic records and pull out the necessary information to build upon. When the Spirit workers take on the work of helping people who are mentally challenged, they have to be advanced enough to be privileged to know what that person has been through in order to help them. Not just anyone can go to the akashic records and find out whatever they want about another person. The records are very, very well protected. This is private information. And so it requires that it be treated very confidentially. The helpers are not just curious, rather they are committed to really helping the person to look at the past and try to connect it with the present, or their last incarnation. It takes time. It is not done overnight because the person is not always strong enough to be able to look at their past, and to face what has happened. So we deal with their last incarnation on earth and encourage the individual about having done a good job. As most of them have such a sweet disposition, they have accomplished a great deal. And it takes on average about two years of equivalent earth time, depending on the severity of the retardation, to work through it all and function normally.

As we work on the soul of the mentally challenged, their etheric body takes on changes. And we can actually see the progress we are making. They don't just suddenly get a new body at the end of treatment. The body changes as we move along. The spirit looks like that spirit did on earth because the etheric body is just exactly like the physical body one had on earth. The facial features are the same, but the form becomes brighter. It starts out as dark, not elevated, but as the treatment progresses, it becomes lighter and lighter and more animated. It has a light of its own that is much stronger and brighter than the physical body had.

And another thing, when they do finally take a look at the akashic records, they can choose to go back to that life in which they committed wrong acts and pick it up while in Spirit, or they can stay in the present one. Going back and picking up that previous life can *only* be done while still in Spirit. That is the choice they can make. In any case, they will have the same recovery of their abilities which then can be used for benevolent purposes. Some make the choice to come back to earth more quickly than others, but it is recommended that they stay on this side for about two hundred earth years so they can work through a very detailed and fine plan that will include relatives and friends and others from past lives with whom they have karmic connections.

It has been a very rewarding experience for me to work with the scientist—a very, very sweet and gentle man. The sweetness was there, but as he tells me now, the frustration of never being able to express himself as he could observe others doing was also there. Perhaps some day he will come through and talk to you and tell you more about this.

This experience has not only been a two-fold opportunity in that it helps individuals to come out of their cocoon, but enables the helper to gain in patience, kindness, and other soul attributes.

Comments by the Master Teacher

As mentioned above, at the end of therapy, the spirit makes a choice. The soul can elect to stay with the present etheric body, or return to a former life when that soul was more productive, that is, when the major problem occurred so the soul can really work from that point on. It is almost like another challenge in a sense, going back to that former life with a different attitude—same experience, but different attitude and much lighter body. The decision of if or when to take on a former etheric body depends a great deal on whether the spirit has love ones still on earth that he or she is close to and loves. If they have ties to earth, they probably will delay any change, deciding to keep the same type of etheric body so their people would recognize them.

Dr. Alan (first name) in the above case, elected to go back to the knowledge that he had as a chemist so that he could work with someone on earth, but the attitude and the direction of what he is now doing is totally different. By his thinking, Dr. Alan has stepped back into his former life, taking on a different shape to his etheric body and assuming the appearance of the scientist he previously was. His body is now lighter and he is able to move and get around faster. He very graciously came to the author when she was in trance and the following is a transcription of what he said.

Dr. Alan describes his experience with Down's Syndrome

This is quite an experience for me. Charles and others very patiently and kindly worked very, very hard to help me through my last life on earth when my body was functioning as a moron. As I think now in my previous incarnation as a scientist I was a moron then, possibly more so, for having done the things that I did in that life.

I chose to reincarnate to a family with five children. They were very, very loving to me and I wanted so much to do the things that my siblings were capable of. One liked to construct things and he would let me help him sometimes. I thought he was the greatest because he could figure out how to put all the parts together. It was frustrating to me. When I goofed up something, he got a little annoyed, but then he would give me a hug.

My mother was very good to me. She was a angel, always making sure that I was included as much as possible. She spent time trying to help me learn. I knew I was different because I went off to school in a special bus without my siblings.

I passed to Spirit when I was about 32. I had always had a heart problem, and so I had to be watched. I learned on this side that it was understandable that I had a heart problem because it represented a love problem in my previous life. That was karmic. It worked out fine so that when I finished my karma from my experiments, I had an opportunity to suffer a heart attack and go quickly. I also developed a few other physical problems, as well.

I loved my family, but I did not understand, nor did my family understand why God made me different. They always told me that I was very special and that God had special children.

When I came to Spirit, I was approached by teachers who asked me if I would like to be more like my brothers and sisters on earth. I said yes, if I could learn to do the things that they did. They told me I would be given a great deal of help, and that no one would expect me to do anything that I was not ready to do. Charles came into the picture pretty early, I believe. And we started working in a very simple way. There were times when I would say, *I don't want to do that now. I want to do something else.* So they would be patient with me and they would take me where I wanted to go, such as to see the animals, or some entertainment. In retrospect, I realize they were very subtle in helping me to progress. If we went to a concert, they would tell me that the musicians had to practice and practice and practice. If they were to succeed, they could not decide they just no longer wanted to practice. And with the animals, they would talk about how the animals were trained. Gradually, Igot the message that it was better for me to work at regaining my mental functions at our therapy sessions, and then take a little rest, instead of taking a rest before we even started.

It was all very much as Charles described to you, and finally I did get to the point where I had unleashed that bottled up potential. I was given the choice of continuing on in that body, or going back to the earlier life when I was the scientist. I chose the later and now I am working on this side, trying to come up with something that will be of benefit to earth. I work with a young man on earth who is very sensitive to my impressions, and I am trying to inspire him. Hopefully, I will be able to communicate something of value. Instead of working on the human body, I have changed my interest to working on materials that will benefit people as we move more into the New Age.

It has been a very interesting life. Believe me, I know that we build up karma from wrongdoings, and we certainly pay for it. My debt is now satisfied. Eventually, I will return to earth, and hopefully, will not make the same mistakes again. Charles has been a wonderful friend to me. It took a little adjustment to go back to a former life while still in Spirit, I was able to do it. Now I am Dr. Alan again, and no longer Little Billy.

Comments by the Master Teacher
It is the same soul going back to what happened in the past. His soul wants to go back to the scientific part. There will be another incarnation here and he will come back and do great things.

Charles Bostwick working with Sally Ann
After Dr. Alan moved on, I began working with another mentally challenged individual name Sally Ann who passed to Spirit

when she was eighteen years old. She is absolutely precious, very bubbly and affectionate. She was raised by her aunt and uncle who doted on her. While running an errand, she was hit by an automobile and fatally injured. The fact that her life on earth was so short indicates she had less karma to work out.

(Author's note: Charles wanted her to come through me while I was in trance.)

I think she understands that you are like a telephone and that she can come and talk through you but it is not going to reach her uncle and auntie who took care of her. This is a big change because she knew on earth that a telephone would connect with the person you want to talk to, not just a call to the "telephone" itself. So I told her she could come and talk to you, my wife, and I think she is going to do it. She is right here beside me giggling a little bit. I told her she could not talk long, but she could come in and say hello. And so I am going to let her try right now.

"This is Sally Ann and I am glad that I could come and talk to you. I like Charles very much. He is a very nice man, trying to help me to learn more and do all the things that everybody else can do. I am eighteen years old and I am learning and I am having fun. I dress very pretty. I have lots and lots of pretty dresses. If I want to wear a pink dress, then I have a pink dress. When I want to wear a red dress, I have a red dress. So Charles tells me that since I can think these things and make them happen, I can also think another way and make myself perfect like everybody else. I was so special and I don't want to be special anymore. I want to be specially well and everything. And so I am going to tell you goodbye. I will talk to you again sometime. Bye bye."

Do you see how she is beginning to make a little connection that thoughts are things and that by different thinking, she can develop her thinking powers on a stronger and higher level and really use her potential. She is truly a joy to work with. She is a fun loving, enthusiastic little girl, affectionate and eager to learn. Sally Ann does indeed like to dress in frilly clothes. The materials are noticeably of a somewhat finer vibration as she progresses.

Sally Ann is coming along beautifully, and I am really going to miss working with her when the time comes for her to be more on her own. I told her that the day would come when she would be so much like everybody else and so independent that she would not need me, but she said, *I love you and I want to be with you.* I said that is just fine. You can be with me even after your family comes over, but you are going to find that you will want to do more and more things on your own. She said, "Well, we will see." That is her favorite expression, *we'll see.*

Sally Ann loves colors. We praise her and she laughs and she hugs us. She is really one of the most loving little creatures you could possibly imagine. She is the epitome of sweetness.

I have not been told what Sally Ann's karma is based on. They want us to work for awhile before they tell us that because they do not want us to be prejudiced in any way. They want us to know that this is just a little soul who is eager to be made whole again. In time we will know, and she will know about the past.

I am the head healer for Sally Ann and others help. We have a facility here where the mentally challenged live together if they have no close relatives, so that is how we take care of them on this side. In some respects, it is almost better because the ones who come to our facility are the ones who really want to work on themselves. They are more motivated. Sometimes when they go to relatives, the relatives will protect and shield them instead of encouraging treatment. They can get the same kind of treatment living with a relative as if they were coming to the facility. The difference is that they support each other when they are in a group. And so I think they move along maybe a little faster. They help each other and they have a lot of fun together. And so I thought you would like to know about that.

I take Sally Ann to events and she wants to join in with the entertainers, and I have to tactfully tell her she cannot always do that. Sometimes the entertainers will bring her right in and she has a great time. I tell her each person has his or her own time, space, and they are there because they have practiced and they know how their performance should go. She is not backwards. She does it in such a cute way that she gets by with it. She is so loving and sogiving of herself, it is just incredible. I think if the world were populated with people like her, we might not make any technical advances, but we certainly would make some spiritual oncs.

We not only work on the karmic cause of a particular condition that a spirit has, we have to help them in other ways. That is why we take them around and show them different things that other people are doing. So they are not isolated. They are out in the world. In Sally Ann's case, I don't know whether she will elect to go back to a former life, or whether she will remain as she is although functioning normally, whatever that is. So when her aunt and uncle who took care of her come over, they will be able to recognize her, and then she can make a change if she desires. She is a little handful but so full of life, so loving and sweet. She is moving along beautifully.

I do take her back to earth to see her aunt and uncle, but they do not acknowledge that she is there. In a way, they do because one will say to the other, "You know, I was thinking about what we used to do with Sally Ann," or something to that effect. But it is as far as we have gotten. She is trying to comprehend why they don't just open their arms and hold them out for her.

We will keep working on it. It takes an enormous amount of patience, which I never thought that I had, but I am developing it, and repetition. Patience and repetition, a lot of tolerance, understanding and love, too.♦

Lucy, the new patient

I am now working with a young woman named Lucy who is about 25. She is more mature in some respects than Dr. Alan and Sally Ann, and from a more serious and less loving background, so we really have to reach out to her more. Lucy was more of a "drag" to her people. She was shunted from mother to her auntie and grandmother. She learned some skills with her hands— needlework which is really old-fashioned tatting. Her grandmother did some of that work and was patient enough with Lucy to teach her. Lucy has a good sense of color so she was able to actually design some of the things that she did. I went to look at them and I could see that she had put a lot of imagination into her work. It was really very nice. Doing this needlework was of great benefit to her. She didn't always get the stitches just right, but her colors were nicely chosen. She is doing some of that work now, and we have encouraged her to do so because as she develops she will be able to see how the materials she is working on will become finer and more brilliant. Lucy had been an artist in her previouus life. •

33.

POSSESSION

Enlightening Voices from the Other Side

Dr. Ramsey on his work with Possession

These possessing spirits are very young, young souls. And some of them have only been on earth once or twice, and they have not a clue as to what they are doing. They want to come back before they are ready to come back. And so they figure if they can possess a body, they can do pretty much what they want with that body, Also young souls usually have no idea about disciplining themselves and they are not reaching for a higher state of consciousness.

I know that Jesus did heal a young man (The Demoniac of Gerasa: Their name is Legion) Matt 8:28:32 Mark 5: 1-16 Luke 8:26-39) and he was more developed. The man was so grateful he wanted to follow Jesus and Jesus gave him a job of witnessing to the people in and around Decapolis. I would say in that case he was a much more evolved person but just did not know how to protect himself. None of these people do and they do not understand. He allowed any spirits that wanted, to come into his body. It was not a matter of like attracting like as much as not knowing how to protect himself. I don't think he realized these spirits were as bad as what they really were. He was trying to help them by letting them come in.

We do as much as we can to get those possessing spirits out, but because there is free will it is a very difficult thing to do. Their conscience is not developed to the point where we can reach them that way. When the thousand years of peace is upon us, this will simply not be permitted. I think that we will have to bodily wrench these souls away and provide greater protection. It is very sad to see this happen, and so in time there will be a moratorium on free will, as far as things like that go.

I have worked with those spirits who come over here who were possessed while on earth, and they are in a state of confusion, especially if they have been possessed by several entities. They are very confused. And it is like we have to begin almost in kindergarten in getting them to really be acquainted with their real self. They do progress rapidly, and some of them have been pretty upset and have gone after the culprits. And they have really talked to them pretty strongly, because I have witnessed this, to make them understand that they have to stop doing that, and for them to come with the spirit who was possessed, and that he or she will get them help to know a better way of life. So I have found this to be very helpful to those who want to play those games. They do not always come for help, but the effort is made to reach out to them. And it is usually gratitude that the possessed spirit feels when he or she comes to know his or her real self. It is through that gratitude that they find forgiveness and they vow to help those who have wronged them. Sometimes that touches that spirit who possessed them, and we are then able to step in and pull them up and help them climb a higher ladder. We tell them that we will help them to understand why people go to earth. They go to learn and that the real purpose is to elevate the soul, not to make life miserable for someone else. Sometimes we succeed and sometimes we do not, but at least we have tried. Possession could be a karmic thing in some situations, but usually it is simply a lack of discipline, a lack of understanding that they must work on themselves while on earth so they will not attract undeveloped entities. I think the material you are gathering will be extremely helpful to many in this work. Mediums, especially, and those in mental health fields.

Comments by the Master Teacher
It is always hard for some of these spirits to get through the very difficult possessions. It docs not take place as frequently as it once did. It is related so often to people who play with the ouja board, and in some of these cultures where there is a great deal of vodoo and black magic going on. It does attract the lower spirits. People also open themselves wide open to these low entities by engaging in other activities of a lower order.

When they come to this side, of course, they are free of these entities. They are no longer in a physical body for them to take over. The damage that is done is really that these people have been deprived of their opportunity to grow on their own. Possessing spirits are never of a higher type, so it goes without saying that they do not help a person to evolve. They encourage them to do the things that are harmful, and it is sad indeed, because the guides try so hard to get these possessing spirits to leave the person alone. They are not always successful. Yes, they can wind up in a mental institution, and no one really knows how to help them. When

Jesus worked with a true case of possession, he was very strong in calling that spirit out. The Catholic priest probably knows more about exorcism than the psychiatrists.

There is free will here. And if a spirit's soul is not evolved to the point where they have a conscience, if that is not actively working, then they only laugh when it is pointed out to them what they are doing. They do not care. Truly they do not care. We have worked with some of these low possessing spirits, and in time they have become like little angels. But I can assure you, it does not happen over night. It takes an enormous amount of work. Perhaps some day, one of them will come and talk to you and tell you about it. It is not a pretty thing.

In the experience of Paracelsus, the Swiss physician:
It is very difficult to get the entity to leave, especially if the person is clinging to the entity. Let us say, somebody is possessed and letting the entity totally control them. Then it is very difficult to get them out because the person has to want them out. Sometimes they enjoy it in the beginning, but then when they are so totally controlled, they cannot do anything about it. About the only thing that we can do is use the power of prayer, actually, and the power of exorcism to get them out. Sometimes it works and sometimes it does not. The entity is playing a game and they have no conscience; so there is no incentive or reason for them to leave on their own. They are having a good time. About the only thing that a person can do is to just tell them they have to leave. Sometimes that takes a long time. Holy water does a great deal. If you constantly are saying, *In the Name of Jesus Christ*, and I believe in that thoroughly, *leave this individual.* Use holy water and also use salt from the ocean. That will do it sometimes. The possessed person has to be willing, has to realize they are possessed and want help.

Dr. Redmond shares his experience as a possessing spirit
This is a very cherished and most appreciated opportunity to come through and share. I was requested by you and then Master Joseph spoke to me also about explaining to you from both sides of the coin, so to speak, what it is like to be a possessing spirit and how I came out of it. This happened actually centuries ago. It was during the time of Jesus when I had possessed a young woman. She was very pretty. I was a male then. She was very pretty and I was very attracted to her. She was not on a very high level of

consciousness. She was what you would have called in that day a harlot, and so it was easy to take over. I admit that I gained a great deal of gratification through her sexual activities. I dictated to her and she was completely under my control. I do think that I led her to being a harlot or prostitute though she was a bit promiscuous and it was an easy thing to do.

I controlled her soul and it was the wrong, wrong thing. When possessing spirits take over, it is for their own gratification. It is very different from a high spirit trying to impress one in order to guide them. It was common at that time for spirits to take over.

I had been a eunuch in a harem that belonged to a very wealthy man. I, of course, being a eunuch, was safe to be around the women, but I was deprived of sexual pleasure, though I had watched it. After working as a eunuch in a harem, I had an incarnation in which I was a male prostitute in a temple. Only a few years passed before I came back again. This time I was supposed to live a good life in which I was to straighten myself out as far as the sexual problem was concerned; however, I didn't. I didn't. So after going back to spirit, I wanted to actually possess someone and seek pleasure that way. That is when I possessed this beautiful woman to get my kicks that way. I never seemed to be satisfied, and I drove her and drove her and drove her to do more tricks. Somehow, she heard about Jesus, and when he came to her little town, someone managed to get her to him. This is not recorded in the Bible. Jesus freed many people of possessing spirits as it was common, as I mentioned before. He freed her. He sent me on. I had been with her for probably ten or fifteen years. I had robbed that person of her opportunity. Fortunately for both of us, Jesus came and freed her.

When she came to Spirit, she looked me up, and she really blasted me. I did not possess anyone else, but I did not grow. It was not until this lady, named Elizabeth, came and told me how I had deprived her of her opportunity for spiritual growth. She had gained a great deal from the teachings that Jesus had brought. She had elevated herself considerably while on earth, and when she came to Spirit, she studied further. She became aware of what I had done to her and she really went after me. Somehow, it was so strong an impact that it touched my conscience enough for me to go on a spiritual path. She did forgive me. She did forgive me. And she helped me to grow. And, you know, we came back together as husband and wife in a later incarnation. We worked out the karma. Hers for her loose behavior, and mine for what I did to her. We had a very happy and good relationship, and we are great friends. And we have been back together several times since then.

I have been in Spirit now for probably two hundred years or more and I have grown a great deal. I feel that because I know that one should never, never take over another's body, I have worked hard to get possessing spirits to leave. And if they don't, when the possessed persons come to this side, I try to reach these possessing spirits and to work on them because it is all in ignorance that this is done. It is so selfish. Together with the person who has been possessed, and perhaps with others, we go to that lower entity, and we really just, I would not say blast them as I had been blasted, but we are very strong and very, very persistent in telling them how it is so that they do not do this to someone else. We have eliminated much of this. It is not near as common as it was when I did it centuries ago.

I hope that I have given you a little insight into what we do and how it had affected me. As I rose in consciousness, I felt terribly, terribly remorseful. And it was through that remorse that beautiful Elizabeth really decided she would help me, and that we would grow together. She actually was on a much higher plane, and she would come down and get me and bring me up to a higher realm where she was studying; so we could study together. In between the classes, I had a lot of individual help. And it was very wonderful to have this help. I needed the support and forgiveness in order to really make it. Elizabeth is a beautiful lady today, beautiful inside and out, and she is my dear, dear sweetheart. And so I leave you. I thank you for finding me. It is rather remarkable how we can pick out someone with all the millions and millions to sort through. May your book do very, very well.

Comments by the Master Teacher

I think that Dr. Redmond gave you a very interesting perspective. It also shows the power of remorse and forgiveness, because that is what is so prominently played out on this side of life if one is to grow. I don't think that forgiveness is stressed enough, but it must not be limited to asking forgiveness of another, but also forgiveness of oneself. We know that God will forgive, but make sure we forgive ourselves. ◆

34.

MULTIPLE PERSONALITIES

From a psychiatric standpoint, multiple personalities is described as a psychoneurotic disorder, a dissociative reaction to stress in which the patient manifests two or more complete relatively independent personality systems. Each system has distinct, well-developed emotional and thought processes and represents a unique and relatively stable personality. The patient may change from one personality to another at periods varying from a few minutes to several years. The personalities are usually dramatically different; one may be gay, carefree, and fun-loving, and another, quiet, studious, and serious. Usually the patient alternates from one personality to the other and cannot remember in one what happened in the other.

In truth, multiple personalites does stem from a personality disassociative reaction to stress. A person deals with that stress by living in a fantasy world which then attracts spirits of a lower order. It is similar to Possession as described in the previous chapter in that spirits do actually take over. The difference between the two is in the way an opening is provided a possessing spirit to take over a person.

Enlightening Voices from the Other Side:

Dr. Lochier explains how he works with victims of multiple personalities

I work on this side of life with people who had multiple personalities. From a clinical standpoint, it is a very interesting disorder. From a spiritual standpoint, it is sad. With multiple personalities it means that a person on earth has allowed a number of different spirits to come in and take over their body, usually for short periods of time. I say interesting from the point because these possessing spirits work as a group. Some like each other and share the time; others don't like each other and vie for the opportunity to take over the body. It is very difficult to route these individuals out. Jesus was strong in telling them to get out.

Without some professional help, that is, a professional who understands, the person is caught in a terrible prison. They do not know how to free themselves, they don't know what is going on, they don't know what is the matter with them. It is difficult for them to hold a job, or even to concentrate long enough to prepare for one.

When they come to this side, they are free of those possessing spirits over here because we build a wall of protection around them, and our vibrations are so much higher than the possessing spirits, they cannot penetrate. Then we work with them to help them understand. Eventually, we explain to them that much of that time was lost, they were robbed of the opportunity of their own soul growth. When an entity first comes in, it may seem glamorous to have contact with a stranger or spirit. As a person becomes controlled, it is anything but glamorous. We help them to become very, very strong so if and when they go back to earth, they will not attract this again.

Comments by the Master Teacher:
Sometimes when a person has been very badly abused, emotionally or physically, he or she tries to live in a fantasy world. When that happens, they can attract lower spirits to them. It starts out having its basis as a personality disassociative reaction to stress and then attracts spirits; so it becomes a dual kind of thing. They attract those spirits to them; so it is another personality that is taking over. The spirits do not get complete possession. They are only in maybe for a few minutes and others will stay for years. Whenever the opportunity is there for them to take over, they certainly will.

Truthfully, if you attract the lower realm of spirits, there will be more than one, yes, but not necessarily coming together as a group. It is a group as far as several different entities, not a group as people of like mind working together harmoniously. No, that is not usually the case.

When your soul comes over here, the personality that you have on earth really comes with you. If you have attracted other entities, entities that have been controlling you will be with you because you are going to be on the same realm as those spirits. Like attracts like; so you are not going to be on a higher plane. To get up to a higher plane, you are going to have to be worked with and helped to evolve to a higher plane. When you come over here, your thoughts, your desires come with you, and in that sense, we have to put up a wall of protection so that you know that it is only you. You cannot stay with the other band of entities if you want to progress. The wall of protection is not to keep them away from you. It is to keep you away from them so that you will get to know yourself. It is a very deep subject.

People have the idea that when you pass on everything is going to be nice and rosy and beautiful. They should stop and think they are making their house over here by what they do on earth. They are not realizing that. So when they come over and there have been multiple personalities, they are going to be really confused. They are going to be down in a realm where those other spirits are—not on a high plane.

And if they have been abused, they are going to have to work through that part of it, and to forgive. If they can get rid of it on earth, that is the best way. There have been some cures on earth. It goes along with spiritual evolvement. These people do know that they are living with multiple personalities. If they get the right psychological help on earth and raise their consciousness, they will no longer attract the lower entities. That is anyone's best protection. You do not attract something if you are not on the same level. You cannot just say, *I can't help it.* But you do have to do a lot of your own work on earth before you come here to get rid of that kind of stuff.

Dr. Lochier returned to introduce Pollyann
I came to you once before and talked about multiple personalities. I have worked with a lady named Pollyann who would like to tell you a little bit about her experience.

Pollyann explains how she attracted multiple personalities
Hello, yes, this is Pollyann and I do want to tell you a little bit about it. I am aware that you know that multiple personalities does usually start with someone living in a fantasy world because they find it difficult to live in the real world. I had a step-mother who was very, very unkind to me. I would fantasize that a fairy

princess was with me and was doing so many nice things for me. I never knew my biological mother. She died in childbirth. I did not know about the Spirit World. But I fantasized so much about how beautiful my life was when I was in my dream world.

Fantasizing over a period of time, I opened the door for spirits to come in and take over. First, there was one, and then another, and another. I think I had 9 or 10 different spirits that would come in and possess me. It just increased my fantasy world. It expanded it.

In time, I no longer wanted that, but I didn't know how to get rid of the spirits. There was no one really to help me. I went to my minister and he did not know what to do. He sent me to a Catholic priest that he knew. He had asked him to exorcise me. He did a ceremony, but the spirits did not leave.

It wasn't until I came to this side—I wasn't on a high level. I was on one of the lower realms of the third plane. My guides and teachers were able to get to me. They did build a wall of protection to keep me from reaching out and to keep those spirits from coming near me and influencing me. I did realize that I did not grow while on earth because of being possessed. So I wanted no part of them again. I worked very, very, very hard on this side to raise my consciousness many realms. I am now on the fourth plane, free of all of that.

When I did the review of my life, I thought, oh, my goodness, my goodness, how I was just trapped by these low possessing entities. Eventually, I went through the akashic records and learned that I had been very unkind to my mother in that life. She was an invalid, pretty much, very sickly, and I did not help or do things for her. So we came back into this life. She was my step-mother. I really got my just dues. If I had been nicer to her, despite her rejection of me, it would have been a better life for both of us because I think she would have responded. But we have worked it all out on this side and we are great friends now. ◆

35.

AUTISM

Classic autism is a devastating neurological disorder. It has a strong genetic component and is marked by rapid brain growth during early childhood. Autism is a disorder that severely impairs development of a person's ability to communicate, interact with other people, and maintain normal contact with the outside world. Males account for more than 80 percent of the million-plus Americans with autistic disorders.

It is often noted that as a baby, they were not particularly cuddly or outgoing. Head banging, rocking, teeth grinding, engaging in repetitive activities, difficulties with language, difficulty in expressing emotion, may be observed. In its classic form, the condition leaves people virtually devoid of social impulses. Although many are mentally disabled and require institutionalization, about 10 percent of autistic people are famous for collecting facts, and many can recall them with breathtaking precision. Even when they lack such savant skills, autistic people often excel at mundane, detail-oriented tasks.

Enlightening Voices from the Other Side

Dr. Lewis speaks of autism from the standpoint of one who suffered from this disorder

I was autistic when I was on earth. This was a long, long time ago and they really did not quite understand what it was as much as they do today. As I look back at my life, I was banging my head and I was very aloof. I showed many signs of just not wanting to socialize. I had no interest. And it is a brain or neurological disorder.

I was very bright and I grew up learning some things at my own pace. I was a savant in that I was very musical and could remember tunes once I heard them. It was a blessing that my family had a piano, otherwise, I think I would have just driven everybody around me crazy. I got out of banging my head when I was around 5 or 6 and I got more into the music. I would be able to remember dates and just speel those off. I could do multiplications and things like that, but I wasn't social. I didn't want to be close to people. I grew to adulthood and was about 37 years of age when I passed over. I was never able to work to earn a living. I had a heart problem and I died of cardiac failure.

On this side I was helped by being taken back to a previous incarnation. I was helped to change my feelings toward people. In a past life I was very cold. When people reached out to me, I did not respond to them. I was very intellectual but I was a very cold— really a very cold person. I think I made people shiver to be around me. And so when I came back autistic, I was a cold aloof person because I could not really be any other way. They did not know how to work with me. So in a way, I mirrored that previous life. I could have done something about it in the previous life, but in this last life on earth, I could not.

In reviewing the akashic records of that former incarnation, I think I was cold because my parents had died when I was very young and I was put in an orphanage and not given much care. It was more like being warehoused rather than being given love and care. It was a very harsh environment. I was never a warm person. I was bright and I managed to get a job in that previous life. I worked as a bookkeeper. My employer liked my work because I was efficient with figures, could work quickly, and I did not spend my time socializing. But when someone could have used a listening ear or a little empathy, I did not make myself available. It just didn't occur to me to reach out. I know I had no training, no examples. But the people that I worked with were nice and they tried to reach out to me, and I rebuffed them. And I think sometimes I really hurt them because I was so cold and indifferent.

I was grateful when I got to this side and was worked with very diligently to go back to see how I had gotten myself into that situation. I have made great strides on this side. I have learned to reach out by first working with animals. They gave me so much love. I could reciprocate without having a problem with my ego. Then I graduated to working with children. Later, I worked with autistic children and adults who come over. I did become a doctor over here. I worked very, very hard to qualify myself to work with autistic people.

I think we need to help people on earth to realize that autism is a karmic thing, but to give the patient as much help as possible. Autistic people need to be worked with one on one for a very long time, and then we put them in groups when there is a breakthrough. As I mentioned earlier, we do have to take them back to an earlier incarnation when they were functioning well and that helps a great deal in the treatment process. I have gone back to an earlier life. I am in the etheric body of the one when I was very cold because I now can use that body to be very warm. Some people do not go back to another body. They stay in their present etheric body but it is no longer malfunctioning. All etheric bodies are perfect. There is no longer a neurological problem. Over here, it is a matter of straightening out the thinking pattern.

Comments by the Master Teacher

Only a small percentage of autistic people are savants. That is unusual, but it is true that it is a karmic condition. And it is true that more than one child in a family can be autistic. When they come to this side, that can be reversed because the etheric body is perfect. I thought it was interesting that you were told about working first with animals and then with children because those are wonderful steps to help a person relate more warmly.

Blind Tom (Thomas Greene Bethune) describing his life as a musical savant

I am very happy to be able to come and tell you about my life. This is the first opportunity I have had to come through a medium.

I started my life with a lot of obstacles. My mother was sold as a slave to General Bethune. I was her 14th child. They didn't sell me. I went with her because they thought I was of no value to anybody. And I really wasn't at that time, as far as they saw it. I was autistic and severely mentally retarded. I was born in 1849 completely blind. Even at the age of six, I could not speak. I had a very hard time walking. When I was older, I was able to walk, but always had difficulty. I gave no sign of intelligence at all.

It was not so awfully bad being with the Bethunes because I had the run of their very big place. General Bethune was a wonderful, wonderful person. When I was four, they would sit me at the piano because otherwise I would just lay in a corner, really dejected. It was Spirit that impressed someone to put me at the piano and put my hands on the keys. Anything that I had heard I could play. It was like Spirit was moving my hands. Honestly, I was not moving them. They were being moved. This is true of most savants who are musical. Spirit works through them.

It was the Bethune daughters who really got me going because they played the piano very well. I couldn't talk at first. I couldn't say a word, but I could sing. The family would get together and the daughters would play and the family would sing, and I would sing right along with them. I think in my whole life there were only about 100 words in my vocabulary. I was very mentally retarded. I had no real intelligence and never went to school a day in my life. That was just the way it was. I was a very explosive child. I was so frustrated. I couldn't do what the other children did. I couldn't talk very well even when I was older. I had to have constant supervision, but the Bethunes put up with me. I was supposed to be there. It was by preincarnation plan.

When I was five, I was outside in a thunderstorm. So I sat and composed a song and I called it "The Rain Storm." It was well liked and I could sing it. From the time I was four or five years old, I was creating songs and doing some work at the piano. But by the age of six, I could repeat very complex compositions. I could play whatever the girls had played on the piano. I remember one time they had been playing and quit to go have dinner. So while they had dinner, I got up at the piano and I started in. I played every single note that they had played. The people could not understand it because there was nobody in the parlor. They didn't know what was going on. They came running in and there I was playing the piano. With the Bethunes, I had a lot of backing, but I guess this was the way it was supposed to be.

My mother was not freed but she did have it very well with the Bethunes. She worked very hard but she was very well taken care of. They appreciated her and me. They were very, very wonderful people. They turned the whole house over to us. We could do anything we wanted. My mother died happy. She really did not want her freedom. She would not have known how to take care of herself on the outside. I know you people think of slaves as somebody out there doing all the work and not getting any kind of appreciation, but the Bethunes were very different.

In the year 1857 when I was eight years old, I gave my first concert in Columbus, Georgia. It was such a success that General Bethune decided that we were going to go on a concert tour. I became more sociable and well liked. I learned to talk but had only about 100 words in my vocabulary. I performed almost daily. We were gone for a whole year. I earned $100,000. Of course, that was for him, but he did take very, very good care of me. There were over 7,000 pieces that I knew and I could repeat them at any time. I was taken over by Spirit. I was almost possessed by three or four wonderful spirit musicians because I could do all different types of music. It wasn't just the same type. When I went to Spirit I met them. And, of course, in Spirit I was helped to reverse the mental retardation and become normal.

I think the most important thing was when I was eleven years old and I went and played for President James Buchanan. The musicians there thought that I had really tricked the president and that I was tricking people. And so they gave me a test. They came to the hotel and they played two compositions, one was thirteen pages long. The other one was twenty pages long. And I repeated both of these from beginning to end without any errors. Then they knew there were no tricks.

After General Bethane died, then his son John took over my care. I did do a few concerts in New York in 1904. Then for about the last twenty years, I was semi-retired. I played for myself. I certainly did.

Do you know Leslie Lemke? Have you noticed how he plays? We are very much alike. I am working with him because we are both musical savants and we are really musical giants. He is exactly like me. We work together. I don't know if he realizes who is working with him. He plays some of my compositions. He likes them. I did not have to study on this side in order to help him because what came to me while I was on earth is a part of my memory. I took that memory right back with me. It is in my soul memory. It is a treasure in my soul. Now, if I didn't want to use it again, I wouldn't have to, but I did want to. Leslie wasn't quite as willing as I was. He really needed help to do the things his soul wanted done; so I asked if I could jump in there and work with him. I am not doing it all, but I am there. I planned to work with

Leslie Lemke before he came into this life. His is a little more for karmic reasons than mine was. He is doing fine, and I believe that we are accomplishing something by showing people that you can come with all kinds of handicaps and you can still create something that is very wonderful.

In a previous life, I was a composer. But I really did not want to do this kind of work in that previous life. But I was actually meant to come into this life like I did, not so much to work off karma, but to show people that despite a handicap it is possible to be productive. Today, you call it being an autistic savant. It is really wonderful to be able to do this and to give the kind of hope and help that goes to people when they think about it. You are certainly not seeing too many musical savants today. There are more mathematical and technical savants who can take care of the technical things of today. You are going to find more and more of them. There are spirits who can do mathematical calculations very fast and they impress the knowledge upon the savants. Autism is more rampant now as a way for people to work off their karma.

I am so happy that I was given the opportunity to come back the way that I was and accomplished so much. I brought a lot of joy. My soul wanted this. I don't think I actually needed it, but I do know that it was not all karma with me. For some reason my soul had chosen to do this in order to show people what can be done, even if very mentally retarded. I have chosen to stay in the same etheric body as on earth, rather than go back to the body of the previous life. Now, of course, I can walk and talk. The mental retardation has been completely reversed. I still don't have a large vocabulary because I never learned it. I still have trouble sometimes saying the words because I don't talk that much. Over here, it is mainly through thoughts. I am in a perfect body.

I have met all the great composers over here and I am in the same group with them. We work together, but I am doing a lot of my work on the earth plane with Leslie. I am very happy that I got to talk to you. ◆

36.

DEPRESSION and BIPOLAR

Enlightening Voices from the Other Side

Manic Depression—Comments by the Master Teacher

A bipolar or manic depressive is one who has a definite chemical imbalance. They chose a body that was going to produce an imbalance. At the time they chose it, they thought they would be able to conquer it, so to speak, and work off their karma. Manic depression can be controlled with medication. It is the result of something that has happened in a past life. The reaction would be the same only worse. A bipolar can very often go into schizophrenia. And it is very easy for them to attract the wrong spirits to influence them. All guides and teachers who are a part of the inner band are good and dedicated. Others come in to influence negatively.

Nowadays with the kind of medication and the therapy and the help they can get, there is the possibility of getting through it. Then when they go to the other side, they are fine. They are not going to attract that again. However, there are some who will not take their medication or do anything about helping themselves.

Dr. Merriweather on Depression

I was a captain on a merchant ship while on earth. When I came to this side of life, I wanted to do something very different. And so I chose to work with people who were artistic in various ways, not just drawing but in the various arts who were frustrated because they never thought they reached their potential.

So I had to learn a great deal about spiritual law, how the soul evolves, before I could work with them and, of course, I began under supervision. In helping these people who were so terribly, terribly frustrated, I saw how they were very depressed. Of course, we did not always limit it to people who were trying to use their creative ability because you can use your creative ability in many professions. You could use your creative ability if you were a street sweeper in how you went about doing it a little better than

351

somebody. But mainly, we worked with people who just felt they wanted so much to be good and yet they just did not have it in their own eyes. (Like attracts like to bring them together) There are many others who may not be very good artists who are pleased with their efforts.

I am talking about the ones who are very, very dissatisfied. And there is a difference between wanting to strive to be better, and those who are just plain so caught up in failure. They do not recognize or appreciate the efforts they are making. It takes much practice and through many incarnations that we refine an artistic ability so that it reaches a high level of achievement. We should not put it down. So it is these people that I work with to help them to know that it is through effort and desire that they are able to produce something that goes out into the universe in a very positive way and that is very important to make these deposits in the universe, deposits of beauty. A child may scribble something with crayon and has not stayed within the lines of a drawing, or the picture of something they are trying to illustrate does not look well formed. Children usually are very pleased with what they do until an older person, maybe a sibling or parent or teacher, criticizes and puts them down. They develop an inferiority complex about their ability. They want to do well and try but do not quite make the grade in their own eyes. So we are trying to help them to get out of this attitude that they are not producing.

It is much easier on this side of life to produce something of beauty than it is on earth. Over here you see something more clearly in your mind and you can think it. So we help them to develop that clarity. If they want to draw an apple, they see it to the point of almost tasting it. And then they can reproduce on paper or whatever. It is a matter of trying to help unlock those thoughts or ideas.

By doing that they feel better about themselves and can be at peace and help others. So we do a lot of work in groups and have critiques where we only look for the good. It is a matter of practicing here so they get to the point where they can see for themselves that they are creating beautifully. This does help with their self-esteem and to know that they are expressing their soul talent which is uniquely their own. And we work with them maybe in doing some acting, putting more expression, because everything over here is felt more intensively, more deeply than on earth. And by expressing, they can feel more life coming into their bodies and feel a greater sense of connectiveness to God's beauty. Their bodies take on more light. And then, of course, they teach others who don't need this kind of expression, but simply have an interest in learning artistic skills. They are well qualified because they have suffered through each step of the way and are able to help others. When they come back to earth they will have artistic ability that they can produce.

Comments by the Master Teacher

Dr. Merriweather describes a facet of depression different than bipolar. People can be depressed for many reasons. Some of it is karmic and some can be helped by medication to restore chemical balance.

When a person has been artistic in a past life, that is what their soul wants them to do when they again come to earth. But maybe they just can't seem to produce because teachers, parents and sibling will say, *Oh, that is terrible. That does not look right.* So they just don't do it anymore. Then when they come over here, they realize they have not done what their soul wanted them to do. That is where the problem comes in. So as they prepare over here, they can come back to another life later on and they will be artistic. They have freed their inhibition. On this side of life, you just think something in detail and it will appear on paper or the surface of whatever you are working on. If a newcomer comes over with these problems that they could not fulfill their talents, we have like parchment and paper and they actually draw and paint. Then as they progress, it just seems to appear on the paper, but they have to progress themselves to the point where they can see it in all detail. Anyone could advance himself or herself to do this if they had the interest and that was what they were supposed to do.

Your soul has certain things that it wants to accomplish on both sides. The soul has a plan of what it wants to do when it comes to earth. If it does not do that, then it is brought over here with them to complete. When they go back again to earth, they will fulfill it. In other words, if you had artistic ability in a past life, that ability was to be used upon the earth. That was your purpose for coming back, but if you couldn't or didn't use it, or you thought you failed in it, then you come over here and you realize that in your whole earth life you did not fulfill what you were supposed to fulfill. So then you work on it over here. What you are doing is advancing your ability while you are in Spirit so that nothing is really lost when you go back to earth again to work on your soul talents.

Many times it is those who were artists in a past life who did not use their talent correctly. Therefore, it was an ability that you were given when you came back as part of your earthly contract. It was what you were supposed to do but you did not do it, you did not fulfill it. You felt like you couldn't. Then you are going to work on that over here so that when you do come back again, you are going to be able to do it. If you used your talent to produce ugly, immoral art, then you would be using it wrongly. You will have to learn to express more beautifully in Spirit.

Molly K. discusses her earth life suffering from Bipolar Disorder

I am very happy to come and talk about the experiences I had when I was on earth. They were pretty hectic, weird, and wild at times. I look back and I think that I acted more like I was in a frenzy than a normal human being. Well, that is the nature of this manic depressive or bipolar disorder. We did things in our past, usually, to bring this condition on. We were not stable individuals in a previous life.

In a previous life I was involved in all kinds of cult things. It wasn't exactly voodoo but I tried to get into the occult in a weird kind of way. So I was working more for power experiments than I was out to try to help people. I did all kinds of things. When I went into the akashic records and reviewed my lifetime prior to this time, I could not believe what I was doing. I was shocked. I was working with some animal parts. I tried to put hexes on things. I was not using some clairvoyant power that I had. It was not great; however, I was not connecting with any advanced group of spirits, by any means. They were lower entities that I had attracted, and I was encouraged by them to do things. We would sit around a fire which should have purified, but didn't because of our chants and crazy doings. We would take up a cause or a person we did not particularly care for and send thoughts out. So, in a sense, it probably was a semi-voodoo activity.

I had totally misused my mental and psychic abilities, so I came back into this life with bipolar possibilities. I had come into a family where the potential certainly existed for my chemistry to become unbalanced. If I had lived a very great life, I probably could have avoided becoming bipolar, or having such a severe case of it.

My parents were religious people and I learned a great about ethics, what was right and what was wrong, but I didn't practice too much of what I gained. In my twenties I was working in a business and I was very, very ambitious and got promoted very rapidly. The more money I brought in for the owners, the better they liked it, and the more they paid me. So the temptation was very great and I did some things that I should not have done, but I did them.

When I was about forty, I started to notice some real strong mood swings. I would just get depressed. Sometimes I would get depressed when the business was very good, and sometimes I would feel very manic when business wasn't as good. So, it just didn't make any sense to me what was going on. I would go on real shopping sprees and I would invite everybody over to my house to a party. I loved parties, loved to be around people when I was manic. I did some crazy things. The condition got worse as I got older. It affected my decision-making. I had been promoted to a position of authority. I was trusted and I made some very, very poor decisions. I bought heavily of the things that I liked but they were not very practical. It became very noticeable that I was out of control. And then I went into a depression. It just seemed that nothing was right. I had no hope. I would realize that I had purchased the wrong things—things that were not easily resalable and I felt very badly about this.

And the time came when I got so depressed that I opened myself up for someone from Spirit, who was not developed, to walk into my aura. It was very, very difficult because I really got down, down, down and down. I was controlled by a spirit who apparently was angry that she had gone to Spirit when she did. She had wanted to stay on earth longer. She was angry and she was feeling depressed. And like does attract like, and in she walked. She really kept me down. This was after I had gone through a number of manic depressive cycles. I was feeling very down. It got so bad that I was called into the office for the tenth time to ask *what was the matter? What was the matter?* And I honestly could not say what was the matter. I really could not say. All I could say were things that were negative. I would tell them that business conditions were poor, this was a bad time of the year. I would tell them all kinds of things. I got to a point when they called me in that I did not know what to do. I didn't know what to say because I just was very negative. I was depressed. So my boss said, *Why don't you take a little time off? Take a month off, go on a nice vacation and see if you will feel better.*

So I took a vacation and then the manic swung in again and I attracted a different spirit who wanted to have a great time and I spent so much money that I had saved. I just squandered it and I had a great time. But when I came back and I took inventory of my assets, it absolutely depressed me and I went back into a depression. Finally, I reached the point where I had to ask for State Aid. I could no longer work. I could not control myself. I did not know what was wrong. I did not know that medication might help. It was a sad situation because you know, I was really very bright and very capable, but I was paying my karmic dues and I really did not get any help. By this time my parents were deceased and relatives thought *why should they take care of me?* They thought I should just straighten up. I lived in a small area where there was not much sophistication, truly. I saw my doctor but he did not diagnose me. It is not like today. I have been away from the earth plane some seventy-five years or more. A psychiatrist would no doubt have made a correct diagnose, but I didn't get to a psychiatrist. People didn't think I was crazy, they just thought that some of the things that I did were crazy because they did not make sense.

So I came to this side eventually and it was very hard for me to get out of the depressed cycle. Many worked with me in a group to try to help me to see that this was karmic. And that I had paid a price and I should be very grateful that I didn't do more damage to the business that I worked for. I did cause them some considerable financial loss, but someone came along who was able to turn things around. So I felt good about that. But they really had to work hard on me on this side to get me out of the depressed state. They told me I did not have to be there. Depression is rather difficult to get out of. You don't just find yourself in a different spot and say, *oh everything is great!* It doesn't work that way.

When I found out that I was in Spirit, I could not believe that literally it is a structured world. When they told me I was dead, a part of me said, *Thank goodness, I am out of it.* But then when they told me that I was really alive, it made me more depressed. They told me that I had life eternal. I thought, *Oh my goodness, I have to continue on this way forever.*

I did get out of the depression eventually through a great deal of help. I think being part of a group helped me immensely because there were others there like me. Then others who had recovered came back and they said, *Look, I got through it.* I remember one person coming and saying that she had done a lot of damage. She was on the manic cycle and had been very destructive because she had opened herself up to an entity who was just on a rampage, in a sense. She did things that hurt people. So I was glad that I didn't hurt too many people. I hurt mainly myself and my employer.

It is an awful thing when you don't have medication because you realize that you have no control. You just shoot up and down. You think when you are depressed that you simply do not want to live. It gets that bad. I thought many times that I did not want to live. That's why when they told me that I had life eternal and that I was alive, it sent me further into depression. When you are on a high, you don't realize that what you are doing is wrong or unwise. It makes you feel good that you can spend and go places and bring everybody together for parties, and do all this stuff. And it is crazy, because we bipolar patients have misused our brains in a past life. And the brain can be misused in many ways. Then we come to this life and we don't have control over properly using it. We had control in the past life and we chose how we were going to use it. We had conscious choice. In this life when the chemistry is not balanced, then we do things without any real control. To some extent, yes, I look back and I see that I could have controlled myself more, but I just went with whatever direction it took me.

Now on this side, I am working to help people. I have become very interested in the chemical makeup of the physical body, especially the brain. The mind uses the brain, but the mind can't use a brain that is not functioning properly. If not chemically balanced, the mind can't use it properly. We can honestly try to control our mind to some extent, if we know what is going on, and if we know what is right and practical. It is difficult to do. I am trying on this side to gain a greater understanding.

I have acquired a real interest in chemistry; so I am actually working here to help chemists on this side of life to develop medication that will help people on earth. We have to get that through to a chemist working at a pharmaceutical company to be able to do it. What we would like to develop would be herbal compounds that would work as well as manufactured chemical ones to eliminate side effects. We can work a little faster over here in getting something than a person could on earth. We have so much more available to us in terms of equipment and ability to see effects, and so forth. It is hard to get through to a medium who has the background who can receive. And so that is where we are with this, but the day will come when there will be an introduction of herbal compounds that will be effective. Of course, we would like to be able to do this with all diseases and get away from the medicines which have side effects because they are not natural. What we want to do is to bring herbs that will stimulate the body to manufacture its own remedies. I want to leave that with you.

Bipolar is a very serious and increasingly common disorder, and there are certainly reasons for it. It does go back to the past life when we deliberately misused our mental abilities. I want psychiatrists and others to understand that they are not just working with the current lifetime. And there really is no cure for it at the present time. What can be offered is some amelioration.

Comments by the Master Teacher

I think that Molly has given you a picture of how difficult it is to carry on a normal day literally without being balanced in your thinking, acts and doings. It is like a demon, but it isn't a demon, and this is why many people have felt that they were demon-possessed. It does open the door for undeveloped spirits to come in. There is no question about it. She has told you correctly that it is a karmic condition, worse in some people than others, depending on what they have done in the past. We do have to work over here to break that cycle. Most of them are very grateful to get the help. •

37.

DOMESTIC RELATIONS

Enlightening Voices from the Other Side

Dr. Pittman describes the dynamics of domestic abuse

There are so many, many, many, many, many—I cannot give you enough many's—to describe the dysfunctional families on earth. So many, many families start out with a very poor foundation. The love is just not there. It began with a sexual attraction and because of that, there is no basis that is needed for stability.

There are men who delight in abusing their wives. It goes back to a past incarnation, and usually it is with the same person, not women in general, but with the same spouse. Or, it could be that the woman was a wife or sister or friend, but not a woman in general—a very specific person that the man is getting back at in this lifetime. And more frequently than not, she ran around or did things that were very distasteful to him that really called into questioned his manhood, and he has exceedingly deep resentment and anger over something that happened in that past life and he wants to literally beat it out of her, and sometimes actually kills her. It never seems to abate. There will be a beating and then the soul seems to rise momentarily and there is regret. What happens is that he sees that she is a good person in this life. He does not separate consciously that she was not that great in a past life. But he sees that she is good and he feels remorse. Then the cycle starts over again and it is very, very difficult to break.

It can happen at the beginning of marriage with newlyweds. It can extend for the entire length of a marriage. It is wrong, but it is understandable that a wife may wind up killing her husband because of her fear and really reaching the point of no return with his abuse. The intensity of the abuse is related to the seriousness of whatever rejection occurred in a past life. It is ever in proportion.

They come to this side and we have to take them back to whatever life it was that things went awry, and try to help them to understand the dynamics of what was going on between them. When a wife kills her husband and spends time in prison, sometimes the governor will pardon her. Sometimes not. It really depends on how soon the karma is worked off. When she comes over, she is regretful but usually feels she had no choice because society did not protect her from his abuse, nor did they keep the man in jail long enough or give him counseling to help. Because your counselors do not understand that this is related to a previous life, it is very hard to get through to them completely. I am not saying that many counselors are not very helpful, because they are, and they are continually improving in their skills. I am saying that if they understood the whole picture, it would make it so much easier to get a breakthrough.

When the husbands really accept what has happened and can forgive the wife, and the wife can forgive the husband, then they frequently become friends because they have had an intensive experience in growth. There is a bond that forms. This has been going on since time immemorial. It has only been in recent years on earth that so much attention has been directed to this problem. It is good to bring it out because in the past so many wives have had to hide their bruises and suffer and not let on. It was an embarrassment. It is difficult.

I, myself, was an abuser, and that is how I got into trying to help others. I have been on this side of life for many, many years. Once I got some resolution for my problem, I then began working to become a doctor to try to help others. My wife, because she understood so well both sides, has worked with me for a very, very long time. We do love each other very much. Our relationship goes back many lifetimes, but it got off on the wrong footing in one of those times. We had resolved to come back in this most recent life to work out our differences. I was supposed to come back not to physically harm her, but to be unloving and cold. Instead, I came back really loving her but not having the control when my anger and resentment flared up as glimpses from the past floated in.

It is a very, very difficult thing for families to go through, and for the children to live in fear and to witness brutality. And sometimes it is taken out on the children rather than the wife because the husband will see them as part of her, and this is especially sad. Children have been killed and it is wrong. There is a great deal of work to be done with a whole family when that happens. And, of course, sometimes the children are from a past life and a relationship of some sort that was not a very loving one.

There are many people who reincarnate who are not mature enough to really take on the responsibilities of a family, and the cycle simply repeats over and over and over. In some societies domestic abuse is more acceptable than in others. But it must all change. With better education and more spiritual help, individuals will learn more self-control. It is awful when we have to face what we have done to another human being, and death does not end it.

A doctor talks about divorce
People get divorces on earth and they think that is the end of it. And for many, it is. The karma is worked out and that is it.

A marriage takes place sometimes to work out karma, or there is a deep attraction and love. Some people marry because they are lonely, and being two nice people, they stay together but not always very happily.

I would say it is almost invariably a karmic relationship when there is a divorce, or the couple separates and goes their merry way. I am speaking of relationships that are not amicable. Where the partner just walks off and leaves, it is usually a karmic thing. If the divorce is nasty, it is usually karmic. It is so much better when the couple receives counseling, even though it works toward a divorce. But it really and truly needs to be worked out. The relationship needs to be worked out. There has to be that understanding of why they got into the marriage and why they want out of it. Many want out of a marriage because they do not want to work out the karma. They have no understanding there is a karmic relationship involved. After this has been balanced, and they no longer want to be together, then only religious denominations opposed to divorce would want to hold them in the marriage.

We are here to grow, and when there are relationships which become tainted and damaged, then they need to be repaired so that the soul is freed from that experience and can move on. When no effort has been made to really work out the karma and they get to this side, some still carry a great deal of hatred or ill will. Some think they are free and have forgotten about their past. In order to go ahead, they do have to face this and work it out. Many come to this side not wanting to work out anything, and after spending some time in the Spirit World, they want to go back to earth not having worked out anything. So, they attract the same situation over again. We do the best we can in trying to help them.

It does come as an enormous surprise to many couples to learn that they still are a couple in the sense that they have unfinished business. When they become free, it is a load lifted off the soul. Sometimes, they actually become friends. So we do our best.

What I came this morning to stress is that it is so important to work out as many of your problems as possible while still on earth. Get rid of that garbage so that you are free of it. When you come to this side and you go through your review, you will not have all of that to face. You will not have the frustration and torment for you will have gotten rid of it.

Daniel R. On adultery

I was a Catholic when on the earth plane. My wife and I became estranged. We lived in the same house for a long time because there were children, but we did not get along. Our relationship was very cold. We did reach a point where we felt it was wrong to fight in front of the children. I stayed there to be the breadwinner, but I did carry on an adulterous relationship with someone that I truly, truly loved. I felt that it was wrong to get a divorce because of my religion, but I realize now that it was worse to commit adultery.

When you commit adultery, you are being unfaithful to your own soul because that is where a commitment is first made. You also made a commitment to someone else. A couple should try very, very, very hard to work things out if the relationship is not going well. If they are together to work out karma from a previous life, then it is so important to stay until it is worked out. You can tell when the karma is finished for there is no longer any emotion. You feel a sense of freedom.

When you commit adultery, you are sneaking behind someone's back. Maybe they do find out eventually, but you have really broken that commitment. You are not trustworthy. You are not being honest. I don't think there is anything wrong with separating or getting a divorce if you really cannot work it out after trying very hard. So many marriages take place because there is a karmic situation. But there are too many divorces on your earth today because they have not tried hard enough to work it out. They have not tried at all; so they are going to have to come back and do it all over again.

With my wife, we did try to be civil to each other and I did respect her for many things that she did very well. She was a good mother and good housekeeper. We came back to be together because in a previous life we were brother and sister and we did not get along well at all. We did come back to work it out, and I suppose in many ways we were almost like a brother and sister in this marriage. My real love was on the outside.

I just want to say that I think people should really give deep, deep thought to their relationship before they get married. Truly, I believe that a good astrologer, a good numerologist, a good premarital counselor, maybe all three, should be consulted to see what is going to be gained from the relationship. Had I not married my wife, I think we could have been friends and worked it out that way. There are just too many bad marriages and there are too many children that are upset by the breakup. ◆

38.

SUICIDE

Enlightening Voices from the Other Side

Ernest Hemingway on taking his life

I know that you know who I am. I did commit suicide. I just reached a point in my life where I did not feel particularly productive. I was not feeling well and was depressed. I drank too much. I did all the things that were wrong. I think I did have a spiritual side that showed itself occasionally. In my characters I did try to bring through something of depth beyond the personality.

It is not a pretty thing when we commit suicide because we leave behind people who are shocked, who grieve, and we cannot reach out and comfort them. As I look back, I should not have done that. I realize that now. I should not have done it. I could have held on. I could have turned my life around to some degree. What bothers me the most now is the weakness that I showed, the cowardice—that is what really gets to me, in addition to hurting others that I left behind. Had I been so terminally ill that I could not stand the pain that would have been one thing, but I certainly had not reached that point at all. I deliberately took my life thinking I would simply end it all.

I did somehow have a feeling there was an afterlife where you just float in the stratosphere, kind of a vapor-like figure floating. I did not realize that the afterlife was so structured in its own way and that the Spirit World is our real home. The Spirit World on each planet is the real home for that planet.

I have learned a great deal since I have been here, and thoroughly enjoyed the sessions which Dr. Baker gave you on the cosmic rays. I have spent some time with him privately. He has been very kind in helping me to better understand the relationship between earth and the other planets, and what we gain from the rays that come. That has really been the most interesting aspect of my education on this side. Yes, I have learned many things and I do attend Master Joseph's classes along with going to other schools. I want to help a writer on earth to really somehow weave into the story something about the invisible influences from the universe. I do not think Star Wars type, but something that is more realistic— not the mechanical kind of people, but something more realistic that will help educate people.

I was really shocked when I got to this side to find out what it was really like. And, boy, that is when I thought how stupid I was because I was talented as a writer, and I brought a lot of entertainment to people. It took them away from everyday thoughts for awhile. I know I will have to come back, and hopefully, if I have afflictions or I am tired, that I will have the fortitude to stick it out. Again, I say I understand when people are not well and when there is no hope for them, to receive a lethal injection— assisted suicide.

I have been to visit Dr. Kevorkian in his jail, and I do not know whether he really understands what I am trying to say to him. Many of us have visited him. It would be wonderful if you could write to him and share a bit of the spiritual side to bring him some comfort. By being in jail, if he had any karma, he is going to be working it off, so that is one thing to his favor.

But I wanted just to share that with you. Master Joseph invited me because he thought I would be willing to come in, and I certainly was. I have enjoyed my experience here. May God bless you with your work. I am not really that kind of writer, but if I can help you in anyway, call on me.

Thomas Youk
(Dr. Jack Kevorkian's last assisted suicide patient)

I am very pleased to have been invited to come here today. I was in terrible, terrible, terrible pain when I was on earth. I had Lou Gehrig's Disease, a heart problem and cancer. There was really no hope for me. I was not getting any better, and I went to Dr. Kevorkian begging to be put out of my misery. And he did examine me very thoroughly. He wanted to know what tests had been taken, and what treatments I had gotten. I simply was not responding to the medications the way one normally would, I suppose. But I was in terrible, terrible, terrible shape. There was no real hope of recovery. I had multiple problems and I don't even like to think about all the pain and suffering that I was going through. And so I was so grateful when Dr. Kevorkian agreed to help me, and I had the necessary things put by my side that I could do what was going to take my pain away permanently.

It was some concoction that I drank. And I don't know exactly what he had in there. He did not tell it. I knew that he was giving it to me so that I could go. And he did not reveal what he was doing to people. He did not reveal that because he knew he would be arrested if it was found out. Well, I guess he was trying to test by admitting on national television that he did this and it backfired. But he always made it to where it would be a death that you did not suffer. I went very quickly. And he was never alone in the room with you. He always made sure there was somebody there that witnessed it.

And it was a simple death. I mean, you took it and you were alive for a little bit, and then you just went to sleep. I knew that Dr. Kevorkian was very good at what he was doing, and he did not do wrong. He helped people to pass who could not get better. He got all of your physical conditions and all of that. He did research it all. He made sure that you were not going to get better. Because there were many cases that he refused because there was a chance that they would get a little better.

I want to talk more about death and coming to this side of life. I thought that death was the end of it all and there would be nothing else to face. After taking the drug, I found myself in almost what I would call a dream-like state. And I saw the famous tunnel of white light, and I heard voices telling me to go on toward the light. And so I walked on and finally came out to see people there. I had family. My wife from a former marriage was there waiting to greet me. She had passed on much, much earlier. I was glad she was there. It helped me to get somewhat oriented because she immediately told me that I had passed over, and what we think of as death was really a new beginning of life. I really thought that when you died, you just—well, I don't know what I thought. I did not think it was like this at all. I didn't think you lay in the ground, but I just figured you were dead, and you were dead and that is it.

I was taken to a hospital and strange, but very nice people were trying to help me. I later learned they were the guides and teachers like everyone has who come to help us, to guide us and to try to keep us on our soul's path. At first I could not believe that I did not feel all that pain. It was like my body was numb. Then an interesting thing happened. As I began to realize that I was dead, all of that pain returned because it was in my head at that point. The doctors over here worked hard on my mental attitude. It was all such a shock to me that death was really life anew. I had heard about the tunnel and all that business, but I did not believe it. I was, I guess, so identified with my body and its pain that I did bring it with me mentally. And it took a long time for me to get over it. I wanted to commit suicide all over because of all that pain. And I was told that the body that I was in, the etheric body, was indestructible and I could not get rid of it, but what I could do was to change my attitude and just know that I was now perfect and whole and absolutely well. Gradually, very gradually, I did change. It is amazing what the mind does to a person, but I did change. When I finally accepted that I did not need to feel sick, I started getting more energy. I saw people around me who were active and I wanted to be as active as they were. My guides were wonderful, really wonderful, teaching me many things about the Spirit World. And as I began to progress, I got out of that sick bed, never to return. I am very grateful to Dr. Kevorkian, Jack as we knew him. He was a friend, a saving angel. He did not assist me simply because I asked. He did it because he was thoroughly convinced I would not get better.

If you do not have the understanding, and it is really atrocious that people do not have this understanding, that the churches do not teach anything about life after death. You know, it is very, very hard, and it is hard on the people left when they think their son, daughter, whoever is just laying somewhere. Or, think they are in the grave waiting for Gabriel to blow his horn. You know, I have had such a desire since I have come over here to go to these graves and blow a horn so they would get up, but I know I can't do that. Some of them are just not ready, and it is so sad really. It is very hard, too, on the parents, or sister or brother to see somebody go and really think they are just dead. It is harder on them than on the person who comes over. But most of the people who go to Dr. Kevorkian honestly believe there is life after death, at least 70% believed there was life after death, or they wouldn't have wanted it. I just wanted out. I didn't care how, where. I just wanted out. My wife, my second wife, was very understanding. She was right there with me.

I am working now, trying to help people the best I can. I go to groups that are helping suicide victims. I tell them about my experience. I have met many of the others that Jack assisted. And I try to work with them. We have a club here. We call it "Jack's Group." Sometimes we go to visit him and tell him.

Well, I am working with those who come over, trying to help them to understand that there is life, that we can do as we want to do. We are not limited anymore. And I take them around and show them places over here that I think they may enjoy seeing or doing. Let's say that somebody was a fisherman on earth. They really loved to fish. All right, he comes over here and he doesn't exactly know what to do or where to go, or what's happening to him. So, I'll take him to fishing ponds here. The fish we catch, we just let go. We don't use hooks like on earth. Everything is spiritual. It looks like a hook but it doesn't penetrate. We have fishing, we have golfing, we have anything we want on this side. I was very unaware of that, but I certainly found out soon. And I will take them and I will show them that what you did on earth you can do here, if you want to. You can sit by the water for days if you want to. But you see, you have to show them. You have to almost take them by the hand and get them to understand. It is very beautiful here, and I am so happy that I am here. Well, I would have come over by now anyway. I know I would have. But I am so happy that Jack helped me to come sooner.

Well, you know, we had a gentleman come over here and talk to us about how he left. And he was in a very bad physical state. He was on life support, yet he was aware of things. He could talk to his wife and his children. He did know them, but he was in very bad shape. He had to be on a respirator and the whole thing. And so he made up his mind that he was not going to live that way. And so he talked to his doctor, and his doctor said, "I cannot do anything to help you to go." And he said, "Well, I'll tell you what I am going to do. I am going to have my wife and children here tonight. I am going to tell them I will not be here tomorrow. I am going to pull everything off myself, and I don't want you to come in. I don't want you to let the nurses come in. I just want you to tell everybody I am all right. I am going to sleep. You come tonight and you see that I am going to sleep. Tomorrow I will be gone." And the doctor went along with him. But, of course, he did not admit it, but he went in that night and he made sure that everything was tight, and that everything was the way it was supposed to be, told the nurses to go in and give him his nighttime medicine, and then not to go in any more because he wanted a good night's rest and did not want to be awakened. And the next morning he was gone. But he, himself, had taken everything off. And his wife and his children, he told them not to come back. He did not want them there. And he told them goodbye and they were all for it because he could have lived a long time in that state. He had been in the hospital, I think he told us 3 months. He knew he was not going to get better. But you know, they took the insurance away from his wife. They would not pay the insurance because they called it suicide. His wife really suffered. He knew what life after death was all about. So he kind of looked forward to it. He was very religious. He prayed to die, but nothing happened, so he took care of it himself.

I think it is wonderful that I can talk through somebody. I think that is really wonderful. I am very happy that I got this opportunity.

A spirit message from Tony Kervorkian
I am a distant relative of Jack. I really had little or no contact with him to speak of. But I feel he was honest, sincere, and very helpful to many who were suffering terribly. I don't think he did anything wrong. I just want to thank you for letting him know how spirit feels about that and how grateful his patients are for what he has done for them. I am aware of what you have sent him and the contact you have had with Mr. Kouk. I just want to come in and thank you for that.

Father Donovan tells about his life and suicide
I was a Catholic priest when I was on earth. And I had a very difficult time because I was a very heavy drinker. I was so intoxicated at times that I do not know how I managed to get through the service. It was pretty shameful as I look back.

I had become a priest to please my family, and probably because I was not ambitious enough to do anything else. I had gone to a Catholic school and I knew a lot about Catholicism from early childhood. And I fudged around. There were several of us in our large church, and they sort of took care of me. I finally reached a point where I had to be helped so often that I managed to get some pills and overdosed. So I can tell you a little bit about suicide and what it was like going to the other side.

When I arrived at this side of life, I was very, very surprised. I wanted to die and that is why I took the pills with the alcohol. But I did not think I would be in some low, dark place because I had hoped that because I was a priest and, therefore, God would honor me with a very beautiful home and all the amenities. Instead, because I had not been too sincere in my work, I went to a shabby place and it depressed me all the more. I wanted to continue drinking and would go wherever there was drinking to get the essence.

I have been over here between 25 and 30 years and I am just now ready to respond to the help that is all around me. I felt extreme frustration that I had taken my life and it did not relieve that pain. It only caused me to have more. I was depressed while on earth and I wanted so much to end it to come to this side to bring some happiness where Jesus would come and touch me and heal me, but that did not happen. The spirit angels tried to help me and I rebuffed them. I am finally looking at it and realizing that people who commit suicide simply because they cannot cope with things emotionally set themselves back. If they commit suicide because they are terminally ill, that is another situation altogether. But when one ends one's life just to get out of something they can't face, it only makes it worse. They lose that opportunity, that precious opportunity while on earth to work it out. It was kept very quiet what I had done.

It does not happen too often among priests, but once in awhile. And, of course, with my background and all those teachings, many of which are not correct, I had great remorse and guilt. Guilt for doing this to my family and my fellow priests. I intended to end this remorse about leaving without working on myself, but I am seeing things more clearly now. God never gives us anything that we cannot handle. I thought at the time it was too much because each day I just sank deeper into depression, and probably could have been helped a great deal with medication. If somebody came to me for counseling, I could have cared less about their problems. I wanted to say, *Let me tell you how I feel. You are not in bad shape.* So I feel guilty about not having helped those who came because they were hurting and in need of what I could offer as a priest—words of comfort.

I arrived over here in my misery until finally my teacher said to me, "You will never get better if you don't make a change. We cannot do it for you and neither can God do it for you. But if you decide, if you have had enough, I will help because God is on your side and we will all help you." And so I thought, *all right, I will give it a try.* And they took me to a beautiful little school where others who had committed suicide were there. Some had recovered and were working with the new arrivals. And a very beautiful lady helped me and has continued to help me to see that my thoughts must be directed to the good, to the positive. And she assured me that I would have an opportunity to help others through their depression because God will forgive me. I know that God will forgive me if I make the effort to change, and I am doing a pretty good job of it.

I am working right now with children because they are so wonderful, so full of life, and it is a blessing to be around them. As far as the drinking, I have totally recovered from that. I no longer seek the essence. I am glad that I did not cause anyone to go back to drinking who had quit. I just enjoyed the essence until I was strong enough to give it up. I hope I have helped to bring you some idea of what hopelessness can do. It is the very opposite of what to do to elevate us.

The Master Teacher's Comments:

The question was asked, do they incur a karmic debt for committing suicide? That depends on the reason. Let us take an ill person, terminally ill, one can't stand the pain any longer and commits suicide. That is taken into consideration. There is no karma concerning that. So there really was nothing wrong with what Dr. Kevorkian was doing in assisting the terminally ill. He was doing something actually to help them to leave. They were in terrible pain. We do not want that pain. Spirit does not want anyone to have to suffer like that. We let animals go.

In the case of passion—a break up with a girl friend, or a wife leaves you, that is totally different. Then there will be karma with that. Some think you will go straight to hell if you commit suicide. There is no hell. You will reach hell within yourself, and then you are responsible for what you have done to the people left on earth. They will all come back together to work out the karma.

M. Marsh talks about suicide

I was invited to come today because I was very, very ill on your earth plane. I had many, many things wrong with me that were very painful. I had cancer of the leg bone, the femur. I had emphysema. I had an ulcerated stomach. I had pancreatitis, and I had coronary heart disease. I was a mess! I had so many pills to take, and just so many pains and problems trying to breathe. When it came to the point where they wanted to amputate my leg, I wanted to die. And so I had a friend who was a pharmacist, and I also had a friend who was a veterinarian. I begged them both to tell me how to do it. Actually, the veterinarian was the more helpful of the two. He did not do it, but he did tell me how he did it with animals. And I managed to get what he used, and I did it.

After I got to this side of life—this was a long, long time ago—probably 50 years ago. Since I have been on this side of life, I became aware of Dr. Kevorkian and his work, and I truly applauded what he was doing. From this side of life, when a person on earth truly has no quality of life left, it is wrong for them to continue to suffer. It is really cruel for them to continue to suffer. I do not believe in taking the life of someone healthy, even though they have committed murder. Let them serve out their time. It is no punishment to take their life and send them to this side. And I think that when people are more elevated to know there is an afterlife, they will stop that capital punishment sentencing. That will cease to be. If we put animals out of their misery, why don't we relieve human suffering as well?

So when I came to this side, I really had no idea, absolutely no idea, there was an afterlife. I just thought we died and that was the end of it. I did not know that life was continuous. I still would have done it, but I would have had the awareness of knowing I would be coming to something instead of going to nothing. Coming to something was really a shock. I thought I was dreaming. I thought that maybe the injection I gave myself didn't work. I wasn't in pain. I did not know what had happened to me. Every once in awhile, I would be aware that somebody was around me. Something was around me. There was life and activity going on. I began very slowly to awaken and to see figures around me. I wondered why I was not moving, but I was not in any pain, either. I just was in an inert state. Gradually, I became aware enough to see my mother and father hovering over me, and I was very surprised because they looked so real. They told me that I had died and that I was in an etheric body, a spiritual body, and that I was very much alive, and that as soon as I had rested a little more, I would be up and moving around just as they were. And so, of course, this did happen. And the more I learned about where I was and why, and more about the Spirit World and gained some understanding, then the more mobility I would have.

I really wanted to learn more about this wonderful new world which, I guess in the *Book of Revelation* they call New Jerusalem. And so I was really a very enthusiastic student. I acknowledged my guides and teachers and they helped me a great deal. They were really wonderful. They helped me to understand that the soul does go on, and that I should not feel any guilt about having taken the life of my physical body. This was because I could not have really done much to have gone on in that old body. My soul was ready to come to this side.

I think suicide is wrong when people are just not willing to face their problems, and I get very upset that these young teenagers, especially boys, are taking their lives more and more. We hear about it on this side of life. If only someone could reach them and help them to get through whatever it is that seems so dreadful at that time. They do come to this side and realize after awhile that they have thrown away a wonderful opportunity for their soul to grow while on earth, then they become despondent and they really have to be worked with a great deal here. They can't take their life here, they just have to suffer through. And when they see how their parents and their loved ones on earth have suffered because of what they have done, it is heart wrenching, truly. Truly it is. I have talked with some of them and I have tried to help them, but they have their own helpers. They have teachers who are trained to help them, and they do work with them very intensely to pull them through that. In those cases, they may go back to earth a little sooner than some of us who are here and have had a long life on earth. But those young people may be guided to go back sooner and to try to plan to be stronger to go through whatever it is.

One young man came over because his close friend had been killed in an automobile accident, and he did not want to live without him. The friend was supposed to come over. His time was really up. That is all that he needed in that particular incarnation. It wasn't meant for this young man to take his life. And so the two friends are together, and the one is trying to get through his automobile accident and to understand that he is supposed to be over here, but he is also trying to help his friend who took his life prematurely. Those things do happen, and we just wish the information was out there for people to understand that life is continuous, that there is karma that we need to work off and that is why we need to go back to earth to do it. It is better worked off there. We can work off much of it over here, but it is better to work it off on earth. It can go faster.

And so I just wanted to let you know that in extreme cases, absolute extreme cases, where there is no hope for a reversal of physical problems, assisted suicide is perfectly all right. But one should never take their life unless there is that extreme condition, otherwise, they are not working off their karma. And you do not want to have to come back and do anything again that you could have taken care of in the first place. Do it while you are there, if at all possible. It is just when the conditions are so bad the soul really cannot function to accomplish anything more the way it should. All of the energies are going into trying to alleviate the pain, but it is not good to take it too soon. Eventually, this will come to pass.

The teachers here tell me we will all grow to the point where we will no longer need to have such awful things happen to us. I just was a very miserable negative person and what I didn't have the propensity for developing, carried over from a past life, I developed while on earth through the karma I accumulated then. And so I think I have said as much as I can say. I really have enjoyed this opportunity to come through and talk. May your work go far and wide and reach many, many souls.

Elizabeth tells how her suicide was part of her preincarnation plan to help her father work off his karma

This is Elizabeth. Thank you for inviting me back again. I love it. Since coming to this side I have learned a lot about my past life. My dad was involved in some business dealings of some sort. He was an artist then and things were just not going right and he was getting very, very discouraged. He felt that he was worthless and that he simply couldn't make it. He was so involved in his own thoughts, and he and my mother were just not getting along at all.

I adored my dad. I thought the sun just rose and set in my dad. I know he really did love me, but he was so distraught that one day he just decided to take a gun and end his life. I was absolutely devastated. I found him. He had gone out away from the house. I found him. It was so hard. It was so very, very hard. I was 13 years old. I cannot tell you how much it hurt me. I never really got over it. Life was hard for us. We sold some of dad's paintings and relatives took us in. But I grieved for my dad for years and years and years.

I finally went to Spirit when I was in my 40's. I had some medical problems. Eventually my mother came over. She was very angry, very, very angry at dad that he had committed suicide and had left us. Even though they were not getting along, at least he was trying to provide. He felt like he wasn't doing a good job. It was a bad situation.

I was the go-between and I convinced my dad and my mother, with the help of the guides and teachers, to come back and try it again. And so we did.

In this life, my dad was so very happy when my mother was pregnant with me. His soul knew that I was going to be very special to him. This was not a conscious realization but his soul knew. I was so loved. Again, my parents just didn't get along. But somehow they managed to be civil to each other so that their time with me could be shared. I just adored my father, and I know he adored me. I know he did. But the karma for causing me so very much pain in the previous life had to be paid by him. And I, too, committed suicide at age 21.

I paid for things I had done in other lives by having my illness when I was so small. I was very precocious and talkative until I was about four. Then I was stricken with Landau Kleffner Syndrome, which was karmic. This seizure disorder completely wiped out my ability to receive and express language. For awhile I was unable to communicate. My dad helped me with games involving drawing, but I was ridiculed by other kids. I received highly specialized education. When I was eight I had brain surgery and the seizures ceased and I began to recover language skills. Because I missed out so much on normal education and socialization during the early years, my parents decided to sent me to regular school. Junior high school was very difficult and high school was a disaster. The stress of boys, drugs, and being a teenager was too much. I dropped out of school, ran away from home and lived on the streets for awhile. I nearly died of a heroin overdose. Then I gave up alcohol and drugs. I had a very difficult life. I really paid for some of the stupid things I had done in previous lives. I had been very materialistic and didn't use my brain in the right way, and I paid. I did a lot of things. I got pregnant in this life and had twin boys. I was in no position to take care of them; so I arranged an open adoption.

I had periods of real depression. The psychiatrist that I saw gave me Celexa, a drug that had been banned in England. I cannot blame her because this was karmic and it was supposed to happen. That drug should not be used and I hope it will be banned here in the U.S. My psychiatrist probably had a heavy caseload, and I was not good about taking it on a regular basis. I was off and on it. And the time came when my soul apparently was saying, *It's time to go.* I verbalized this to my roommate. I think he just did not know what to do and didn't take me too seriously. And so I made up my mind that this was it and I walked into the commuter train station and right into the path of an oncoming train. I wanted to end my life quickly and I knew this way would do it.

I didn't want to hurt my dad and yet the plan before I came to earth was to commit suicide in order help my father erase his karma for having taken his life and for having hurt me so deeply. My dad has grieved terribly. I myself may still have karma to work out.

At 21, I thought stepping into the path of the train would end it all, but as my etheric body rose from that scene to view my mangled physical body lying on the ground, I realized, *Hey, I'm still alive.* I was around the earth plane for three days. I went to dad and I told him, "Dad, don't judge me. And don't judge others." And he heard me very, very clearly. When someone close to you first passes over, you tune in more clearly than you ordinarily would. You can pick up these things.

I went to my mother. She wasn't as upset as my father. It wasn't because she loved me less. It was because she was aware of my pain and was more accepting that I wanted to get out. I really had reached a point in my life where I honestly could not cope.

So I came to this side and a wonderful, wonderful spirit came to me and has helped me. I have met all of my guides and teachers and they all work with me. It was a shock to know that life continues. I thought, *Well, since I am over here, I am not going to just sit around and twiddle my thumbs. I am going to get busy.* I always loved children and animals. I started first working with children doing little skits. We would dress up. Sometimes we would be Indians, and at other times, Chinese, Greek, and so forth. We could make all our costumes and things because we could think them into existence. The children looked so cute. I loved it. We had a lot of fun. And I still do this some times.

Then my interest centered more on young people who have committed suicide. So many of them have done it because of certain drugs that they were on that made them so depressed. Others have done it because they just felt they were alone emotionally. Some were the victims of bullying and they just couldn't take it any longer. Some because a friend had committed suicide and they wanted to be with them. So I work with them to try to help them as best I can. I am not working alone by any means because I work with very advanced teachers. Because I am a young person, they can relate to me. I especially try to help young people who have come over because of drugs. I know that feeling and emphasize with what they went through.

Part of our therapy is to do art work and to go down and help with the animals. One young man said he was not going down to the animal realms and be a pooper scooper. We laughed and laughed because he didn't understand that just like our etheric body, the etheric bodies of animals also contain organs which are non-functional. There is no poop to scoop. We still kid him about that. He has really become one of the best animal keepers. In his life on earth, he had little close contact with animals, but now he relates to them beautifully. It is wonderful because it helps him to feel that he has an important place to work.

So this is what I am doing and I am really very, very happy here. I do wish my dad would accept that this was all supposed to be. If he had stopped me from walking into the commuter train, I am sure I would have found another way to take my life because I just could not have coped much longer the way I was going. This was supposed to be the way it happened. I hope my story helps someone to see that everything that we do has karma attached to it. It is either good karma or it's bad karma; so we must be very mindful of what we think and what we do.

Comments by the Master Teacher

Elizabeth did a very fine job in telling you from beginning to end about her life. And it is true that everything has karma attached to it, good karma or bad karma. And her advice to be mindful of our thoughts and actions is sound indeed. ◆

39.

LEARNING TO BOW THE EGO

Enlightening Voices from the Other Side

Sidney Walker on helping actors to bow their egos

I am working over here with people who were actors on earth. When they come over, many times they still have a terribly strong ego and still want to be the center of attention. It is called the Pedestal Syndrome. The first thing we do is to tell them that everybody is equal. They want to be waited on so we talk about that and we show them that we are all the same, regardless of what we do. They think they are supposed to get the gold out of St. Peter. Depending on how advanced they were in the work determines how long it takes to help them. I had a little difficulty at first, but I had an understanding which helped me a great deal.

We start out individually, and as they begin to understand and know what is going on, then we work in groups. They will put on little skits and things like that over here. It's fun. We have a whole group watching them, but they are not doing it in the same way they would do it on earth. It is not for money— just doing what they love to do and we encourage that. It is their expression. You should see, there will be so many people on the outside of the group watching and laughing and clapping, just the same as they would do on earth. But if they have the idea that they are better than someone else, they are out of the group and we work with them individually again. We work with actors and actresses from all nations.

In putting on little plays, I have tried to teach them to put on something for children. It is very hard to get an actor of any accomplishment at all to do that. And I work very hard at that because I try to tell them, you have got to humble yourself, you have got to come down to their level. Those children need it, children who have been deprived on earth and come over here.

You have to take the actor all the way down before you can get him or her to do it. It's the high priced ones that made a lot of money who think they are just the greatest. They are the hardest ones.

I wanted you to know that I scouted around and found that Raymond Massey was very, very willing to come and talk about his attitude. In fact, he was truly, from the depths of his heart, grateful for the opportunity to come and share because it has bothered him a great deal that he was so arrogant. I don't think he did show it so much on the outside, but he felt it inside, and he is very happy to have you use his name because he wants others to know that this can be a serious problem when we have been put on a pedestal, and then we come to this side of life—I, myself, felt it—and we are not so important. We are just like everybody else. We do have to recognize this and to gain some perspective as far as humility is concerned. And when we do, we are happy because we are not putting ourselves above anyone. We truly begin to realize that we are all God's children. We are all One, some having expressed their spirituality a little better. And those that have do have the opportunity and are qualified, really should give back by helping those who are younger on the pathway.

It is difficult to get them to understand that they are here to serve now. Serving their own soul is their first duty, and that they can bring great happiness by using their talents to help others. It is a "come down" for many. And it is not unusual for some to say they wished they could go back to earth for it was much better there. Where possible, the guides will get permission to go into the akashic records and to see the fuller picture of what they were trying to achieve on earth. Anyone who has been on center stage— politicians, anyone who has been in the limelight has to understand that they are not going to get that here. What we respect over here is the contribution that they have made. It has truly helped. We do respect our more advanced brothers and sisters for making a different kind of effort than many make on earth.

Raymond Massey on reviewing his ego needs as an actor
I was an actor on earth, and I have been on this side for a number of years. I guess I was one of those who had a pretty big ego. And when I came to this side, I did want a lot of recognition which I did not receive, because we do not grow that way. I was

told early on by my guides and teachers that humility was something that I must work on if I were to grow. And it was one of the most difficult things to do. When you have portrayed Lincoln and your ego was boosted, and you played in a number of movies and were very well known, received a lot of fan mail, and to come over here and find you really are nothing that amounts to anything. What did I bring with me? A big fat ego! I don't think I showed it a lot when I was on earth, but I was all puffed up inside.

So I had much to learn, and I did go through a review of my life. By honestly looking at it, and knowing my inner feelings and reviewing them, I thought, "My goodness, some of that has got to go." You know where I went for help? I went to a group of Catholic nuns over here who were still very, very much in their Catholic way of thinking. I asked them to work with me, to help me to develop or unfold humility. And these humble sweet ladies did work with me. Truly, they did work with me. They said, "You are not humble when you think you are humble, because that is still the ego talking. You are humble when you just are humble, and you don't think about being humble. You just are humble. You respect others, and you certainly realize that you are just a little speck. Your soul is just really a little speck of God, and you are not any better than anybody else. That little soul is the same. It comes from the same source of every other soul in existence."

I took away a real feeling from the nuns that maybe I was unworthy. I probably perceived that they were teaching me incorrectly because I don't think we are unworthy of anything that is good if we are good. Like does attract like. I have had to really work at this, to think that I am a good person and to love myself so that I can show love to others. We have to put it all in perspective, and be guided by that soul which is beautiful in everyone. It is just a matter of expressing it and bringing that goodness out.

When I got myself a little straightened out, then I did connect with some in the old movie colony, as we call it here. Many had come to me when I first passed, but I had to do work on my own. I am grateful to those nuns for helping me. I have progressed and I do work on this side in various theatrical performances, which I enjoy very much. And I try, as I run into someone who has a problem similar to mine, to willingly share my story and the fact that we are not quite as big as we think we are. That old mind, that old ego, has to bow. It has to really bow. Eventually, we put it in its place and then things are so much lighter and brighter for us.

I have progressed to the point where I went through the akashic records. One thing that stood out was the fact that I had an ego problem in a former life, and I came back to a family where the body structure was large; so I was a large man, a rather towering figure. That was to help me to get my ego down. I thought I was so big that I literally towered over others. I tried to keep it a little bit in check, but inside I knew exactly that I was a big, big man, figuratively and literally. It was the figurative part that really got me into trouble. I am not saying that every large person feels that way, because many of them have told me they feel rather awkward. They wish they were shorter because height does call attention to yourself. That was the very thing that I was to work through, so I flubbed that. But I had many other things to work through as well. Some of them I did; so by no means did I go to a realm of darkness when I came over. I was pretty average. I bring this out because people really must know that being egoistical doesn't count for anything here. It is something that is really obnoxious to oneself and to those around them.

I am very happy that I had this opportunity to talk to you. I have really enjoyed coming and talking about that. It frees you to be able to talk about some of the things that we did that were not in our soul's best interest. But ignorance is ignorance. It is not bliss by any means.

Chet Atkins shares his perspective on bowing to the soul

I give concerts on this side to the children and to those in a rest home, and I had difficulty because of my fame and fortune to make the initial adjustment over here. But I did learn to do it. And I am so happy that I am not somebody so special. I am simply one of God's many, many, many workers, and that is what we all should be. I have tried to impress other musicians on earth to give freely of their time and talent, and never to forget to be grateful that they have that talent to give to others. Because music especially does lift the soul. It is a very, very important part of every day life. Just because one person has a talent does not make him better than one who does not. Maybe that other person has elevated his soul to a higher level and that is really what is important. I leave you with this and I am so pleased that I had an opportunity to come and talk to you.

Sir Cecil explains how difficult it is for the privileged to bow their egos

Good morning, this is Cecil. I was known as Sir Cecil. I was knighted by the British royalty and I served in a capacity where I was in command. I gave orders. I expected people to follow them without question. I left many, many years ago. It is hard to keep track of what went on earth. When you come to this side and you make your adjustment to things on this side, then the things of earth do not matter as much unless we are really trying to work with someone on earth and help them.

I had many privileges. I really had royal privileges with servants waiting on me; so when I came to this side I expected to have a castle, to be waited on hand and foot, to have my butler, to have my secretary, to have my footman, and for my wife to have her maids, etc. It was very difficult for me to suddenly be told that I was just like everyone else. I had so elevated myself in my mind that I was above the commoners and it took me a long, long, long time, and it required much help, both individually and attending groups, for me to realize that what was important was not social position, but what was in one's soul, and how that was expressed. It was a real come-down, and the teachers did go to the Bible and give me the teachings of Jesus that had to do with humility. Jesus himself demonstrated humility by washing the feet of his disciples at the Last Supper. *He who is last shall be first.*

And so they told me these things, and I thought that was fine for someone else, but I was born into a fine position. I should not have to abide by any degradation of my position. They suggested, after going through the akashic records, taking a look at how I wasn't unkind to my servants, but I kept them in their place. They were always to treat me with the respect and the deference, especially, that would be shown a master. And so it was quite an experience for me when my footman who handled my carriage was brought to me. I saw his beautiful aura. His light was bright. And believe me, it was immensely brighter than my own. At first, it made me very jealous. Why should he, one who just had a menial little job, who did not have to carry the weight of making important decisions and doing the things in government that I did, have such a beautiful aura? I had totally the wrong perspective. This man chose to develop his soul faculty of humility in his life by the position that he took, and he did it beautifully. He never complained. He never was surly. He was always loyal. He was always there. He was always respectful and courteous. And he loved God. I went to the Church of England but I thought because I did have the social status that I had, that God had chosen to put me in that position and I showed very little humility or true acceptance of a higher and divine power. I did not understand at the time that I had made a plan prior to incarnation to be placed in a position where I would have the opportunity to learn humility.

It took quite some time to break down the walls of resistance to the spiritual teachings, and I believe that being in a group and listening to those in the group, as well as having some come back who had elevated themselves to share their experiences, helped. They could empathize with us and they convinced us because they had been through it. You can stay where you are as long as you like, or you can change your thinking and find peace and love and joy. You have that choice. Eventually, I decided on the latter. And now I am working as a group leader, and some of those in the group are pretty tough and they have been here a long, long time and they do not want to give in.

I hope that your Dr. Cranston can persuade a king or queen to come and tell his or her story because thousands and thousands bowed down to them. I only had a small group. And there are some over here and some are still struggling. Some are very kind and I am sure would be willing to share with you the jolt they received upon arriving in this new world. So I hope I have given you a little understanding of that. It would be wonderful if you could reach the haughty, the pompous, and the so-called socially elite to let them know they are directing their energies to the wrong goals. The true gold should be to unfold the beautiful soul faculties of love, understanding, humility, tolerance, peace, joy and all the other soul treasures.

King Alfred, the Great on bowing his ego

Good morning. My, my, my, this is a most unusual invitation, and one that I accepted with open arms. I am very happy to come and to talk to you. I was a king, yes, and it goes way, way back in England. You can look me up. This was a time when we thought we were absolutely above God. Yes, we talked about God because the Catholic Church made sure that we had churches, but I really thought I had more power because I had direct authority and control over my subjects. And one of my wives was Evangelene.

My subjects could never do enough for me. I treated them as though they were subhuman. There were only a few who were close in my court—my advisors and a few others.

There was a great sickness that came upon my subjects, an epidemic. And so I lost many, but I think that was karmic to help people end their existence on earth. They had served their karma. I did nothing to help the families who had been devastated. For example, if the husband had died of the plague, leaving the wife penniless with children, I offered no help. They could have died of starvation and I could have cared less. My feeling was they could scramble like rats. They could eat the rats and scrounge up something. I was very harsh, very cruel in punishment to those who did not obey my laws. I cannot imagine how I could have been so demanding and so cruel. Believe me, I paid for it. I took money from people who could not afford it and squandered it on jewels, marble floors, and things that were not necessary.

And you know, when I went to Spirit, I expected to go right to a castle over there, if there were an afterlife. I had no worries about it. I would be well taken care of. But when I got to the other side, yes, there were people who came to greet me, but they didn't bow down to me. They didn't bow down at all. I went eventually to my home in Spirit and it was a shack. It was worse looking than some of the worst houses of my subjects. Some of them were able to cut down trees on earth and build shelter which was far superior to what I had in Spirit.

I was not really on a realm of light. It was very dim light. I went to the highest realm on the first plane. I could barely see. Where are the candles I asked? But there were none. I was told that you create your own light on this side. Well, how do I do that? I don't have any tallow. How can I make a candle? And they told me that you make a candle, not by physically making one out of tallow or wax or something that will burn. You have a candle already within, they said. What you must do is ignite it. Let it burn. And as you feel some sense of remorse and you ask for forgiveness of your subjects, that candle within will burn more brightly. And it will eventually burn so brightly that you will leave this plane and you will go to the third plane. And as you continue to make amends, restitution for what you have done, you will find yourself with a body of light. But first, you must do what you must do. Well, I thought, I'm not going to go to all those people. They are not worthy of it. Why should I as the king go to them and tell them I'm sorry? Huh! Forget it!

But, you know, I got tired of being in such dim light. I really got tired of it. And they showed me a little bit of what it looked like in a little higher realm. And I thought and I thought and I weighed it all out. And begrudgingly, very begrudgingly, I admitted, well, I guess that is my only alternative—to bow my ego. So I went to the first person that I had sentenced to death, and he called me all kinds of names. He was in a bad way. He was so full of hatred, so full of hatred that he just laughed at me and said, " I will never forgive you. I will never forgive you." So I retreated, but my guides—I did not really understand who they were, but they were kind men and they were persistent in their efforts. They said for me not to give up on one, to go to another. And so they directed me to someone that they thought would be more forgiving— someone on a little higher plane. And that person did forgive me. And that broke the ice, so to speak. I became more comfortable in seeking out the others. Some rebuffed me, so there was nothing I could do at the moment. But I went on and I went to all of my subjects, every single one, and I asked for forgiveness. I found that as I worked at this, my body became lighter or illumined and I was going to a higher realm. I finally worked myself up to the fourth plane. And I thought this was wonderful. With the light and the knowledge, the understanding, that I had gained, I went back to those who would not forgive me and I explained to them how difficult it was for me to bow my ego to ask anyone to forgive me and that I understood they didn't want to change their attitude. But I said, look at me now, I am a living demonstration of what change of attitude can bring. And your proposed book on attitudinal healing is exactly what has to take place. I worked and worked and worked. I would not give up. And I managed, with the help of others, to change every single one of my former subjects. And then I was free to come back to earth and work off karma.

Now I had gotten into all of this because prior to being king, I had been raised in a noble family and was very haughty in that life. I looked down on the serfs. I thought they were nothing. I chose to come back as a king to not only be different, but in a position to help many souls. I had a good many serfs, but that was a small number compared to the number I would have as subjects as a king. And, therefore, if I were a very good king, look how many people I could help. But I was not a kindly king at all. I did the same things as in the previous life; so I didn't learn. In fact, I got myself into more hot water. So there was a goodly amount of karma.

I have been back a few times and I have paid off my karma. I am working on this side to help people who have been in positions of power. I am helping them to really understand that we are given positions of power to help us with our spiritual growth, and to help others grow by influencing or providing the kind of environment that is necessary for raising the consciousness of all. Mainly what happens on this side is a review of the damage that we have done, and thinking, oh my, if I had only known. Well, we pay dear prices, don't we, for thinking that we can get by with anything that we do. I hope your book reaches many, many people to help them to understand that it is better not to do it, than do it and have to pay for it.

And so I leave you with that thought. This actually is the first time I can remember coming through any medium on the earth. I have thoroughly enjoyed my visit, and I hope you will invite me back again sometime because I could tell you about some of the people that I have helped over here, or I could ask them, some of them, to come and talk to you. Maybe you could do another book on how to "tame the ego," as your Wayne Dyer says. There are many egos to be tamed, believe me.

Comments by the Master Teacher:

I am very grateful that King Alfred was willing to come and share his experiences. He is doing a fabulous job on this side, because, you see, he qualified himself by his position on earth to talk to some of those who come over who think they are so high and mighty. When they tell him that they were so and so, he says,

"Well, I can top that. I was King Alfred." And you know, it helps them to just stop. It is interesting. I checked into King Alfred's work since I talked to you last night, and learned that he does a wonderful job.

King Alfred's return visit

(**Author's note**: After channeling the above from King Alfred, I checked online "The Life of King Alfred, by Asser." In this biography, Asser wrote: "King Alfred the Great (born 849, ruled 871-899) was one of the best kings ever to rule mankind. He defended Anglo-Saxon England from Viking raids, formulated a code of laws, and fostered a rebirth of religious and scholarly activity. His reign exhibits military skill and innovation, sound governance and the ability to inspire men and plan for the future, piety and a practical commitment to the support of religion, personal scholarship and the promotion of education, etc." King Alfred himself wrote: "Desire for and possession of earthly power never pleased me over much, and I did not unduly desire this earthly rule. . . I desired to live worthily as long as I lived, and to leave after my life, to the men who should come after me, the memory of me in good works."

Having read the glowing portrait painted by Asser especially, I found his perception of King Alfred's "good deeds" to be in stark contrast to what King Alfred said about himself. For that reason, I invited King Alfred to come again and elaborate upon his motives for his "good deeds." King Alfred consented to come.)

Good morning. This is King Alfred. Well, I did not think I would be so fortunate to have another invitation to come so soon after our first visit. I am delighted. I can understand the dilemma you may have experienced. Yes, when I first took over the reigns of the monarchy, my ego soared so high that it was absolutely impossible for me to have cared for my subjects in any way shape or form. They would come begging and I would just want them out of my sight. I wanted to have nothing to do with them. I wanted them to go away and never see them again, but, of course, that is not what happened.

Yes, I was a better king later on, in a sense, but let me make it very clear. What I did, I did for my own satisfaction. The motive was not pure. I rebuilt cities destroyed by the wars with the Danes and others, yes. And London was one of the cities that I rebuilt. I am very proud that I did this work because it did help people although that was not my real motive. I think I wanted monuments so that people would not forget me. Yes, I did built two monasteries. But I felt that these monks and nuns would take care of the people so that I would not have to bothered with them. If these people wanted to come sniffling and crying to me, they would have some place to turn—someone who would work with them and help them and really get them off my back, so to speak. That was my real motive.

I did want education for the more educated people, not the ignorant ones on the bottom, but the noble and upper class. We would evolve and improve our country and this would make for a better country in the long run. It would also keep people busy.

I can assure you that I did not, nor would anyone else, find themselves in a dim light who did not deserve to be there. Divine justice is unfailing. I stated that I wanted to be a good king in my writings of that time, but I was not a compassionate king. I was tied up a lot in fighting off the Danes. I was determined they were not going to take over my country.

So I am going to leave you. If there is anything else, I want you to feel free to call on me. I will be very happy to come back and just talk. It is a wonderful opportunity to be able to come through. There are so few on this side who have that chance. In fact, there are so many over here who do not realize that it is possible to communicate. I am sure if more knew, the line waiting to come in would be very long.

Comments by the Master Teacher
I think perhaps you have received some understanding how difficult it is for people to recognize why they are in situations that they are in. If the incarnation carries with it a preplan, then that person is exactly where he or she should be in order to work out whatever is necessary. ◆

40.

COPING WITH PANGS OF
GUILT, REGRET, GRUDGES AND BULLYING

Enlightening Voices from the Other Side

W. M. on the sins of ommission

We think about coming over here and how wonderful it is, but the truth is we can go through a hell over here. It is a hell of our own making when we have been very selfish, thinking only of ourselves. I left a spiritual responsibility unfinished because I did not want to give up my material comfort. I could have worked it out in a different way. I realize that now, and I carry on my back that terrible pressure that I let everybody down because I was selfish. This is my karma. It weighs heavily on my mind.

I want people to understand that you should not do things for selfish reasons. You should not think only of yourself. I think sometimes metaphysics emphasizes that we can have the things that we want. Yes, we can, but we are to help those less fortunate than us. When we come over here and we leave loved ones on earth, and we look down and we watch them suffer, we watch them go without, we watch them in really miserable conditions, we realize *I could have changed all that*. And that is very heavy on my heart because I could have done so much because I had the money, I had the ability to change things and I did not do it. That is hell for me now. It is hell because we have to watch the loved ones on earth suffer.

I procrastinated way too much. I always was a procrastinator. You should not be a procrastinator. We should do what we know we should do. I was a very good teacher. And I left a lot of good thoughts, but I think people should be made aware that when they come over here, it is not just beautiful sunshine all the time, no, it is not. We bring the garbage with us that was with us on earth. That is something that we have to go through. We can talk to the guides and teachers and they can help us, but they cannot remove the scars. We have to do that, and we cannot do that until the people we love come over here with us. Because we are going to see it every single time we look at them. It is truly a hell. Not a hell of pitchforks and all of that stuff, no. It is a hell within us. I would like to have people understand, do your good on earth. Don't put it off. Do for those that you love what you can do now. Don't wait. Don't say I have all kinds of time. No, you do not. You never know how much time you have.

Yes, we always have another chance to do it over. The more elevated souls know this. We are talking about the average person. Someone less elevated will not be that concerned. Those who are elevated will be. They know the law and they know that law has to be obeyed. We do have to go through those things. We do not come over here and lap it all up and go about our business. Many come over with grudges. It is very hard to do anything about it from this side. You can go to those still on earth but they are not always aware of your presence. They do not receive the impression.

We try to help others, but we still have that inner feeling of what we should have done and didn't do. You do not always think about those things. You may think you are great because you haven't gone out and killed anybody, or stolen anything. Maybe you have done many things just as bad.

It is always a struggle to progress. When you are over here and cannot do anything about the things you know you could have done or should have done, how do the guides and teachers help a person? They tell us that we have to go through it. We have to understand what is causing this within us. There is really nothing that we can do as long as our people are still on earth. When they come over and forgive you, then it is over. They do not really have to forgive you, but it is over then because you no longer have to see them suffer. As soon as they come over, you go them, you tell them that you are very sorry. You could have helped them and you did not. Most of them will be forgiving, but some won't. But you then can **forgive yourself**.

When you come back to earth will you attract situations where you will have the same opportunities? Very definitely, yes. You will attract those same kinds of circumstances and hopefully you have learned enough by the terrible misery you feel in your heart over here. You will understand that is not the way to do it, and you will be much less selfish and much more willing to help others cope with their karma, if you are standing behind or beside them as they go through their karma. It will help alleviate your own karma.

Sins of omission are just as bad as sins of commission. You have to understand that, because you are going to suffer when you get over here and you are watching your loved ones. The realization comes to you, I could have changed that. I could have done much differently. I could have made things easier.

Lets say you are a very, very selfish person. All you are thinking about is the money you can make, a nice house, a nice car, a nice this and a nice this. If you are thinking that way, you are not helping anybody. It is the neglect of those you really love that evokes the real hell within yourself. Not just money, but other help, taking out the garbage, calling a person who is lonely, offering words of encouragement to someone who is down, giving financial aid and so forth. It depends a lot on the attitude of the person.

I did not help others in my field that I thought could be as good as me. Heavens no, I would not do that. That hurts now because I look down and see how I could have helped. And another thing, never want what someone else has. Greed and jealousy only bring pain.

Luther Burbank, Horticulturist, on grudges and resentment
I would like for you to consider some of the experiences I had on earth with people sending me negative thoughts, groups of people sending such negativity accusing me of defacing God's beautiful flowers by offering hybrids. I don't think they stopped to consider that cross pollination and hybridization do occur as a part of natural phenomena. I simply was directing it in the way that I thought would produce the greatest beauty. I did not feel at that time I was doing anything wrong, and I still know that I did absolutely nothing wrong. It was people who did not understand, who were Fundamentalist in their views and they really did send daggers to me. Being a sensitive person, I felt and absorbed and allowed those thought forces to literally wreck my health. I had various disturbances of my stomach and intestinal track.

I really grieved that I could not do more work and stay longer on earth. But I was open to those low vibrations and was not aware of what was happening to me until after I came to this side. When

I got over here, I really wanted to confront some of these people, but they were so believing that they were right in what they did, that I simply left it alone. It was not worth it. I contented myself with taking care of me and growing on this side, and trying to guide my wife who did many things that were absolutely correct. They were under my guidance. She was able to receive my impressions and she did a very nice thing to leave the home and land in Santa Rosa for a park. I was very pleased that she did this. The grounds were improved a great deal after she came to Spirit and I think a very nice job was done.

I just wanted to tell you that we have to make decisions in life, whether we want to hold grudges, resentment, or if we want to forgive and move on. I am able to do some work from this side. I work with herbs in trying to get across to people how these can be used effectively. I have many interests, not only in plant life. It has been a real pleasure over here to see the beautiful, beautiful plants and flowers. I have tried to suggest a few possibilities to those on earth, but never on earth, as long as you have such low vibrations, will you have the brilliance you have on this side of life. The plants and flowers on earth pale beside the flowers over here. Perhaps in the thousand years of peace we will see some change, but I don't think it will ever be the same quality of life as on this side.

Rodney W. on sharing what it is like to be a bully

I am Rodney W. Yes, I was a big guy and I delighted in picking on innocent, helpless little kids that by no means could have defended themselves. I could have just flattened them. I started doing this when I was little. I did it to a younger brother who was smaller. He didn't have the physical structure that I had and I always came on to him like *I'm the giant*. And, you know, when you are big and you are taller than everybody else, and you are stronger than the average person, and very athletic, you just think you are something, you are the king of the walk. My father was a bully type and it just came naturally how to do it.

I bullied everybody at school. We had gangs in the school and I was a gang leader. The leader of the other gang was a big guy but he wasn't as big as me, so I finally convinced him to join forces. I do not understand to this day why the teachers and the principal tolerated this kind of behavior. I observe it now from this side of life. To the kid who is much smaller, who is more delicate, when

And it happens not only boys doing this to other boys, but grown men doing the same thing. It happens with girls. The girls would have gangs and just literally tear down somebody. That's part of bullying, destroying their self-confidence. I did it in every single year of school. In high school I particularly picked on a boy named Dennis. He was in many of my classes and I always picked on him. I always made him feel so little, so inadequate. I tried to pick fights with him and he couldn't stand up to me. I thought that was great. It gave me a sense of power. It reached a point with Dennis that he could take it no longer. One day his parents walked into his room and found him hanging from the ceiling. He left no note. His parents were heartbroken. They did not know why or what drove him to suicide. This young man, who had good potential, left feeling so inadequate that he could not tell his parents what was going on. That would have made him feel more inadequate to admit that he could not handle the situation. I know this because I have talked to him on this side. And so he left without his parents' knowing and carrying that heavy, heavy burden throughout the rest of their lives, wondering what did they do wrong. What could they have done to have prevented that? Well, it didn't bother me. I don't think I had a tinge of guilt that I might have been the cause. No one thought my bullying serious enough to have stopped me or anyone like me.

I went through my life always working in some capacity that required my physical strength. I worked on a loading dock in order to earn money to go to college. I was a bully there because I was good at it and I demanded a lot of some of the guys who were smaller. I would give them jobs that should have required two average individuals to lift. I was always dealing with them with a threatening attitude, demanding and teasing in a mean sort of way.

I did get to college. It didn't seem to change my disposition. I had trouble keeping a job because I was such a bully. And I finally went to work, outdoors again. There was a problem with a crane and somehow I was severely injured and I lingered for quite awhile partly paralyzed. I never recovered, so I died in my 40's. I think it was a good thing that I was taken off the earth plane without doing more damage.

When I look down at earth, it is so sad to see how devastating this behavior is, not only to the person being bullied, but to the bully himself or herself. What it does to the soul! I accumulated karma aplenty. When I got to this side, I thought I still could just order people around because I was big and strong. But I found out that they just ignored me. *Who are you, Buster? You are going to have to change your ways.* I found that I was being isolated. Once in awhile these really nice men would come to me. They introduced themselves as guides and teachers and I didn't have a clue about them. They told me what I was doing to myself. Bullying just didn't work over here, and that I should consider some counseling. That didn't go over too well at first. But I found that people didn't want to have anything to do with me. So, I finally said, *Okay, I'll go to one session and see what it's all about.* I went to that session, which was a group session with all bullies. We were either all big guys or women who had positions of power when on earth and who had threatened their employees or subordinates in a bullying way, demanding they do this or that or they would not get a raise, and so forth. They would make life miserable for those under them.

When I started listening to what these guys had done, I found they had done everything you could think of—some things I had done, some things I had not even thought of doing. I not only listened to them, I listened to one who had been bullied. And he came back as a strong individual because he had been given much therapy. He told how being bullied had driven him to the brink of despair and he had shot himself in the head, and how he had awakened, so to speak, on this side of life to find that he had not ended it at all. He received wonderful therapy. He wanted to come and tell us, *Look you guys and women, straighten up. It is a cruel thing to do to anybody. It leaves scars that are very, very difficult to erase. Instead of being bullies, why don't you use physical stature and positions of power to comfort, protect and help those who are of a smaller stature or who are helpless, instead of bullying a dwarf or midget, or someone smaller, or maybe a little retarded. Reach out and help them. They are working off karma in their own way.*

And so, that woke me up when I listened to him. I learned that if I wanted to be free, I not only had to be kind to people, but I had to go back to those I had really hurt and ask for forgiveness. The first person that I went to was Dennis who had committed suicide. On my knees I begged for forgiveness. He is a gentle soul and we had a good cry, and he did forgive me. It makes me cry now to think how kind he was in forgiving me. He helped me to go to others. He pointed them out because he knew, having gone through so many grades of school with me, many that I had hurt. I did go to those who had come over and they told me what they thought of me. They really read me off. They finally did forgive me. And the people that I had worked with—a couple have still not come over, but those who have—I have gone to.

I would like to come back again, and to work off my karma, I would like to be a fragile little boy to really experience what it is like to be on the receiving end. Either that, or come back again to and try to put a stop to this bullying business. There is a law pending in one of your states. Parents are tired of this, and we are working on this side to get a law against it in every state. We want it done all over the world. This has to stop. No one is so high and mighty to get away with this. We want therapy for the person who is a bully. We want group sessions with a good supportive counselor where the bully can sit with those who are being bullied and have some meaningful dialogue. The law should require that this kind of counseling take place. It should be mandatory. Those who have been bullied should feel free to speak out without feeling there will be repercussions. They need help in dealing with this, not to feel more inadequate in asking for help, but to feel that it is okay, that it is helping the bully also, helping him to learn to socialize. This is a serious situation that is going on and it has gone on from time immemorial, but it must stop. I am so grateful that you want to include this in your book to help people to become aware that it is a psychological problem that must be dealt with.

Comments by the Master Teacher
With bullying, it is true this is a very damaging thing to happen to someone who feels helpless. We cannot take advantage of helpless people. We must help them. And so we are grateful to Rodney for sharing his story. He is doing a very, very fine job over here working with bullies.

Jane Doe on carrying over guilt feelings
I want to tell you about my situation on earth and how it was finally worked out on the spirit side of life. I was involved in many activities on earth. Some of these activities were on the shady side. It is difficult for me to talk about these things. I'm afraid it will bring disgrace to my family, if you used my real name. I robbed a bank and was not caught because I had no prior record, nor any

fingerprints on file. I stole from my employer and covered it all up. It remained so until my sudden death. I was a bookkeeper and kept covering up year after year after year until the books were in a complete mess.

Then I had a heart attack before this was discovered. When an auditor came in after I died, it was exposed. I felt terribly, terribly guilty because my employer was really a very, very, very fine man. And to have taken from him or anyone was not the right thing to do, but I was so tempted. I had full responsibility and he trusted me. I did actually go in and rob a bank. I disguised myself and because of having no prior record, I was never caught.

I came to this side feeling guilty. I always intended to put back the money that I "borrowed" from my employer. I had children who needed more than I could provide for them. I always thought I would pay him back, and of course, I did not live long enough to do it. I am not terribly certain I could have done it, or would have done it.

When we are on this side and we bring problems like that with us, we cannot solve them. We cannot reach the people we hurt and say we are sorry. When my employer found out that his very trusted employee had done this to him, he was very disillusioned. He still has not come to this side so that I can go to him and ask forgiveness. And so, as I have progressed, my conscience hurts terribly. It is very painful. The waiting is awful. So I try to do things on this side that will be helpful to people so that I don't torture myself.

My guides and teachers have worked with me and I know that I will have to go back to earth, and possibly will be in a reverse situation so that someone will do the same thing to me. And you know, I wish it could be right away so that I could get over this thing because it truly bothers me. And to think I left a son and a daughter, both in their late teens, to be so ashamed of their mother and to be without support. My employer was concerned about them, but his wife was not sympathetic.

I am going to leave now. I hope this gives you some understanding of the terrible feelings that we can have over here for the wrong things we have done when on earth. We cannot rectify them immediately, and maybe never completely erase them from soul memory. ◆

"People are like stained glass windows.
They sparkle and shine when the sun is out,
but when the darkness sets in,
their true beauty is revealed only
if there is a light from within."

—Elizabeth Kubler-Ross

ROBERT D. REED PUBLISHERS is proud to offer you special pricing on additional copies of this book and other books listed below. The more you order, the more you save!

Call in your order for fast service and quantity discounts:

(541) 347-9882

OR order on-line at www.rdrpublishers.com using PayPal.

OR order by mail: Copy this form, enclose check or payment information, and mail to:

Robert D. Reed Publishers
1380 Face Rock Drive
Bandon, OR 97411

Feel free to make copies of this form and share with others!

Send indicated books to:
Name _____
Address _____
City _____State _____ Zip _____
Phone: _____
Fax: _____ Cell: _____
E-Mail: _____
Payment of $_____by check / / or credit card / /
(All major credit cards are accepted.)
Name on card _____
Card Number _____
Exp. Date _____Last 3-Digit number on back of card: ____
     Note: Shipping is $3.50 1st book + $1 for each additional book.

What Goes On Beyond the Pearly Gates?   *Qty.*
Communication with Angelic Healers
by Miriam Bostwick .... $17.95 _____

The Conquering Soul: The Key to Understanding
Spiritual Psychology
by Miriam Bostwick.. $14.95 _____

More on the Conquering Soul: The Key to
Understanding Spiritual Psychology
by Miriam Bostwick.. $14.95 _____

All You Need Is HART! Create Love, Joy, and Abundance - NOW!
by Helene Rothschild .... $14.95 _____

Other books from Web site: www.rdrpublishers.com:

_____ $ _____ _____

_____ $ _____ _____